# HINDU TRINITY

Devdutt Pattanaik writes, illustrates and lectures on the relevance of mythology in modern times. He has, since 1996, written over forty books and seven hundred columns on how stories, symbols and rituals construct the subjective truth (myths) of ancient and modern cultures around the world. He consults corporations on leadership and governance, and TV channels on mythological serials. His TV shows include *Business Sutra* on CNBC-TV18 and *Devlok* on Epic TV. To know more, visit devdutt.com

# HINDU TRINITY

21 Life-enhancing Secrets Revealed Through Stories and Art

# DEVDUTT PATTANAIK

First published by Westland Publications Private Limited in 2019
1st Floor, A Block, East Wing, Plot No. 40, SP Infocity, Dr MGR Salai,
Perungudi, Kandanchavadi, Chennai 600096

Westland and the Westland logo are the trademarks of
Westland Publications Private Limited, or its affiliates.

Image on Page 314 ©Sri Balambika Divya Sangam, who can be contacted at
editorial.bds@gmail.com

ISBN: 9789388754712

10 9 8 7 6 5 4 3 2 1

Typeset by Special Effects Graphics Design Co., Mumbai
Printed at Thomson Press (India) Ltd.

MIX
Paper
FSC  FSC® C010615

*I humbly and most respectfully dedicate this book to those hundreds of artists, artisans and photographers who made sacred art so easily accessible to the common man*

# Contents

*Introduction*                                                    *xi*

**7 Secrets of Shiva**                                      **1**

1. Lingeshwara's Secret                                    7

2. Bhairava's Secret                                          35

3. Shankara's Secret                                         67

4. Bholenath's Secret                                       101

5. Ganesha's Secret                                         135

6. Murugan's Secret                                         169

7. Nataraja's Secret                                         199

## 7 Secrets of the Goddess     227

1. Gaia's Secret              231

2. Kali's Secret              273

3. Gauri's Secret             311

4. Durga's Secret            343

5. Lakshmi's Secret         387

6. Saraswati's Secret       433

7. Vitthai's Secret          457

## 7 Secrets of Vishnu       489

1. Mohini's Secret       495

2. Matsya's Secret       531

3. Kurma's Secret       553

4. Trivikrama's Secret       585

5. Ram's Secret       621

6. Krishna's Secret       651

7. Kalki's Secret       689

*Symbols in this book*       *713*

*Acknowledgements*       *715*

# Introduction

*T*hese books — 7 *Secrets of Shiva*, 7 *Secrets of Vishnu* and 7 *Secrets of the Goddess* — were written to help people in India and around the world understand the meaning of artworks in India that have a mythological theme.

Art historians generally try to explain where, when, how, these images were made, by whom, for whom, with what material, but they generally ignore the significance of these images to the common man, the consistency of this imagery for thousands of years, and the way it has shaped the Indian way of life.

The purpose of this book is also to draw attention to the concept of the Hindu Trinity. This is commonly considered to be the male trinity of Brahma, Vishnu, Shiva, who create, sustain and destroy the world. However, at the practical ground level, the trinity comprises of the Goddess who embodies nature, and Shiva and Vishnu who embody the cultural response to nature as hermit and householder. Shiva is the hermit who becomes the householder, and Vishnu is the householder who lives like a hermit. And the Goddess enables both their transformations. Together, the Goddess with Shiva and

Vishnu form the cornerstone of the Hindu worldview.

The Goddess is often visualised in yellow, as she is smeared with turmeric (*haldi-mukhi*); Shiva is white as camphor (*karpura gauranga*) and Vishnu is dark as a monsoon cloud (*ghana-shyam*). In Tantrik art, Shiva and Vishnu become Gora Bhairav and Kala Bhairav, the white and the black consorts of the Goddess. These have to be taken symbolically, as the human attitude towards life — some of us want to withdraw from the world, some of us want to engage with the world and, like Hamlet, we are confused. Shiva and Vishnu embody the wisdom that enables us to deal with these two extreme reactions to life.

These ideas can be been traced to the Upanishads which are three thousand years old. They started being transmitted as stories and art, two thousand years ago. Scholars often focus so much on the form that they miss the meaning. This omnibus focuses on the meaning underlying the art. It hopes to remind the reader how the common Indian developed his worldview, and faith, based on oral stories and art, not elitist texts alone.

These books present my way of seeing things. I do not claim to have an objective or perfect understanding of a culture which is three thousand years old and spread over a vast subcontinent. I contextualise things based on history and geography. What I have is an overview: a trend that is unique to the subcontinent. Hence, please read this omnibus keeping in mind that:

*Within infinite myths lies an eternal truth*
*Who knows it all?*
*Varuna has but a thousand eyes*
*Indra, a hundred*
*You and I, only two.*

# 7 Secrets of Shiva

*Smeared with ash*
*Draped in animal hide*
*He sits atop the snow-capped mountain*
*Skull in hand*
*Withdrawn, with dogs for company*
*Destroying the world with his indifference*
*He is the God who the Goddess shall awaken*
*His name is Shiva*

Locked in his stories, symbols and rituals are the secrets of our ancestors. *7 Secrets of Shiva* attempts to unlock seven.

# Author's Note
## On Context and Structure

*I*magine a Western scholar. He, or she, is typically from Europe or America. All his life, he has been exposed to Judaism, Christianity or Islam, religions that frown upon any overt display of sexuality. To him, sexuality is almost always an act of rebellion, an expression of defiance against the establishment. It is seen as being modern.

So imagine his surprise when he comes to India and encounters temples embellished with images of men and women in erotic embrace. Imagine his bewilderment when he finds Hindus worshipping an image shaped like a phallus called Shiva-linga. This is what his ancestors, a hundred years ago, also encountered, and condemned as pre-modern, licentious and savage. The scholar finds them vicariously liberating. Keen to study and understand these images, he hunts for a suitable academy. He finds none in India. So he enrols in a Western institution, where he is guided by Western academicians and is expected to follow methodologies developed and approved in the West. He starts reading texts as he would read the Bible, not realising that texts do not serve the same purpose in Hinduism. He decodes scriptures and images using his own cultural frameworks as the template. His conclusions are published in respected academic papers that win him accolades from Western academia, but they discomfort, even horrify, the average Hindu devotee.

Most Hindus become defensive and, like their 19th-century ancestors, go out of their way to strip Hinduism of its sexual heritage. A few, especially those with political leanings, react violently, outraged by the conclusions. Accused of cultural insensitivity, Western scholars strike back saying that Hindus do not know their own heritage and are still viewing Hinduism through the archaic Victorian lens. Battle lines are drawn. They are still drawn. Who is right? The arrogant academician or the stubborn devotee? It is in this context that I write this book.

I have noticed that the divide between Western academicians and Hindu devotees exists in their relative attention to form and thought. Form is tangible and objective, thought is intangible and subjective. Western scholars have been spellbound by the sexual form but pay scant regard to the metaphysical thought. In other words, they prefer the literal to the symbolic. Hindu devotees, in contrast, are so focused on the metaphysical thought that they ignore, or simply deny, the sexual form. The Western preference for form over thought stems from their cultural preference for the objective over the subjective. Hindus, on the other hand, are very comfortable with the subjective, hence can easily overlook form and focus on thought. This book seeks to bridge this wide gap between academics and practice.

• The first chapter looks at the meaning of the Shiva-linga beyond the conventional titilation offered by a phallic symbol.

- The second chapter focuses on Shiva's violent disdain for territorial behaviour amongst humans.
- The third and fourth chapters deal with how the Goddess gets Shiva to engage with the world out of compassion.
- The next two chapters revolve around Shiva's two sons, Ganesha and Murugan, through whom he connects with the world.
- The final chapter presents Shiva as the wise teacher who expresses wisdom through dance.

This book seeks to make explicit patterns that are implicit in stories, symbols and rituals of Shiva, firm in the belief that:

*Within infinite myths lies an eternal truth*
*Who knows it all?*
*Varuna has but a thousand eyes*
*Indra, a hundred*
*You and I, only two.*

# 1. Lingeshwara's Secret

### Imagination makes us human

Icicle Shiva-linga

Carved Shiva-linga

River stone Shiva-linga

Natural rock formation Shiva-linga

*O*ne day a sculptor was given a rock and asked to carve an image of God. He tried to imagine a form that would best encapsulate God. If he carved a plant, he would exclude animals and humans. If he carved an animal, he would exclude humans and plants. If he carved a human, he would exclude plants and animals. If he carved a male, he would exclude the female. If he carved a female, he would exclude all males. God, he believed, was the container of all forms. And the only way to create this container was by creating no form. Or maybe God is beyond all forms, but a form is needed to access even this idea. Overwhelmed by these thoughts, the sculptor left the stone as it was and bowed before it. This was the linga, the container of infinity, the form of the formless, the tangible that provokes insight into the intangible.

The name given to God was Shiva, which means the pure one, purified of all forms. Shiva means that which is transcendent. Shiva means God who cannot be contained by space or time, God who needs no form.

Shiva has been visualised as an icicle in a cave in Amarnath, Jammu; as a natural rock formation rising up from the earth, as in Buda Kedar at Tehri, Uttarakhand or Lingaraja, Bhubaneswar, Odisha; as a smooth oval stone from the river bed of Narmada placed in a metal trough as in Kashi-Vishwanath, Varanasi; or a sculpture of a smooth, cylindrical, free-standing pillar rising up from a leaf-shaped base, as in Brihadeshwara, Tanjore or the Chandramouleshwara temple at Unkal, Karnataka.

In the 12th century, in the land which is now called the state of Karnataka, lived a man called Basava, who encouraged everyone

Ishta-linga of the Lingayats

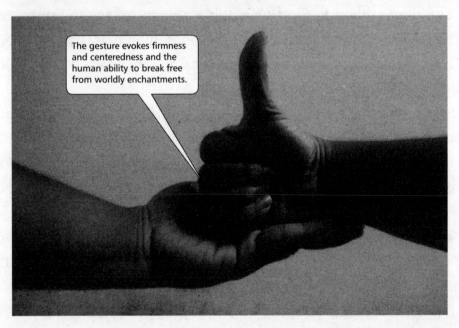

Hand gesture of a dancer showing Linga-mudra

to worship the formless, limitless divine in the form of a personal image, the ishta-linga, placed in an amulet and tied around the neck. The ishta-linga had no particular form and reminded Basava of the formless divine. He believed that by adoration of this idea through the formless form of the linga, humans would be able to break free from all divisions created by man on the basis of lineage, gender, profession or wealth. He inspired the Lingayat and Virashaiva movements.

Only humans can conceptualise the idea of infinity. Only humans can communicate such an abstract idea using various forms, such as words and symbols. This is because humans are blessed with imagination. It is the one thing that separates us humans from animals.

Humans can imagine because we have a highly developed brain, the cerebrum, with an especially large frontal lobe. This anatomical difference separates us from the rest of nature. So much so that in Samkhya, the Indian school of metaphysics, humanity or Purusha is seen as being separate from nature or Prakriti. This difference is seen as fundamental in the study of metaphysics. Because humans can imagine, the notion of a reality beyond the senses, a reality beyond nature, has come into being. Without the cerebrum there would be no imagination, and hence no notion of God!

In nature, all things have form. Each of these forms is limited by space and time. To sustain these forms one has to feed and one has to procreate. Eventually all forms are destroyed and replaced by new forms. Nature is thus a self-sustaining, predictable wheel of events where forms come and go. Only humans can imagine a

The pillar linga indicates absence of forms.

The human head is a reminder of the human ability to imagine all forms.

A stone Mukha-linga from Ellora

Masks make the rather abstract linga more accessible to a devotee.

Masculinity is reinforced through moustaches.

Brass masks that are placed over Shiva-lingas

world where all these rules are subverted: a world without forms, a world without limitations, a world without the need for action, or the obligation to experience a reaction, a transcendental world beyond feeding and procreating, creating and destroying, a still world, with no restlessness, only serenity, only bliss. In other words, humans can imagine a world beyond nature. This idea is contained in the linga.

In many temples of India, a head or multiple heads are carved on the linga stone, or a brass mask representing a head covers the linga-stone. This head is identified with Shiva. It is a reminder of the human head that is unique from all other heads in the animal kingdom. It houses the highly developed brain that can imagine and hence forge a path to the divine. This is the very same reason that sacred marks are placed on the forehead of devotees: to remind them of the critical role our brain, hence our imagination, plays in defining our humanity.

From imagination comes our vision of the world, our vision of our future, and most importantly our vision of ourselves, who we are and what we want to be. These visions may have nothing to do with the reality of the natural world around us. They may be improvements on what we remember or have been told. It is imagination that makes us realise that we are distinct from nature. In other words, imagination makes us self-aware. It is also imagination that makes us feel unique because no two humans can imagine the same thing. Imagination therefore makes us wonder about who we are, compelling us to analyse, synthesise, create and communicate. It is our imagination that will not allow us to stagnate. It propels us to improve. It propels us to grow.

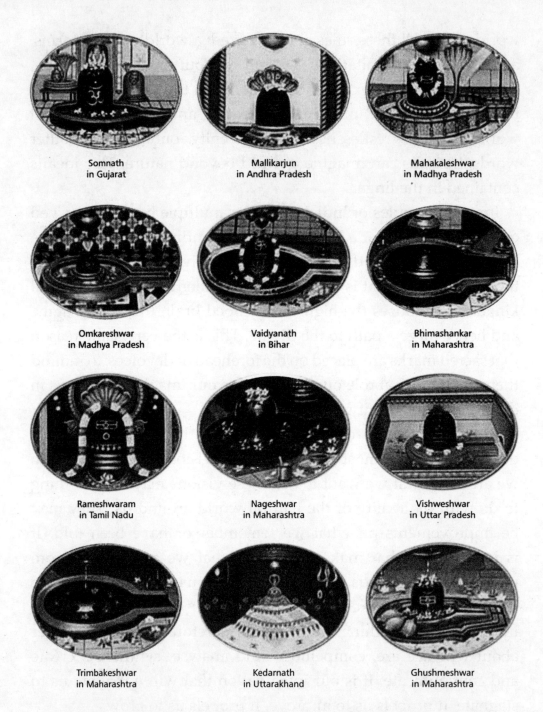

Somnath
in Gujarat

Mallikarjun
in Andhra Pradesh

Mahakaleshwar
in Madhya Pradesh

Omkareshwar
in Madhya Pradesh

Vaidyanath
in Bihar

Bhimashankar
in Maharashtra

Rameshwaram
in Tamil Nadu

Nageshwar
in Maharashtra

Vishweshwar
in Uttar Pradesh

Trimbakeshwar
in Maharashtra

Kedarnath
in Uttarakhand

Ghushmeshwar
in Maharashtra

The twelve major Jyotir-lingas or self-illuminous, self-created lingas of India,
mentioned in a hymn composed by Shankaracharya in the 8th century

In Sanskrit, the sound 'Brh' means to grow, to swell, to expand and enlarge. From this sound come two very critical ideas: brahman and Brahma. The former is a concept found in the Vedas and the latter is a character found in the Puranas. Vedas are the earliest sacred scriptures of Hinduism and are full of abstract hymns containing esoteric concepts. The Puranas were written later and use stories and characters to make those esoteric concepts more accessible. The Vedic brahman is a neuter noun, which means the vast, the boundless, and the infinite. Puranic Brahma is a proper noun referring to a form of God that is, very peculiarly and significantly, not worshipped.

The Hindu idea of God is rather complex. It cannot be explained without referring to Goddess. Most people, using the notion of God in the Bible as template, do not appreciate this and hence get confused. Goddess is nature and God is how nature is perceived by the human imagination. When the perception is incomplete and inaccurate, God is not worshipped, as in the case of Brahma. When the perception is complete and accurate, God is worshipped, as in the case of Shiva and Vishnu. In fact, when perception is complete and accurate, the divide between God and Goddess collapses. There is only one. That one is brahman. Brahma is God yearning for perfection that is the brahman. Hence the Vedic maxim, 'Aham Brahmasmi' which means both 'I am Brahma' — meaning 'I am finite', as well as 'I am brahman' — meaning 'I am infinite'. Every human being is in the process of moving from the finite to the infinite, from Brahma to brahman, on the path forged by the imagination.

Poster art showing three forms of God

The neuter brahman is also called the nirguna brahman or the formless divinity. To be worshipped it needs to become saguna, or possess a form. Brahma is God who creates all forms, hence is called the creator; but he has not yet found the perfect form and is still yearning and searching, making him unworthy of worship. Vishnu is God who has realised that no form is perfect and so works with the limited forms. This is why he is called the preserver and is worshipped in various forms. Shiva is God who breaks free from all forms, having found all of them limited, hence he is the destroyer who is worshipped as the linga.

Devotees need form to understand and seek the formless; through saguna is realised the nirguna. Hence they turn to stories, symbols and rituals of Shiva and Vishnu. Shiva is Hara, who is indifferent to form, while Vishnu is Hari, who is appreciative of form. In medieval times, there was much rivalry between devotees of Shiva and Vishnu as they showed preference for either Hara or Hari. Wisdom lies in breaking free from all differences, divisions and limitations so that infinity may be realised.

One day, Brahma and Vishnu were quarrelling. Brahma claimed, 'I created the world. I must be God.' Vishnu retorted, 'That you seek validation means you cannot be God.' 'Then who is God?' Brahma demanded to know.

In response, a pillar of fire appeared between them. It stretched up beyond the dome of the sky and down below the foundations of the earth. And the fire seemed to be burning without any fuel.

Both Brahma and Vishnu decided to look for the ends of this pillar of fire. Brahma took the form of a swan and flew up to

North Indian miniature showing Shiva emerging from a pillar of fire

find its top. Vishnu took the form of a boar and dug his way down, determined to find its base. Brahma flew for months and years but there was no sign of the tip of the fiery pillar. Vishnu dug for months and years but there was no sign of the base of the fiery pillar. Finally, exhausted, the two returned to share their findings. 'This pillar of fire has no base,' admitted Vishnu. 'It is endless and infinite.' Brahma, however, lied. 'I found the tip. I even found Ketaki flowers on it. I have done what you could not do. I am greater than you. I must therefore be God.'

As soon as Brahma said this, the pillar of fire burst open and out came another god, who looked like a mendicant, smeared with ash and wrapped in animal skins. 'Liar,' he shouted pointing to Brahma. 'You lie so that you can delude the world and dominate everyone around you to feel powerful. You are not God.' He then turned to Vishnu and smiled. 'You admit the truth. You are humble enough to accept limitations. You are curious to know what lies beyond the horizon. You are not intimidated by uncertainty or afraid of ignorance. You are in the process of becoming God.'

Brahma trembled and bowed to this self-assured being. Vishnu watched him in awe. The mendicant identified himself, 'If the formless can be given a form then I am he. I am God, I am Shiva.'

Since that day the stone pillar or linga is worshipped by all, a reminder of the pillar of flames that appeared between Brahma and Vishnu. Those who look at this stone image as merely a stone image are like Brahma, people who lack imagination and who do not yearn for wisdom. Those who look at this stone image as a symbolic container of an idea are like Vishnu, people with imagination who yearn for the truth that exists beyond the tangible.

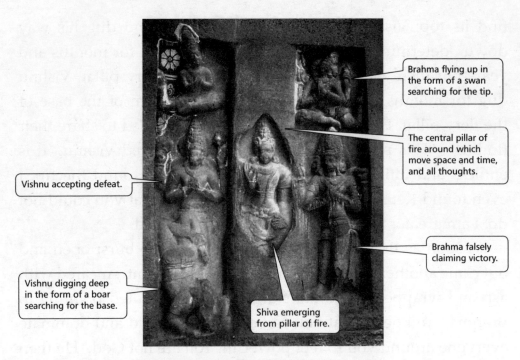

Brahma flying up in the form of a swan searching for the tip.

The central pillar of fire around which move space and time, and all thoughts.

Vishnu accepting defeat.

Brahma falsely claiming victory.

Vishnu digging deep in the form of a boar searching for the base.

Shiva emerging from pillar of fire.

Stone carving of Lingo-bhava, the first appearance of Shiva

Banyan tree indicating permanence.

Pole Star indicating stillness and marking the north.

Snow-capped mountains indicating stillness.

Shiva, the primal teacher.

Rishis, the students of the primal teacher.

Temple wall sculpture showing Shiva as teacher

In nature, everything has a beginning and an end. In nature, fire needs fuel. The idea of a pillar without beginning or end, made of fire that needs no fuel, can exist only in the imagination and is hence worthy of representing reality that is transcendental, existing beyond the senses.

In order to communicate the idea of spiritual reality, one needs symbols. One depends on nature to provide these symbols. But all things in nature are bound by natural laws, hence inherently unsuitable to express the idea of spiritual reality. So one selects those symbols that are less fettered by natural laws, at least in perception.

The Pole Star, for example, is the only celestial body in the sky that does not move at all. It appears fixed. All the stars and the planets move around it. The Pole Star serves as the symbol of a world where nothing changes, nothing ages or dies. The direction marked by the Pole Star becomes the direction of aspiration, the direction of spiritual reality. In the north, lives Shiva, said the wise.

No one has seen the birth of a mountain or the death of a mountain. No one has seen a mountain move. Mountains thus represent the stability and stillness of spiritual reality. Shiva is imagined as living on a mountain. This mountain is located under the Pole Star, in the north. This mountain is called Kailasa. It is covered by snow, water that does not move.

Shiva is visualised seated under the banyan tree. Roots of this tree emerge from branches and anchor themselves in the ground and eventually become so thick that it becomes difficult to differentiate the trunk from the roots. One does not know where the tree starts and where the tree ends, like the limitless pillar of

Stone wall carving showing Lakulesh

fire. It also has an unusually long life, making it appear almost indestructible, defying the laws of nature. That makes it a symbol for Shiva.

Shiva, who emerged from the limitless pillar of fuel-less fire, is therefore visualised sitting under the Pole Star, on a snow-capped mountain, in the shade of a banyan tree. Through this form, the idea of spiritual reality is communicated.

The earliest followers of Shiva were mendicants who lived outside human settlements, in forests, and moved around with matted hair, smeared with ash, naked or dressed in animal hide, carrying cups made of gourds or skulls, and bearing a staff. These were hermits, people who chose not to be part of culture. These men were not interested in marriage or children or society or worldly life. They were interested only in realising the infinite.

The leader of these men was called Lakulesh, meaning the bearer of the staff, or lakula. It is not clear whether Lakulesh was the name of a man, or a title. Eventually, it became one of Shiva's many names.

The lakula referred to two things that are seen in Lakulesh images: either the staff or the erect manhood. Maybe it refers to both. Lakulesh images on ancient temple walls have faded over time. Typically he sports an erect penis, holds a staff in his hand and his eyes are shut.

Ancient Indian artists used the male body to represent the mind. This is because the male genitalia, unlike female genitalia, shows dramatic visual transformation between states of non-arousal and arousal. A flaccid penis indicates an unstirred mind. An erect penis

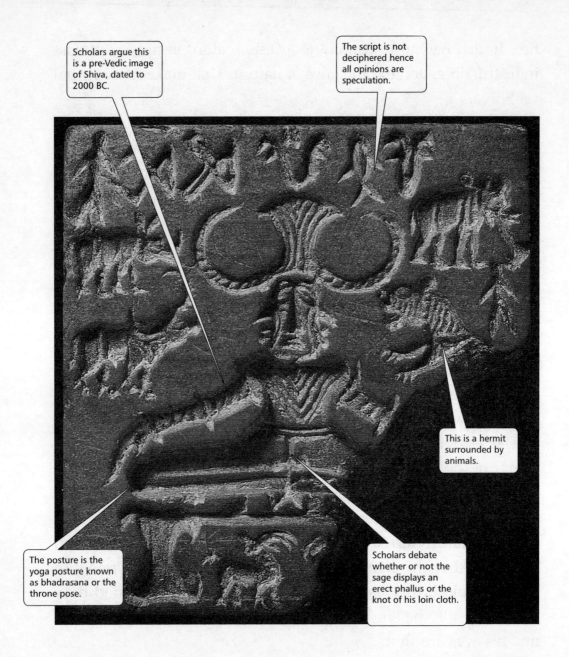

Scholars argue this is a pre-Vedic image of Shiva, dated to 2000 BC.

The script is not deciphered hence all opinions are speculation.

This is a hermit surrounded by animals.

The posture is the yoga posture known as bhadrasana or the throne pose.

Scholars debate whether or not the sage displays an erect phallus or the knot of his loin cloth.

**Indus valley seal showing a sage surrounded by animals**

represents a stirred mind. The spurting of semen offers a very visual metaphor to show the submission of the mind to external stimulus. Eyes represent the senses. When the man's eyes are shut and his penis is flaccid, it indicates a mind that refuses to submit to external stimulus.

When the man's eyes are shut and his penis is erect, as in the case of Lakulesh, it indicates a mind that is stirred by an internal stimulus. Lakulesh's erection is not a product of sensations since he has blocked out all external stimuli. His bodily response is not dependent on a cause; it is causeless, it is not a reaction to something. That is why his aroused penis is considered self-created or self-stirred, swayambhu, hence worthy of adoration.

Through imagination one can experience everything from zero to infinity. Animals and plants do not have this ability; they depend on stimulations and memory. Humans have the power to block all stimulations that stir the mind and purge all memories that contaminate the mind, thereby experiencing imagination that is pure and pristine. This experience is the experience of pure consciousness. Realisation of this infinite power of the human imagination over nature's reality is expressed in the self-stirred erect phallus of Lakulesh.

Lakulesh's staff indicates the human ability to master the mind, stop it from responding to external stimuli, enabling it to cleanse the mind of all memories and prejudices. By doing this, the hermit outgrows dependence on things outside himself for happiness. Liberated from the confines of nature, he becomes master of his own contentment by discovering the infinite possibilities of imagination. Hence, the staff in his hand, symbol of power, authority and autonomy.

**Poster art of Shiva**

The self-stirred phallus of Lakulesh is a physical expression of an idea known as sat-chitta-ananda, which means tranquillity (ananda) that follows when the mind (chitta) discovers the truth of nature and of the human condition (sat) by purging itself of all memories and prejudice.

According to the alchemical principles of the body, a body's energy is utilised whenever the mind engages with the material world around it. To replenish these, we need food, water and breath constantly. As the body is used to generate more energy, it ages and eventually dies.

However, when the mind withdraws from material reality, it does not depend on nature anymore. It does not need to be fed. It generates heat autonomously without fuel. This is tapa, spiritual fire that does not need fuel, unlike agni that is material fire which needs fuel.

Tapa cleanses the mind, purges all memories and prejudices so that it experiences sat-chitta-ananda. It makes the body radiant, youthful and prevents it from aging. Tapasya is the process of lighting this fire. Lakulesh and his followers were Tapasvins, fire-churning ascetics.

Tapasvins hold Prakriti in disdain, because everything in nature is mortal. They seek immortality. In nature, everything is limited by space and time and restricted by form. The Tapasvin wants to break free from all limitations, expand into infinity, achieve what is called Siddha, the ability to acquire whatever he desires, not be fettered by gravity. And so the Tapasvin seeks to fly in the air and walk on water, expand and contract his size, change his shape. He

Literally, the pillar is the erect phallus, but symbolically, it is the alert mind that is aroused by wisdom, not worldly stimuli.

A traditionally decorated Shiva-linga without a mask

The hooded serpent represents stillness of the mind.

The gaze is inwards so the eyes are shut.

Shiva-linga with mask

seeks independence from nature. Withdrawing from nature is the first step in this process.

Detached from nature, a Tapasvin feels no pain, hears no sound, sees no image, tastes no flavour and smells no odour. In art, Tapasvins are shown as seated in cross-legged positions with creepers around their feet, termite hills over their bodies and serpents slithering around their necks. These men are intellectually, emotionally and physically liberated from all things material.

Tapasvins look inwards in their quest for independence and infinity. This inward gaze away from the material world is called nivritti marga, while the outward materialistic gaze is called pravritti marga. The inward gaze seeks the seed from where the tree comes; the outward gaze seeks the fruit of the tree. That is why Shiva is always bedecked with the seeds of the rudraksha tree. Rudraksha literally means 'the gaze of Shiva'. In contrast, Vishnu, patron of the outward gaze, is bedecked with leaves and flowers.

Shiva is the greatest Tapasvin. He spends no heat engaging with the outside world. All the heat he generates remains contained within his body. Naturally, the world around Shiva, unseen by him, gradually loses all heat and becomes cold. As a result, water stills and turns to snow. His mountain becomes Himalaya, the abode of snow.

The Tapasvin practises celibacy, refuses to have sex with women, and father children. Thus he destroys his family tree voluntarily. No other living creature can do this.

Plants are bound by nature to bear fruit and seed. Animals are bound by nature to mate. Humans are the only creatures for whom

Rudraksha tree

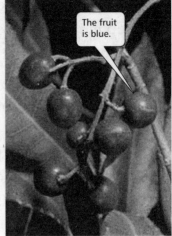

The fruit is blue.

Fruits of the ruraksha

Seeds of Elaeocarpus which grow in the foothills of the Himalayas.

Symbol of celibacy and continence.

The commonly found seed has five grooves and is known as the panch-mukhi rudraksha. The eka-mukhi rudraksha is a rare mutant with only one groove, and is said to be more potent in spiritual power.

Said to be the dried tears that Shiva shed when he saw the world.

Rudraksha beads

reproduction is a choice. A male hermit represents the rejection of that choice; he cannot be forced to make a woman pregnant. Women can be hermits and also refuse to bear children, but they cannot be used to represent the idea of disengagement from the material world because the female body can be forced to bear a child. Artists used the male body to represent the voluntary mind and the female body to represent involuntary nature. If all males chose not to procreate, one can imagine the end of the human race. Humans are the only creatures who can voluntarily make themselves extinct, if the men choose not to act on desire. The male gender of Lakulesh is thus indicative of choice.

Shiva strings the seeds of the rudraksha around his neck, instead of sowing them under the ground. Thus he prevents germination. Thus the rudraksha-mala or chain of rudraksha beads represents celibacy.

In Tantrik physiology it is said that men have white seed (sperms in semen) and women have red seed (ovum in menstrual blood). The two seeds fuse to create a child. The followers of Shiva believed that so long as the flow of seed is downward, living creatures will remain mortal.

Plants and animals cannot control their urge to spill their seed. Women have no control over their red seed. Their menstrual cycle is fettered to nature's rhythms like the waxing and waning of the moon and the movement of the tides. Only the human male has the power to control the movement of his white seed. It can flow downwards in pleasure or to procreate — this results in mortality. It can be made to flow upwards with yoga. This generates wisdom, ignites the spiritual fire of Tapa and results in immortality. This upward movement of semen is described in Tantra as Urdhvaretas.

Miniature painting of woman worshipping Shiva-linga

Reverse movement of the semen is also a metaphor for the reversal of the senses so that they pay less attention to the material reality outside and more to the spiritual reality inside. This reverse movement is also known as the northern movement, towards the Pole Star, in contrast to the southern movement, out of the body, which results in children, family and social responsibilities. It is depicted in art as an erect phallus in a Tapasvin whose eyes are shut.

Shiva's holy city, Kashi, is located at a bend in the river Ganga where it turns and moves northwards instead of southwards. This reverse flow of the river is a reminder of what the human mind can do. Only the human mind, blessed with imagination, can challenge the laws of nature, withdraw from it and even break free from it. This is moksha, or liberation.

Shiva-linga then is at once the self-stirred phallus of the Tapasvin, the reverse flow of his semen, the burning of Tapa, the endless pillar of fire and the form of the formless divine. This is the Stanu, the still pillar of consciousness, the fountainhead of imagination, around which nature dances.

# 2. Bhairava's Secret

*From fear comes all corruption*

The upward palm indicates the promise to remove fear of predation and provide security.

The deer is the symbol of the frightened and restless mind.

The downward palm indicates the promise to remove fear of scarcity and provide nourishment.

South Indian bronze showing deer in Shiva's hand

*B*haya means fear. And the greatest fear of all living creatures is death. Yama is the god of death. We fear him. We do not want to die. We want to survive.

To survive, we need food. But to get food we have to kill. Only by killing a living creature can food be generated. If the deer has to eat, the grass has to die; if the lion has to eat, the deer has to die. The act of killing and the act of feeding are thus two sides of the same coin. Death ends up sustaining life. This is the truth of nature. Shiva is called Kaal Bhairava because he removes the bhaya of kaal, which is time, the devourer of all living things.

Fear of death leads to two kinds of fears as it transforms all living creatures either into predator or prey. The fear of scarcity haunts the predator as it hunts for food; the fear of predation haunts the prey as it avoids being hunted. Nature has no favourites. Both the lion and the deer have to run in order to survive. The lion runs to catch its prey and the deer runs to escape its predator. The deer may be prey to the lion, but it is predator to the grass. Thus no one in nature is a mere victim. Without realising it every victim is a victimiser, and there is no escape from this cycle of life.

Fear of death creates the food chain comprising the eaters and the eaten. Fear of death is what makes animals migrate in search of pastures and hunting grounds. Fear of death establishes the law of the jungle that might is right. Fear of death is what makes animals establish pecking orders and territories. Fear of death makes animals respect and yearn for strength and cunning, for only then

The head houses the brain which is the seat of imagination.

The human gaze gives value to things, and therefore creates hierarchy in nature.

The moustache reinforces the gender of the head.

Humans can imagine a world without fear or a world of amplified fears.

The male head that is often placed over a Shiva-linga

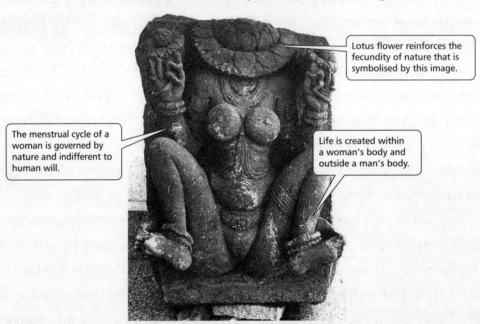

Lotus flower reinforces the fecundity of nature that is symbolised by this image.

The menstrual cycle of a woman is governed by nature and indifferent to human will.

Life is created within a woman's body and outside a man's body.

Stone carving of headless female body known as Lajja-gauri

can they survive.

Such behaviour based on fear is appropriate for the beast or pashu, but not humans. Humans have imagination and hence the wherewithal to break free from animal instincts. Humans need not be territorial or dominating in order to survive. Humans need not form packs or herds in order to survive. Humans can break free from the fear of death, shatter the mental modifications emerging from time. Humans need not be predator or prey, victim or victimiser. Shiva, who rises out of the endless pillar of fuel-less fire, shows the way.

Shiva reveals the power of the higher brain over the lower brain, the human brain over the animal brain. That is why he is called Pashu-pati, master of animal instincts. He offers the promise of a-bhaya, the world where there is no fear of scarcity or predator, in other words no fear of death. Shiva offers immortality.

Because humans have the ability to imagine, humans stand apart from the rest of nature. This division is the primal division described in the *Rig Veda*. On one side stands nature, the web of life, the chain of eaters and eaten. On the other stands the human being who can imagine a world where the laws of the jungle can be disregarded, overpowered or outgrown. Humans therefore experience two realities: the objective reality of nature and the subjective reality of their imagination. The former is Prakriti; the latter is Purusha.

Prakriti is nature who has no favourites. Purusha is humanity that invariably favours a few over the rest. In art, Prakriti is visualised as the female body without the head while Purusha is

Painting from Nepal of Bhairavi, the fierce mother goddess

visualised as the male head without the body.

The head is used to represent Purusha because the head houses the brain, which is the seat of imagination. The body without head then comes to represent Prakriti.

The body's gender is feminine because the head has no control over the natural menstrual rhythms of the female body; the arousal of the male body is, by contrast, influenced by the head.

The head's gender is masculine as indicated by the moustache because the male body can create life only outside itself within a female body, just as imagination can only express itself tangibly through nature.

Nature creates and destroys life without prejudice. Human imagination is the seat of prejudice. It has two choices: to imagine a world without fear or to imagine a world with amplified fears. When the Purusha outgrows fear and experiences bliss, it is Shiva, the destroyer of fear. When Purusha amplifies fear and gets trapped in delusions, it is Brahma, the creator of fear. Naturally, the former is considered worthy of worship, not the latter.

A childless couple were once offered a choice: a wise son who would live for sixteen years or a foolish son who would live till he was hundred. The Rishi chose the wise son. In his sixteenth year, Yama, the god of death, came to claim the son who had been named Markandeya by his parents. Yama found Markandeya worshipping a Shiva-linga. 'Let me finish my prayers and then I am ready to die,' said Markandeya. But death waits for no man or prayer. Yama hurled his noose and dispassionately started dragging the boy towards the land of the dead. The boy clung

Mysore painting showing Shiva overpowering Yama

to Shiva's linga and fought back. Yama refused to give up and yanked the boy forcefully. The tug-of-war between the boy and the god of death ended when Shiva emerged from his linga and kicked Yama away. Markandeya declared that Shiva is Yamantaka, he who destroys Yama. Markandeya became the immortal sage.

In this story, wisdom is intertwined with immortality. One becomes immortal when one outgrows the fear of death. Markandeya does at the age of sixteen when he clings to the Shiva-linga, which is the symbol of Purusha or spiritual reality. This is a metaphor for faith. Faith is not rational just as immortality is not natural. Immortality is an idea that appears in the human imagination in response to the fear of death. When one liberates oneself from the fear of death using faith, one becomes indifferent to death. Death then no longer controls us or frightens us. We are liberated. We achieve immortality.

Shiva's ash draws Markandeya's attention to immortality. Shiva smears himself with ash to remind all of the mortality of the body. When a man dies, his body can be destroyed by fire. What outlives the fire and the body is ash, which is indestructible. Ash is thus the symbol of the indestructible soul that occupies the body during life and outlives the body in death. The soul is atma.

Markandeya realises that only the fool derives identity from the temporary flesh; the wise look beyond at the permanent soul. Flesh is tangible but the soul is not. Flesh is fact but the soul demands faith. Atma defines all laws of nature — it has no form, it cannot be measured, it cannot be experienced using any of the five senses. It is a self-assured entity that does not seek acknowledgment or evidence. One has to believe it. There is no other way to access it.

Brahma has no faith. He refuses to look beyond the flesh. He

Poster art showing birth of Brahma

ignores atma, and so catalyses the creation of aham, the ego.

The ego is the product of imagination. It is how a human being sees himself or herself. It makes humans demand a special status in nature and culture. Nature does not care for this self-image of human beings. Culture, which is a man-made creation, attempts to accommodate it.

Brahma is every human being. He is described as emerging from a lotus. This is a metaphor for a child emerging out of the mother's womb. This is also a metaphor for the gradual unfolding of the imagination.

Birth is not a choice. And survival is a struggle, a violent struggle, plagued by fears of scarcity and predation. This is true for plants, animals and humans. But only humans can reflect on these fears and resent it and seek liberation from it.

Imagination makes Brahma think of scarcity in the midst of abundance, war in times of peace. Though he can rein in his fear, he ends up exaggerating fear. He assumes he has no choice in the matter. Like Markandeya, he can imagine Shiva, but unlike Markandeya he does not have faith in Shiva. He therefore does not discover atma, and finds himself alone and helpless before nature, a victim. Who is the cause of this misery, he wonders. Is nature the villain?

Who came first — the victim or the villain, nature or humanity, Prakriti or Brahma? Objectively speaking nature came first. Nature is the parent. Humanity is the child. Subjectively speaking, however, imagination caused the rupture between humanity and nature, imagination forced Purusha to visualise itself as distinct

North Indian miniature painting showing Shiva as Pinaki, the bearer of the bow

from Prakriti. That makes nature the child. Humanity then is the parent. Thus Prakriti is both parent and child of Brahma. He depends on her for his survival, but she is not dependable. She is the cruel mother and the disobedient daughter. He feels ignored and abandoned and helpless and anxious. He blames her for his misery. In fear, he allows his mind to be corrupted.

Brahma's expectations of Prakriti are imaginary. Nature does not love him or hate him. Nature has no favourites. All creatures are equal in Prakriti's gaze. Because Brahma can imagine, he imagines himself to be special and so expects to be treated differently by nature. This is because of the ego.

Brahma renames Prakriti as Shatarupa, she of myriad forms. Some forms nourish him and make him secure. Others frighten him. Brahma seeks to control nature, dominate and domesticate Shatarupa so that she always comforts him. Unlike the Tapasvin who sought liberation from nature, Brahma seeks to control nature.

The *Brihadaranyaka Upanishad* describes how Shatarupa runs taking the form of various animals and how Brahma pursues her taking the form of complementary male animals. When she runs as a goose, he pursues her as a gander. When she runs as a cow, he pursues her as a bull. He becomes the bull-elephant when she is the cow-elephant; he becomes the stallion when she is the mare; he becomes the buck when she becomes the doe. Shatarupa's transformations are natural and spontaneous. Brahma's, however, are the result of choice — he chooses to derive meaning from her, be dependent on her and in the process loses his own identity. The autonomy of his mind is thus lost, its purity corrupted, as it grows

Poster art showing a hooded serpent around Shiva's neck

South Indian painting of Patanjali, the author of the Yoga-sutra

attached to the world.

Brahma's chase of Shatarupa thus entraps him. It is the movement away from stillness and repose towards fear and restlessness, symbolically described as a southern movement, away from the still Pole Star. To stop him, Shiva takes the form of a bowman and raises his bow, the Pinaka, and shoots an arrow to pin Brahma to the sky. In other words, Shiva stills the mind.

The bow is the symbol of concentration and focus and balance, in other words, it is the symbol of yoga. Yoga is a set of practices that stills the restless mind. It is what can pin the deer down. The word yoga comes from the root yuj, meaning to align. Fear destroys the alignment of the mind; rather than accept the reality of nature, the mind seeks to change and control it. These attempts invariably fail, creating frustration and fear and confusion that blinds one to spiritual reality. Yoga restores mental alignment so that nature is seen for what it is. Witnessing Prakriti will provoke the journey towards Purusha. Rather than blaming nature or clinging to the flesh, one will find refuge in atma. Shiva is therefore called Yogeshwara, lord of yoga.

Seated coiled around Shiva's neck is the hooded cobra. The cobra is unique amongst all serpents as it possesses a hood that it spreads whenever it is still. The hooded cobra around Shiva's neck thus represents stillness which contrasts with the restlessness of nature. Shiva pins Brahma down so that he stops and observes nature's dance, and aligns himself with her rhythms rather than manipulating them to suit his whims.

It is said that the serpent around Shiva's neck is Patanjali who wrote the Yoga-sutra, the aphorisms of yoga. In it, he defines yoga as the unbinding of the knots of the imagination. Brahma creates

Poster art of Batuk Bhairava

these knots as he pursues Shatarupa; Shiva destroys them.

In the *Linga Purana*, Shiva howls when he witnesses Brahma chasing Shatarupa. It is a howl of despair and disgust. He mourns the corruption of the mind. Shiva, the howler, is called Rudra.

Rudra watches as Brahma sprouts four heads facing the four directions as he seeks to gaze upon Prakriti at all times in his attempt to control her. Brahma then sprouts a fifth head on top of the first four. This sprouting of heads refers to the gradual contamination of the mind, its knotting and crumpling with fear and insecurity as the desire to dominate and control takes over.

The first four face the reality of nature in every direction; the fifth simply ignores the reality of nature. It is the head of delusion. It is called aham, Brahma's imagination of himself, his self-image or ego. The fifth head of Brahma declares Brahma as the lord and master of Prakriti. This claim over nature is humanity's greatest delusion.

Hoping to shatter this delusion, Shiva uses his sharp nail and wrenches off the fifth head of Brahma. He becomes Kapalika, the skull bearer. Shiva severs the head that deludes Brahma into believing he created objective reality or Prakriti, when in fact he has only created his own subjective reality, the Brahmanda.

Prakriti is nature. Brahmanda is culture. Prakriti creates man. Man creates Brahmanda. Prakriti is objective reality. Brahmanda is subjective reality. Atma witnesses Prakriti, aham constructs Brahmanda.

Kala Bhairava images from temple walls of north India

Every human being has his own cerebrum, hence is subject to his own imagination of his self and the world around him, which is why every human being imagines himself to be special. Every human being is thus Brahma, creator of his own Brahmanda. Prakriti is common to all living creatures but Brahmanda is unique to a Brahma. As many Brahmas, as many imaginations, as many Brahmandas.

Prakriti is the universal mother of all Brahmas. Brahmanda is, however, daughter of the particular Brahma who creates her. Nature does not consider any Brahma special. Every Brahma believes he is special in his own self-constructed subjective reality.

Every human being compares his subjective reality with nature and finds nature inadequate. This dissatisfaction provides an opportunity to outgrow dependence on nature, hence fear. But instead of looking inwards, Brahma looks outwards. Rather than take control of his mind, he chooses to take control of nature. He proceeds to domesticate the world around him. Every Brahma creates Brahmanda for his own pleasure or bhoga, indifferent to the impact it has on others. This self-indulgent act is described in narratives as Brahma pursuing his own daughter. By equating it with incest, a taboo in human society, the scriptures express their disdain for the pursuit of aham over atma, bhoga over yoga.

The story of Brahma chasing his daughter is taken literally to explain why Brahma is not worshipped. Metaphorically, it refers to the inappropriate relationship of humanity and nature. Rather than pursuing atma and becoming independent of nature, man chooses to pursue aham and dominate nature. This does not allay fear, it only amplifies fear.

Shiva mocks Brahma's delusion by always appearing in a state

Tantrik miniature painting of Gora Bhairava and Kala Bhairava

of intoxication. He is always shown drinking or smoking narcotic hemp. In intoxication, one refuses to accept reality and assumes oneself to be the master of the world. When the reference point is aham, not atma, when the world is only Brahmanda not Prakriti, one is as deluded as one who is intoxicated.

Brahmanda creates artificial value. In Brahmanda, we are either heroes or victims who matter. In Prakriti, however, we are just another species of animal who need nourishment and security and who will eventually die.

Realisation of this truth creates angst. Brahma wonders what is the point of existence then. He finds no answer and a sense of invalidation creeps in. It makes him restless and anxious. A life with imagination but no meaning is frightening. The human mind cannot accept this and so goes into denial. It seeks activities that fill the empty void created by time. It seeks to occupy the mind with meaningless activity so that it is distracted from facing the emptiness of existence. That is why human beings get obsessed with games and recreational activities that enable time to pass.

Shiva recognises this and so holds a damaru in his hand. A damaru is a rattle-drum that is used to distract and train a monkey. The monkey here represents the mind which is restless and angst-ridden. Unable to find meaning, it yearns to be occupied. Shiva rattles the drum to comfort Brahma's mind. He hopes that, eventually, Brahma will realise that meaning will only come by moving towards atma rather than aham, pursuing yoga instead of bhoga, choosing Prakriti not Brahmanda.

Recurring theme of three visible in poster images of Shiva

But Brahma stubbornly refuses to take the journey towards Purusha. He is determined to find identity and meaning through Prakriti alone. Brahma divides subjective reality into two parts: what belongs to him and what does not belong to him. Property is thus created. It is humankind's greatest delusion through which humanity seeks to generate meaning and identity.

Animals have territory but humans create property. Territory is held on to by brute force and cunning; it cannot be inherited; it enables animals to survive. Property, on the other hand, is created by man-made rules; take away the rules and there is no property. Rules also govern relationships in culture, creating families to whom property can be bequeathed. Neither wealth nor family is a natural phenomenon, both are cultural constructions, hence need to be codified and enforced through courts.

Through the idea of property, Brahma hopes to outsmart Yama. A human being can die, but his property and his family can outlive him.

Brahma splits Brahmanda into three parts: me, mine and what is not mine. This is Tripura, the three worlds. Each of these three worlds is mortal. The 'me' is made up of the mind and body. 'Mine' is made up of property, knowledge, family and status. 'Not mine' is made up of all the other things that exist in the world over which one has no authority. Even animals have a 'me' but only humans have 'mine' and 'not mine'. Human self-image is thus expanded beyond the body and includes possessions.

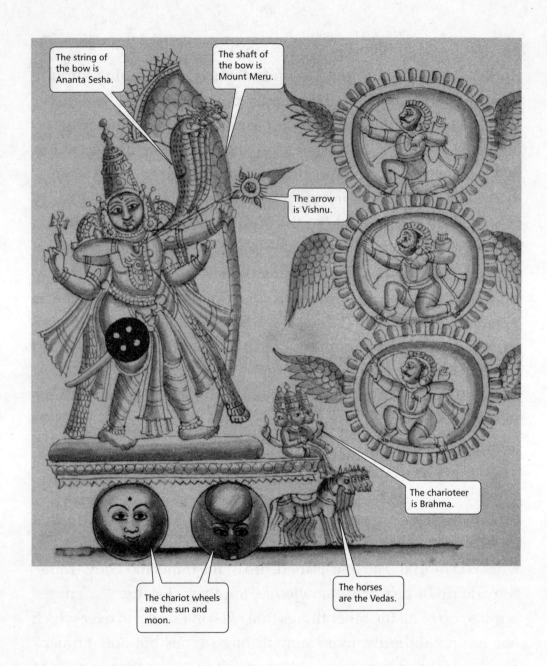

South Indian painting of Shiva as Tripurantaka, destroying three cities

Humans identify themselves with other things beside their body, hence get hurt when those things get attacked. A man derives his self-worth from his looks and his car. When his looks go, or his car gets damaged, his tranquillity is lost. Tranquillity is also lost when he yearns for things that are not his, things that belong to others. Anxiety and restlessness thus have roots in the notions of 'mine' and 'not mine', which depend on imagination for their survival.

At every Hindu ritual, 'Shanti, shanti, shanti,' is chanted. This means peace thrice over. Humans yearn to come to terms with the three worlds. This can only happen when we recognise the true nature of the three worlds we have created. Realisation of the true nature of Tripura will unfortunately reveal their mortal nature and the futility of clinging to it. Shiva is Tripurantaka, who reveals this reality and hence destroys Tripura.

The story goes that three demons created three flying cities and spread havoc in the cosmos. So the gods called upon Shiva to destroy these cities. The cities could be destroyed only with a single arrow. And so one had to wait for the right moment when the three cities were perfectly aligned in a straight line. Shiva decided to chase the three cities until this moment arrived.

The earth was Shiva's chariot; the sun and moon were its wheels; the four Vedas were its horses; Brahma himself was the charioteer. Mount Meru, axis of space, was the shaft of Shiva's bow while Sesha, the serpent of time, was the string. Vishnu was the arrow.

Shiva chased the three cities and waited for the moment when they were all aligned. At that moment, he released the arrow and destroyed all three cities in an instant. He collected the ashes of these cities and smeared them across his forehead as three parallel lines. This was the Tripundra, the sacred mark of Shiva. It

Kaal Bhairava drives away malevolent spirits.

The fearsome Bhairava who protects Nepal

He is known as the Kotwal or the policeman of Kashi, who protects Prakriti from the ego of humanity.

Kaal Bhairava of Varanasi

communicated to the world that the body, the property and the rest of nature, the three worlds created by Brahma, are mortal. When they are destroyed, what remains is Purusha, the soul.

The lines are drawn horizontally. In mythic art, vertical lines associated with Vishnu represent activity, while horizontal lines represent inertia. Shiva's mark is horizontal to remind us that nothing needs to be done actively to destroy the three worlds. Eventually, inevitably, the body will die, the property will go and the divide between 'mine' and 'not mine' will collapse as Prakriti stakes her claim. Shiva has infinite patience, which is why he is able to wait for the moment when the three cities align themselves, ready to be struck down by his arrow.

The number three plays a key role in Shiva's mythology. His sacred mark is composed of three parallel lines. He holds in his hand a trident, a weapon with three blades. He is offered in temples the sacred bilva leaf which is a sprig with three leaves. Shiva holds the shaft of the trident just as the devotee holds the stem of the bilva sprig. What is held is the immortal soul; the three blades and the three leaves represent the three worlds that Brahma creates and values, which need to be given up if one seeks, 'Shanti, shanti, shanti.'

Bhairava or Hara, the remover of fear, is visualised as a child riding a dog and holding a human head in his hand. The childlike form of Bhairava is to draw attention to his innocence and purity. There is no guile behind his actions. The head that he holds in his hand is the fifth head of Brahma, which is full of amplified fear and has no faith. This fifth head constructs the self-image. This fifth head

Southeast-Asian image of Bhairava

constructs Tripura, which Shiva destroys. The dog that Bhairava rides represents the human mind and how it regresses to animal nature when governed by fear.

Symbolically speaking, dogs are considered inauspicious in Hinduism. Dogs are most attached to their masters: wagging their tail when they get approval and attention, and whining when they do not. This makes the dog the symbol of the ego. Like the dog, aham blooms when praised and given attention, and it withers when ignored. Ego or ahamkara has no independent existence of its own but is constructed by Brahma and dependent on Brahmanda in an attempt to outgrow fear. It ends up amplifying fear.

Dogs also remind us of the notion of territory. Dogs spray urine to mark their territory; even when they are domesticated and provided for, they mark territory, indicating their lack of faith. They bark and bite to defend their territory. They fight over bones with other dogs. While dogs do it for their survival, humans behave similarly as they fight over their property and defend their rights. Humans seek the survival not of their bodies, as in the case of animals, but of their self-image, which is a combination of body and property. Property includes not just wealth, but also family and status. Without property there is no meaning, without meaning there is only fear.

Bhairava rides the dog to remind us of our animal instincts and our amplified fears that have constructed the notion of property. Like dogs we cling to 'me' and 'mine' and are wary of what is 'not mine'. We call this love, but it is in fact attachment, as they give us identity and meaning. Bhairava invites us to break this attachment, cut the fifth head of Brahma, cleanse the mind of all corruption, and discover the world where there is genuine freedom from fear.

Poster art of Datta, the gentle form of Bhairava

Many followers of Shiva worship Bhairava in a gentler form, as Datta, the three-headed sage who has four dogs around him and a cow behind him. Datta is called Adi-nath, the primal teacher of all mendicants.

Datta's three heads represent Brahma, Vishnu and Shiva, who constantly create, sustain and destroy. The future is created, the present is sustained and the past is destroyed. Datta does not cling to any construction. He does not fear any destruction.

His four dogs are a reminder of our fears. The cow reminds us of our faith. The cow walks behind Datta; he does not turn around to check if she is following him. He knows she is. The dogs are our fears walking in front of Datta, constantly turning back to see if he is behind them. They do not have faith. They constantly need reassurance.

Datta wanders freely without a care in the world. Nothing fetters him. No property binds him. Having achieved the full potential of his human brain, he has outgrown fear. He trusts nature. Prakriti, visualised as the headless female body, who is Bhairavi, for the frightened Brahma, ends up as his companion, his friend, his mother, sister and daughter. He is at peace with the world.

# 3. Shankara's Secret

*Without empathy there is no evolution*

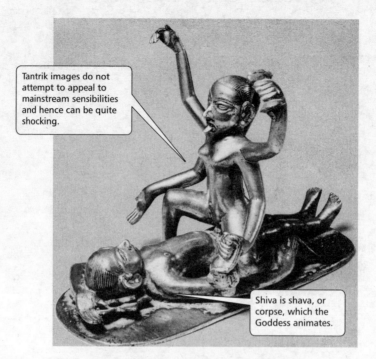

Tantrik imagery showing Kali forcing an indifferent Shiva to copulate

Poster art showing Kali standing atop Shiva, forcing him to awaken

$S$hiva is Rudra, the angry god. He is angry with Brahma because Brahma seeks freedom from fear by trying to control Prakriti rather than by seeking Purusha. In anger, he beheads Brahma, then shuts his eyes and immerses himself in the infinite bliss of an unfettered consciousness, sat-chitta-ananda. Liberated from all things sensory, nature has no effect on him.

Physics informs us that a surface looks white when all the colours in the light spectrum are reflected back. Shiva reflects back all things material. He holds on to nothing. To him, everything is as ephemeral as camphor. That is why he is called Karpura Gauranga, he who is as white as camphor.

But what is the point of wisdom if divorced from the world? Wisdom is meaningless if it does not enable the liberation of those who are trapped in fear. That is why the Goddess stands in opposition of Shiva as both the radiant Gauri, producing light, and as the dark Kali, consuming light. While Shiva sits still in the north, she comes forth swaying from the south as Dakshina-Kali, demanding to be seen. Nature will not be ignored.

The Goddess is naked with hair untied and drinks blood. Her nakedness is an invitation to sex, hence to childbirth and life. Her lust for blood is her acceptance of death. She is both life and death. Her unbound hair is a reminder that she is wild and raw. She is Shakti, energy, constantly on the move. He, on the other hand, is still like the hooded cobra. He shuts his eyes to her.

In Indian philosophy, a thing exists when it is seen. And a creature is alive when it sees. Shiva's eyes are shut, meaning he is indifferent to the fears of those around him. Shakti, the mother,

Shiva with the Goddess who holds up a mirror

will not allow that. If she is Bhairavi, inducing fear, she needs Bhairava to enable the frightened to outgrow fear. Without Shiva, Brahma will remain finite and never realise his divine potential.

Brahma's eyes are open, but he sees only his own fears, not those of others around him. Consumed by his own Brahmanda, he does not realise each one of those around him has a Brahmanda of his or her own. He needs to look at others, recognise that every man and every woman has his or her own subjective reality, his or her own unique way of looking at the world. He needs to have empathy.

Looking at others is called darshan. Brahma looks at others in fear: he pursues them as he pursues Shatarupa. He seeks them when they comfort him; he shuns them if they frighten him. When he looks at them, he wonders if they are 'mine' or 'not mine'. A gaze that is born of fear, a gaze that excludes and exploits is not darshan. Darshan is gaze that is free of fear. Darshan is gaze that looks at the other for its own sake not because it is 'mine' or 'not mine'. Darshan is an empathy-filled gaze. We see people around us as deer who fear predators, or as lions who fear scarcity and seek prey, or as dogs who bark when threatened or whine when ignored. Darshan enables us to see people's thinking patterns or mind-sets. We recognise the Brahma and identify the Brahmanda around them. We see the pashu — dependent on Prakriti, frightened of Yama, lacking faith in atma and seeking refuge in aham.

When we genuinely do darshan, we discover how the other reacts to us. That is, the other ends up as a mirror or darpan, reflecting who we are. If people around us behave like deer, it means we are behaving like lions. If people around us behave like lions, it means they see us as deer. If people around us behave like dogs, friendly or hostile, it means we matter to them.

South Indian stone sculpture showing Shiva as Pinaki, the bearer of the bow

The Goddess wants humans to look at humans as humans. This will not happen as long as fear governs the relationship. Simply cutting Brahma's head will not remedy the situation. Some hand-holding is required. Just as Brahma needs to have faith in Shiva, Shiva needs to have patience with Brahma. For this, Shiva has to first engage with the world, not withdraw from it. Determined to get Pashu-pati to help humans, Shakti dances on top of him. She hopes to transform Shiva, the insensitive, angry god, into Shankara, the god who empathises and is patient.

In the lore of Shiva, Brahma is treated as Shakti's father and Shiva is her beloved. Brahma behaves as a father should not behave, when he seeks to control his daughter. For this act, Shiva beheads him. Shiva behaves as a beloved should not behave, when he shuts his eyes to Shakti. The Goddess negotiates with both father and beloved. The father needs to trust and the beloved needs to pay attention. A relationship is needed for harmony to exist.

The Puranas inform us that Brahma gives birth to 'mind-born' sons, which means sons created without copulating with a woman. This is a metaphor for mental modification, a twisting and folding of the pristine imagination as it experiences more and more fear. One of these sons is called Daksha, the skilled one. His name alludes to Dakshin, the south, the land of movement, birth and death. The birth of Daksha is Brahma's response to nature.

Daksha also means the skilled one. He is skilled at coping with nature's transformation. He does so by establishing culture through the ritual of yagna.

Yagna is all about controlling wild nature and domesticating

Daksha performing a yagna

Devdutt Pattanaik

it so that it comes under human control, becomes manageable, predictable, hence less frightening. Yagna is a metaphor for domestication. Yagna involves domestication of fire, limiting it to a sacrificial altar. Yagna involves domestication of water, limiting it to a pot. Yagna involves domestication of plants and animals; some become auspicious offerings while others remain inauspicious outsiders. Yagna involves domestication of humans through rules, regulations and rituals; everyone has a different role and responsibility with respect to the ritual, hence to society. Yagna thus transforms forest into field, wild animals into pets and beasts of burden, man into husband, woman into wife, and humans to members of castes, clans and communities. Yagna thus creates hierarchy. And, therefore, the *Rig Veda* holds yagna as the core of human activity. It refers to society as a human organism, or Purusha. It refers to dismemberment of this Purusha as hierarchies are established and humans are classified and differentiated.

Through Daksha, Brahma becomes domesticator of nature and creator of culture. In exchange for domestication, yagna grants abundance and security and so promises the end of fear.

But end of fear for whom? Daksha is Praja-pati, master of the people. He is not Pashu-pati, master of animal instincts. Daksha seeks to dominate people around him rather than outgrow his own fears. His gaze is outward not inward. He seeks to control nature around him in order to feel secure. He seeks to domesticate everyone around him. He is not willing to question his own delusions which cause the amplification of his own fears. He is the alpha male, no different from the lion in the jungle that uses force to dominate and control his pride of lionesses. He remains pashu.

Chandra rides an antelope, symbol of restlessness and helplessness.

Poster art of Chandra, the moon-god

Shiva is the source of unending power that helps the waning moon wax.

The moon in final phase of waning sits on Shiva's head

Daksha finds nature inhabited by two sets of divine beings: the Devas who live in the sky and the Asuras who live under the earth. Under the earth, withheld by Asuras, is all the wealth that society needs — plants and metals. The Devas provide the wherewithal — heat, light, wind, fire, rain — to draw this subterranean wealth out. With the help of the Devas, Daksha gets access to wealth hoarded by the Asuras. For Daksha, Devas are therefore 'gods' while Asuras are 'demons'.

Yagna is the ritual performed to make the Devas stronger so as to defeat and kill Asuras. Daksha establishes a relationship with the Devas by offering them his daughters as their wives. This is a transactional relationship. If either the Devas or his daughters do not comply with this arrangement, he loses his temper.

Daksha gives twenty-eight of his daughters, the Nakshatras, to Chandra, the moon-god. The moon, however, prefers only one of them, Rohini, lavishing her with attention while neglecting the others. Upset, one of the Nakshatras, Abhijit, withers away in sorrow, while the other twenty-six daughters complain to Daksha, who curses Chandra to suffer from the wasting disease. As the days pass, Chandra starts to wane, much to Daksha's satisfaction. A distraught Chandra turns to Shiva, the god who defeats Yama. Shiva, who is Mrityunjaya, conqueror of death, places Chandra on his forehead. This contact enables Chandra to wax once again, much to Daksha's irritation. Shiva is therefore known as Chandrashekhara, on whose head sits the moon.

Daksha takes the life of one who does not align to his rules; Shiva gives life instead and expects nothing in return, least of all

North Indian painting showing Sati with Shiva

obedience. The Devas therefore call Shiva Maha-deva, the greatest of gods, he who is God, hence independent of nature's laws.

Daksha does not consider Shiva to be Maha-deva. He views Shiva as the enemy who opposes him. Shiva seems to side with the Asuras by giving their guru, Shukra, the secret knowledge of resurrection known as Sanjivani Vidya. Using Sanjivani Vidya, Shukra is able to bring back to life all the Asuras killed by the Devas. That is why, much to Daksha's exasperation, wild nature cannot be permanently domesticated. Eventually fields and orchards are overrun by weeds and forests season after season, children of domesticated animals remain wild and have to be broken generation after generation, rules once instituted have to be reinforced year after year. Yagnas have to be performed again and again to keep intact the crucible of culture.

What Daksha fails to realise is that Shiva does not distinguish between Devas and Asuras; he is indifferent to their station or their roles. One is not the hero and the other is not the villain. Shiva does not share the prejudices that shape Daksha's thoughts.

For Daksha, obedience is virtue. He excludes those who do not obey him. Asuras do not obey him, Chandra does not obey him, Shiva does not obey him. Asuras are therefore sacrificed during the yagna; Chandra is tolerated only when he agrees to share his attention between all his wives; but Shiva is always excluded, as Shiva remains indifferent to him.

To Daksha's vexation, his youngest daughter, Sati, disobeys him. One day she sees Shiva wandering in the mountains. She recognises him for who he is and falls in love with him. She expresses her

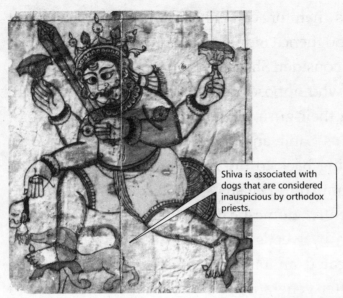

Shiva is associated with dogs that are considered inauspicious by orthodox priests.

Manuscript painting of Bhairava

Shiva is associated with corpses and the ash of the crematorium, hence considered inauspicious.

Temple wall carving of Bhairava

desire to be his wife. Her father refuses to grant permission but she is adamant. Shiva does not pay her any attention, but it does not deter her; she is in love. Daksha refuses to accept Shiva as his son-in-law and include him in his household. So Sati leaves her father's house to become Shiva's wife.

Rather than understanding Sati, Daksha is angry. Sati's defiance makes him feel insignificant. So he refuses to acknowledge her independence. He blames Shiva for Sati's behaviour. To teach both Shiva and Sati a lesson, he conducts a grand yagna. All Devas are invited to Daksha's sacrificial hall to partake the sacrificial offerings. Everyone except Shiva and Sati are called. Through exclusion, Daksha seeks to teach both of them a lesson. He hopes to eventually domesticate them.

Shiva does not care. But Sati is upset. Why has she not been invited? Maybe it is just an oversight, she thinks, and insists on going back to her father's house. Shiva does not stop her. She comes of her own free will and she is leaving of her own free will. He simply says, 'The oversight is intentional.' Sati does not listen.

When she enters the sacrificial hall, she expects to be greeted by her loving father. Instead she is humiliated. 'Why have you come? You were not called,' says Daksha. Sati demands to know why Shiva has not been invited. He is also a son-in-law, one even the Devas respect. Daksha snarls, 'I will not invite a man who does not care for culture and who is even indifferent to nature. Look at him. He wanders around naked, smears his body with ash, smokes narcotics, dances in crematoriums, takes refuge in caves and mountains, has no home, has dogs and ghosts and snakes as his companions. He is filthy and vile and disgusting and unworthy of any sacrificial offering. He is not welcome in my house. And if

South Indian temple wall image of Virabhadra attacking Daksha

you have any shame, you will stay out too.'

Sati knows that her father's insults do not matter to her husband. Daksha seeks control; Shiva lives in freedom. But she wants her father to see sense, recognise the Maha-deva, the god who gives life. She also wants her husband to see sense, realise that engaging with Daksha is critical. How else will Daksha outgrow his desire for control? How else will Daksha outgrow his fears? How else will Praja-pati understand Pashu-pati?

So Sati leaps into the sacrificial fire and sets herself ablaze. She makes herself the offering to the one who is denied offering by Daksha. She burns for Shiva.

When Sati follows Shiva, she does it out of unconditional love. She does not expect him to change. She serves him without asking anything in return. Shiva remains the wandering Tapasvin. She accepts him as he is. This is why the word 'sati' means a devoted wife.

But Sati's unquestioning, undemanding company dents Shiva's indifference. Following her self-immolation, he is forced to look at her. He does Sati's darshan — finds a charred corpse in the sacrificial altar. Sati becomes his mirror, his darpan. Her painful death is a reflection of his indifference and her father's fear of her independence. When he learns that no one came to her rescue, he realises how much fear governs the world of Praja-pati, making people submit to the most unreasonable demands. He decides to show Praja-pati a fear greater than all others fears. His righteous outrage takes the form of Virabhadra, a terrifying warrior.

Virabhadra leads an army of ghosts and goblins, of Ganas and

Modern sculpture of Shiva with the body of Sati

South Indian painting of Daksha with the head of a goat

Pramathas, all inauspicious and wild creatures, into Daksha's sacrificial hall and goes about destroying the precinct. Everything that is holy is rendered unholy. Urine, sputum, blood and vomit are poured into the pots and pans. Screams and shouts and cackles replace the melodious hymns. Order is disrupted. The guests run and scream in fear. There is chaos and cacophony. Dogs howl. Ghosts screech. Virabhadra finally finds Daksha and beheads him.

As Virabhadra, Shiva beheads Daksha just as he had beheaded Brahma in the form of Kapalika. The severing of the creator's head is a recurring theme in Hindu mythology. This follows the abuse of the Goddess. Brahma lusts for Shatarupa and Daksha insults Sati. With the act of beheading, Shiva condemns the misuse of the human mind to control and domesticate nature and to create a self-image that deludes one to justify such action. Rather than exploring the possibility of outgrowing fear, humans are indulging animal instincts. Rather than discovering the infinite, humans are choosing to entrap themselves in the finite.

Shiva lifts the corpse of Sati in his arms and wanders the hills, howling in pain. In sorrow, even Shiva forgets that he who can restore Chandra, he who can give Sanjivani Vidya to the Asuras, can resurrect anyone. Indifferent to her all her life, Shiva misses her in death and so experiences pain and weeps. His howling is so intense that the universe is unable to bear its burden. So Vishnu hurls his discus, the Sudarshan Chakra, and cuts Sati's body into 108 pieces. Each piece falls on earth and transforms into a Shakti-pitha, the seat of the Goddess.

With the body gone, Shiva regains his composure. The Devas beg him to forgive Daksha. They beg him to resurrect Daksha so that the yagna is not left unfinished. Shiva replaces Daksha's head

Miniature Indian painting of Kama

with that of a male goat, which was supposed to be the sacrificial offering. Symbolically, he reminds Daksha what true sacrifice is — the sacrifice of one's animal nature and the realisation of one's human nature. Only then will Praja-pati become Pashu-pati. Only then will fear give way to tranquillity.

Shiva then withdraws to his mountain of snow under the Pole Star. He withdraws into a cave. Like a turtle, his senses once again stop engaging with Prakriti. The endless pillar of fuel-less fire burns again.

The story is far from over as far as the Goddess is concerned. This is merely part one of a two-act play. In Prakriti, death is merely a comma, not a full stop. What goes around always comes around. What went away as Sati will surely return, but embodied in a different form.

As Sati, the Goddess has opened Shiva's heart to feeling. He experiences loss and reacts with passion. But now the Goddess wants his engagement with the world to be more considered, emerging out of concern and affection, not rage. Only then will Shiva truly be Shankara.

So the Goddess takes birth as Parvati, daughter of Himavan, king of mountains. Shiva's abode, Kailasa, is located atop Himalaya, the abode of snow. That is her father's kingdom. He is her father's guest. Just like Sati in her previous life, Parvati decides Shiva shall be her husband. He may be an avowed hermit, but she will make him a householder.

To help Parvati awaken Shiva, the Devas enlist the help of Kama, the god of desire. They tell him to shoot his arrows at Shiva when

Poster art showing Shiva setting Kama aflame

the Goddess approaches him.

Kama is described as a cheerful god who rides a parrot and has as his weapon a bow whose shaft is made of sugar cane and string made of bees. His arrows are made of flowers with which he stirs the five senses. His companions are Vasanta, god of spring, and Rati, the goddess of lovemaking. His entourage is made up of Apsaras, dancing damsels, and Gandharvas, celestial musicians. They hold aloft his banner, which displays his symbol, the Makara, the constellation Capricorn. When the sun enters this constellation, winter gives way to spring, the cold earth is warmed with desire and, like a flower, opens itself to the sky.

With the aid of Kama, Indra has managed to destroy the tapasya of many a Tapasvin. Kama's arrows have made upward flowing semen of hermits flow downwards. Rather than igniting tapa in their minds and throwing light on Purusha, it has flowed out into Prakriti to create a child. They have thus been fettered by nature and denied liberation.

Shiva, however, is no ordinary Tapasvin. He is the Purusha. He is Pashu-pati. When Kama shoots his arrows, Shiva remains unaffected. He simply opens his third eye. Out comes a missile of flames and sets Kama ablaze. Rati and Parvati watch in horror as Kama is reduced to ashes. Shiva remains as tranquil as ever. The phallus remains self-stirred and his eyes remain shut. He remains indifferent to Prakriti. By this act, Yamantaka, the destroyer of death, also becomes Kamantaka, the destroyer of desire, hence life.

The third eye of Shiva indicates transcendental wisdom. Implicit in the idea of desire, is the idea of choice. Desire means the quest

Stone carvings from Southeast Asia and north India showing Parvati meditating

Poster art showing Shiva appearing before Parvati

for one thing over another. To want something one must not want another thing. In other words, one needs two eyes, one that selects and the other that rejects. When both eyes are shut it means nothing is selected or rejected, nothing is approved or disapproved, nothing is included or excluded. Everything is the same. The third eye therefore embodies absence of discrimination and choice, hence absence of desire. Kama is unable to open Shiva's two eyes. He succumbs to Shiva's third eye. Parvati, however, refuses to accept defeat. She is determined to make Shiva open his two eyes — not by force or cunning, as Kama tries to do, but by his own volition.

Parvati, a princess of the mountains, decides to turn to tapasya to awaken the Tapasvin. She rejects her colourful clothes, her jewellery, her cosmetics, drapes herself in bark and proceeds to invoke Shiva. She prays to him with single-minded devotion, standing on one toe in the cold, immersing herself in freezing water, surrounding herself with fire. She does not eat or drink. She tortures her body to demonstrate her determination and her devotion. She becomes the Tapasvini.

Parvati's austerities form the root of the ritual known as vrata, during which women of the household fast and stay awake all night hoping to change the fortunes of their household and bring in luck and health and prosperity. In life, all circumstances are determined by karma. Every event in our life is determined by past actions. So every moment is as it is supposed to be. But it is possible to change one's fate and fortunes. The dance of Prakriti can change if Purusha intervenes. For that, one has to invoke Purusha through acts of determination that demonstrate desire and devotion.

Parvati is as firm as the mountain she is born of. Her determination is a measure of her devotion and her devotion

Mysore painting of Kama

Poster art of Kamakshi

stems from desire. She desires Shiva. She wants him to open his eyes. She wants him to embrace her and engage with the world. She wants to shatter his indifference.

Parvati's tapasya is different from that of other Tapasvins. Many Asuras and Devas and Rishis like Markandeya perform tapasya and invoke God. They ask for boons that benefit themselves. Parvati seeks from Shiva a boon that benefits others. She wants Shiva not for her pleasure but for the benefit of the world. Through her austerities she hopes to evoke compassion and empathy in his heart. Without him, all living creatures are fettered to nature. He will liberate them. They are bound by gravity; he will release them with his grace.

In the *Shiva Purana*, it is said that Parvati's actions stir Shiva. He opens his eyes and moves towards her. At first he tests her resolve. 'Are you sure you want to marry a wandering mendicant, a good-for-nothing vagabond?' Parvati says yes. 'Don't you want a more worthy groom? A more handsome, stronger and richer groom?' Parvati says no. He tries to distract and dissuade her, but he fails.

So intense is Parvati's devotion that he finally succumbs. 'Ask and it shall be yours,' he says. She asks that he become her groom. He agrees. She asks that he come to her house and ask her father for her hand in marriage. She is not willing to run away from her father's house as she did in her last birth as Sati.

Shiva looks at Parvati and recognises Sati. If he shuts his eyes to her, she will once again transform into Kali, wild and fearsome. If he opens his eyes to her, she will become the gentle and demure Gauri. The world is frightening when nature is seen without wisdom; the world is beautiful when nature is seen through wisdom. Parvati holds her mirror to Shiva, and Shiva finds himself reflected in it as the attentive Shankara.

The three-legged Bhringi.

Mysore painting of gods at the court of Shiva and Parvati

Shiva acknowledges the value of Prakriti by marrying Parvati, princess of the mountains.

Poster art showing Shiva's marriage

And so Shiva comes on his bull with his Ganas to the abode of Himavan and asks for Parvati's hand in marriage. It is given, and she goes to Kailasa with him as his wife with her father's blessing. Thus is Shiva domesticated by Shakti. The hermit turns into Shankara, the householder. The Goddess is therefore called Kamakshi or Kamakhya, she in whose eyes resides Kama. She is visualised as holding in her hands all the symbols associated with Kama: the sugar cane, flowers and parrot. In her body, Kama is reborn but qualified with devotion.

Shiva refuses to respond to lust. That is why Kama fails. Shiva responds to prayer. That is why Kamakshi succeeds. She does not force Shiva to engage with the world; she beseeches him to do so. Unlike Sati who followed him rejecting her father, Parvati insists that he come to her and seek approval of her father. The relationship of Shiva, Sati and Daksha is a negative one with an indifferent husband and an angry father. The relationship of Shankara, Parvati and Himavan is a positive one, with a concerned husband and a loving father.

Had Kama established the relationship between Shiva and Parvati, it would have been a relationship based on power between the temptress (Parvati) and the tempted (Shiva); it would have been the reverse of the relationship between Brahma, who seeks to conquer, and Shatarupa, who refuses to be conquered. The relationship between Shiva and Parvati is not based on power. There is no conqueror and there is no conquest. Each one allows the other to dominate. Neither seeks to dominate the other. This is love.

Bengali Kalighat painting of Shiva as half Goddess

In south India, the marriage of Shiva and Shakti turns the Goddess from a wild warrior woman into a demure consort. The domestication is mutual. While he stops being a hermit, she stops being wild. He surrenders to become the householder, and she surrenders to be his wife. From the fearsome Bhairavi, she becomes the pretty Lalita, as Shiva transforms into Shankara.

After Shiva's marriage, Bhringi, a follower of Shiva, wanted to go around Shiva. Shiva said, 'You have to go around Shakti too. I am incomplete without her.' But Bhringi refused. He tried to slip in between the God and the Goddess. So the Goddess sat on Shiva's thigh, making it difficult for Bhringi to pass between the two. Bhringi then took the form of a bee, intending to fly through the gap between their necks, thus completing his round of Shiva and excluding Shakti. Shiva then merged his body with Shakti. He became Ardhanareshwara, God who is half-woman, making it impossible for Bhringi to make his way between the two. Shakti cursed Bhringi that he would lose all parts of the body that come from the mother — the soft flesh and fluid blood. Bhringi was reduced to bones and nerves, parts that come from his father. Bhringi could not stand up as a result of this. So Shiva gave him a third leg. This Gana made of bones and stripped of flesh stands like a tripod next to Shiva and Shakti to remind the world that Shiva cannot be acknowledged without acknowledging the Goddess. By making Shakti half his body, Shiva declares to the world he is indeed Shankara, who empathises with the imperfections of worldly life.

In Shiva temples, Shiva cannot be worshipped without

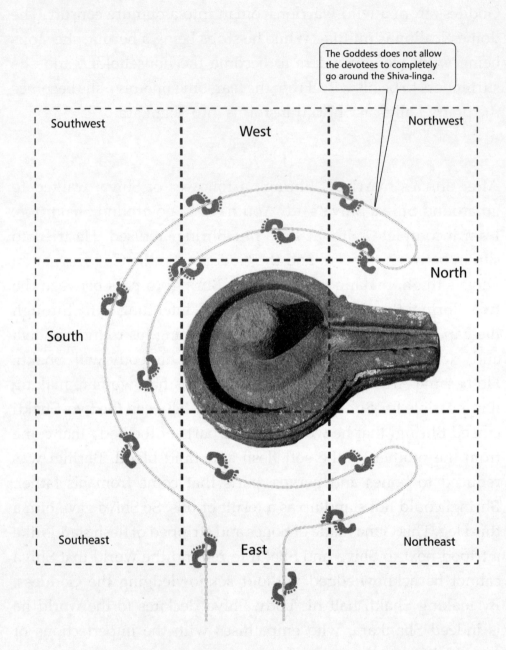

The Goddess does not allow the devotees to completely go around the Shiva-linga.

Southwest

West

Northwest

North

South

Southeast

East

Northeast

Shiva-linga and the directions

acknowledging the Goddess. The linga stone rises from a leaf-shaped trough that points north towards the Pole Star. This is the yoni, the entrance to the womb of the Goddess. The temple, or garbha griha, is the container of the womb into which Shiva has been drawn. She envelops him. Only through her can he be realised. Neither imagination, nor the wisdom that bursts out of it, has any meaning without nature. Wisdom exists for the world. Shiva and Shakti thus form one single unit.

One can go around the Shiva-linga but not completely; the circular path around is blocked by the tip of the trough. After moving clockwise, one has to turn around and move back around the linga once again in the counter-clockwise direction. Thus in a Shiva temple, the devotee moves from northeast to northwest and northwest to northeast, always traversing the south but never the north, a reminder that to reach Pashu-pati one has to live in the realm of Praja-pati. This realm is imperfect and frightening. Here, people often succumb to fears. But Shiva will not abandon them. Coaxed by Shakti, he will patiently wait for man to outgrow these fears until the river that flows southwards will turn to move northwards, pass through Kashi and eventually reach Kailasa.

# 4. Bholenath's Secret

*Culture is a human delusion*

North Indian Tantrik miniature painting of Kali on top of Shiva

South Indian poster art showing Shakti sitting on Shiva

*I*n nature, animals have sex in the mating season to procreate. It is an instinct that ensures survival, governed by hormones and an internal clock. It is not a choice and it is not accompanied by an orgasm. Only in humans is sex a choice and a pleasure-seeking activity that need not culminate in procreation. Shiva is immortal, so does not need to procreate. Shiva is in a state of eternal bliss and so does not seek pleasure-seeking activities. He needs nothing and wants nothing. He is therefore autonomous, independent of nature. So when Shiva opens his eyes and accepts the Goddess, he does so out of grace. But being ignorant of worldly ways, he does not know how to make love to her. So the Goddess sits on top of him and guides him in the ways of the world.

One day, a group of sages paid a visit to Mount Kailasa and found Shakti on top of Shiva. An embarrassed Shakti covered her face with a lotus flower. Shiva, however, innocent of worldly ways, experienced no shame or embarrassment and continued as before. The sages were shocked. They realised Shiva did not intend to shock them: he simply did not know that his behaviour was socially inappropriate. He was ignorant. More appropriately, he was innocent. His mind was pure, untouched by demands of society. They declared he was Bhole-nath, the master who has no guile. He was the simpleton sage.

But culture is neither innocent nor ignorant. Culture's rules and prejudices would not look upon Shiva's activity favourably. It would embarrass, discomfort and confuse devotees. So the sages declared that no one would see Shakti and Shiva locked in intimate embrace, through which the Goddess sought to get Shiva to engage

Shiva withdraws like a turtle into its shell.

Turtle in front of Shiva temple

People clap on entering the Shiva temple to awaken the drowsy Shiva.

Pot represents the Goddess who keeps Shiva awake.

Dripping pot above Shiva-linga

with the world. Instead, this embrace would be visualised as a symbol. That is why the divine couple is worshipped as a linga-yoni combine.

Like the turtle placed before the Shiva-linga, Shiva seeks to slip away into his shell. So the Goddess has to work hard to keep his eyes open and his attention focused on the affairs of man. She turns into a pot that hangs above Shiva. The dripping water from the hole in the base ensures that Shiva does not slip into a trance, and that he is forever gracing his devotees with his benevolent gaze. He is like the hooded serpent: still, alert and aware of those before him. The water dripping from the pot is a reminder that time is running out; as water slowly drains out of the pot, breath is draining out of our body. We have but this lifetime as a human being to discover Purusha, or we will remain pashu despite being blessed with human imagination.

Shiva does not seek to defy or deny the value of cultural rules, rites and rituals. He is simply ignorant of them. He is not a rebel; he is simple and pure. This is most evident during the marriage of Shiva and Parvati.

Parvati insists that Shiva come to her house like a groom and ask her father for her hand in marriage. When her mother, Mena, and her sisters, step out to welcome the groom, the sight that awaits them horrifies them.

Unlike normal grooms who come on a mare, Shiva comes on a bull. Instead of being draped in fine cloth and sandal paste, he comes wrapped in animal hide and smeared with ash. Instead of garlands round his neck, he has serpents. Instead of bearing

North Indian Pahari miniature painting of Shiva's wedding procession

South Indian temple carving showing Parvati seeking Shiva's empathy

a sword, he holds in his hand a trident. Music is created not by flutes but by rattle-drums. His attendants are demons and ghosts and goblins and witches, Ganas and Pramathas and Yakshas and Bhutas. They have claws and fangs and bloodshot eyes. Everyone, Shiva included, drinks bhang, narcotic hemp, not from cups but from skulls.

Shiva's wild, uncouth form can be either frightening or endearing. The frightening form is called Kala-Bhairava, or the dark one. This form of Shiva is offered alcohol in temples. The endearing form is called Gora-Bhairava, or the light one. This form of Shiva is offered milk and sweetmeats and is also known as Batuk Bhairava or Bholenath.

Parvati's mother, Mena, is disgusted by Shiva's uncouth form. Parvati's sisters and aunts make fun of her. Parvati's father, Himavan, cannot understand her daughter's choice of husband. He is a barbarian: a wild, uncouth hermit.

The Goddess realises the tension between her father and her groom. This had happened before when she was Sati and her father was Daksha. She goes to Shiva and falls at his feet and prays to him, 'They are not enlightened enough to understand who you are. But you are enlightened enough to understand where they come from. So only you can salvage this situation. Behave as they wish you to. Indulge them so that they acknowledge and accommodate you. Only when you engage with them will they eventually realise you.'

And so, Shiva, touched by Parvati's sensitivity to him and her family, decides to indulge the world. He transforms into Soma-sundara, the one who is as beautiful as the moon. Stripped of the ash and the snakes and the animal hide, smeared with perfumes

Nandi, Shiva's bull, in a temple

Kalamkari painting of Shiva and Parvati on Nandi

Stone image of Shiva and Parvati on Nandi

and covered with silks, he is the most handsome man anyone has ever seen, graceful and lithe, regal in bearing. In this form, he asks the king of the mountains for Parvati's hand in marriage. It is given. Everyone rejoices at the wedding of Shiva and Shakti. It is the one occasion where eternal enemies, Asuras and Devas, dance together.

The relationship between Shiva and Parvati is best represented by Shiva's vehicle, the bull, Nandi.

To domesticate a bull, he has to be castrated. The absence of gonads deprives the animal of the male hormones that make him aggressive. He then becomes the gentle bullock, a beast of burden, who can serve society by pulling ploughs and carts. A bullock may be domesticated, but he is unable to father children. To father children, one needs to keep the bull intact. An intact bull is wild and aggressive. It will copulate with cows so that they can give birth to the calf and provide milk. An intact bull cannot be tamed. It must be allowed to roam free for the sake of human prosperity.

Nandi the bull represents Shiva's autonomy and capability. Though Parvati sits beside Shiva, he cannot be fully domesticated. His power comes from his being wild. Through Parvati, Shiva engages with the world but never quite assimilates with it.

Shankara is not Vishnu. Shankara merely engages with Prakriti while Vishnu seeks to establish Sanskriti, a culture that is not based on fear. Vishnu participates in worldly affairs, takes mortal forms, and is part of culture. Shiva watches culture from afar and patiently waits for man to outgrow the beast within him. Stories about Vishnu are therefore located in time and space, in particular eras or

Poster art of the marriage of Shiva and Parvati

Dolls showing marriage of Shiva and Parvati

yugas, in particular cities (he is Ram of Ayodhya in Treta yuga and Krishna of Gokul in Dvapara yuga), while stories about Shiva are located outside time and space. Vishnu forges the path of dharma, which will enable humans to outgrow the beast within them even while being fruitful members of society. Shiva prescribes vairagya, renunciation of society itself. For Vishnu, culture is the springboard to outgrow the beast and discover humanity. For Shiva, culture is a delusion that distracts man from outgrowing the beast and discovering humanity. Though the means are different, the goal of dharma and vairagya are the same. They seek to transform Prajapati, he who commands over human society, into Pashu-pati, he who outgrows the animal within.

When Shiva and Shakti reached Mount Kailasa after their marriage, Shakti says, 'I want a house.' Bholenath wonders why. 'To protect us from the heat in summer,' she says. He offers her the cool shade of the banyan tree as an alternative. He simply does not understand the need for a house. 'What will protect us from the winter cold?' she asks, in an attempt to get some sense into him. He takes her to the crematorium and offers the warmth of the funeral pyre; there is not a single night when one cannot find a funeral pyre, he points out. 'And when it rains? No tree or pyre will shelter us then!' cries an exasperated Shakti, realising her husband is not getting the point. He takes her in his arms and flies above the clouds where it does not rain. This is how Shiva gets the name Jimuta-vahana, he who rides the clouds.

Amongst Shiva's followers are mendicants who seek to emulate Shiva's inability to be bound by anything cultural. Like Shiva, they

Cave wall carving of Shiva and Parvati on Kailasa

stay in crematoriums. Like Shiva, they eat anything that comes their way, even human flesh. While cannibalism is taboo in culture, it is not so in nature. Many animals eat members of their own species, and so Aghoras, as they seek complete disruption of social rules, indulge is such practices. They even indulge in sexual activities with the dead, and follow habits that society considers vile and inappropriate. The word ghora means frightening, while Aghora means one who is not frightening. From a cultural point of view, the Aghoras behave in a frighteningly subversive way as they reject all notions of propriety and auspiciousness. But the Aghoras do this not to frighten anyone. They seek to be indifferent to the cultural gaze. They are on a quest to break all social conditioning that divides the world into appropriate and inappropriate, auspicious and inauspicious. They seek to be as transcendental as Shiva.

But Shakti wants Shiva to be more domestic. She wants him to be a husband who builds a house for the wife. Shiva cannot appreciate Shakti's need for a house. He sees it as a burden, an attachment, a cause of misery, but he decides to indulge her, out of affection and respect. He asks Ravana to build her a house.

Ravana is the king of Rakshasas. Rakshasas are considered demons because, though they have the intelligence and discriminatory powers that humans possess, they willingly choose to follow the law of the jungle and deliberately seek to dominate and control everyone around them. Ravana's father is Vaishrava, whose father was Pulatsya, another mind-born son of Brahma. Thus, Ravana is a descendant of Brahma. Metaphorically speaking, Ravana then is a form of Brahma created when imagination is crumpled and knotted by several layers of fear.

While Brahma has five heads, one of which was wrenched off by

Offering the head is a sign that one is reversing the mental modifications that make the human mind attached to material things.

Stone sculpture from Chhattisgarh showing Ravana sacrificing his heads to Shiva

Ravana composed the Rudra-stotra, a hymn to Shiva.

Ravana designed the Rudra-veena, a lute made with his head as the gourd and his nerves as strings.

South Indian painting of Ravana and Shiva

Shiva, Ravana has ten. Ravana cuts these heads off and offers them to Shiva. He uses one of his heads and one of his hands to create a lute or veena. The head serves as the gourd of the lute while his hand serves as its beam and his nerves serve as its strings. This is the Rudra-veena, the lute that is offered to Shiva. It is also known as Ravan-haath, the hand of Ravana, and it is the inspiration for all stringed musical instruments of the world. Using this, Ravana sings a song in praise of Shiva. Shiva is pleased with Ravana's voluntary sacrifice of his heads, which metaphorically speaking, is the gradual uncrumpling and unknotting and purification of the mind. Being Bholenath, he does not wait for all heads to be cut. In his impatience to be generous, he concludes that Ravana is a truly wise devotee.

Ravana is a devotee, but he is not a wise devotee; rather, he is a clever devotee. He seeks from Shiva freedom from fear, not through faith, but through power. When Shiva asks Ravana to build a house for Shakti, Ravana uses his knowledge of Vastu-shastra, or the occult understanding of space, to build a grand palace. It turns out to be the most beautiful palace on earth. After building it, Ravana, becomes attached to it and covets it. So when Shiva says, 'How can I reward you for building such a good palace?', Ravana asks for the palace itself as his fee, and the simpleton Shiva says, 'So be it.' Shakti, who loves the palace and looks forward to turning it into her home, cannot believe it when Ravana declares that Shiva has gifted it away to him. Very cheekily, Ravana invites the Goddess to stay in the palace as a guest or tenant.

Shakti wants to be angry with Shiva but realises he has behaved according to his nature. He did not understand the concept of house or home or property. She has to accept him for what he is.

Ravana trying to raise Mount Kailasa on his head

Once, Ravana uproots Mount Kailasa, intent on taking it and its divine residents south to his island-kingdom of Lanka. Shiva does not mind but Shakti is upset. She requests Ravana to stop. Ravana refuses. 'I am mightier than Shiva. I can carry him, his wife and his home on my shoulders,' he declares. Hearing this, Shiva presses his big toe against the ground and creates such force that Ravana is crushed under its weight. Ravana apologises by singing hymns in praise of Shiva. Shiva, who is quick to anger, is also quick to forgive. So Ravana is forgiven.

Taking advantage of Shiva's gullible nature, the incorrigible Ravana once makes a request to Shiva, 'I want your wife to be my wife.' Shiva replies, 'If she wants to go with you, she is free to do so.' Being Bholenath, he does not understand notions of wife or spousal rights or marital fidelity. Shakti decides to teach the vile and cunning Rakshasa-king a lesson. She takes a frog or manduka and transforms her into a beautiful damsel called Mandodari and makes her sit atop Mount Kailasa. When Ravana reaches the mountain-top and sees this beautiful woman, he concludes it must be Parvati, wife of the hermit Shiva. He picks her up, takes her to Lanka, and makes her his queen. Shiva and Shakti watch with amusement as the demon-king makes love to the frog-woman, arrogantly believing he has tricked Shiva himself.

Shiva's apparent naïveté stems from great wisdom. He knows that power does not take away fear; it only fuels more fear. Shiva's line of sight is infinity; Ravana's line of sight is finite. Eventually, Ravana will realise the folly of his way. Eventually, the smart demon will realise he can never outsmart divinity.

Kerala mural showing Shiva with Mohini

South Indian painting of Mohini

As Shankara, Shiva bestows boons to anyone who approaches him. A blessing is offered even when the offering is accidental. Once a thief and murderer, running from soldiers, climbed a tree and spent the whole night there to avoid the gaze of his pursuers. He was atop a bilva tree and below the tree was a Shiva-linga. Without realising it, he dropped a few bilva leaves on the Shiva-linga. This was enough for Shiva to forgive the thief and murderer.

A woman called Draupadi once asked Shiva for a husband who is honest and strong and skilled and handsome and intelligent. Instead of giving her one husband with all five qualities, Shiva gave her five husbands each with one quality, without taking into consideration the cultural taboo against polyandry.

Culture by its very nature makes room for some practices and some people, and excludes others. Thieves and criminals and ghosts and goblins have no place in culture. But they all find refuge with Shiva. Shiva is surrounded by all manner of creatures that society deems to be demons. He sits with them, dances with them, and includes them. It is not that he excludes members of society, but members of society find it difficult to connect with a divinity who does not discriminate like them.

The Goddess has no choice but to put up with Shiva's behaviour. As nature, she is mother of all creatures. She understands why they are what they are. But she is also the daughter of culture, she knows why culture shuns such creatures. She struggles to negotiate a truce between the mainstream and the outsiders. But she knows that Shiva is who he is because he does not discriminate. He looks beyond the divisions of auspicious and inauspicious laid down by society.

Once an Asura asked Shiva for a boon. 'Let any creature on

Poster art showing Shiva drinking poison

South Indian art showing Parvati squeezing Shiva's neck

whom I place my hand turn into ash.' Shiva granted the boon only to discover that the Asura sought to place his hand on Shiva first. Shiva ran, not knowing how to tackle the foolish Asura. If Shiva is destroyed then the whole world is destroyed. But the Asura was not thinking about the world. He was only thinking about himself and how powerful he would be if he told the world how he destroyed Shiva. Shiva sought the help of the worldly-wise Vishnu, who took the form of a ravishing damsel called Mohini and enchanted the foolish Asura with her beguiling smile. One look at Mohini and the Asura forgot all about Shiva. 'Be my wife,' he begged her. Mohini said she would if he could dance just like her. She began dancing and the Asura imitated her steps. He moved his hands and legs and hips and head just like she did. At one point, she touched her head with her hand. So did he. And in an instant, he was reduced to ash. Thus the boon of Shiva worked against him.

The Asura represents ambitious humanity. Shiva has complete faith in humanity. Vishnu is wary of human cleverness that makes them do foolish things. Humanity therefore ends up inventing technologies and social structures that are short-sighted, hurting humans and nature. Vishnu tries to make humans eventually see the folly of their ways. Shiva, however, is unconcerned. Even if humans destroy themselves, Prakriti will always survive in one form or another, and with her, Purusha.

Shiva's distance from all things socially appropriate is reinforced by what is offered to him in temple rituals. He is offered flowers and fruit of the poisonous plant, dhatura, which is never grown in any house. His favourite drink and smoke is made from the leaves and

Mysore painting showing a devotee sacrificing his eye for Shiva

flowers of Cannabis Indica, a narcotic that is considered illegal by most governments around the world. His choice of refreshments and companions are seen as disruptive. Society demands discipline and alignment to rules. Shiva does not see the point.

One day, Vishnu got the Devas and the Asuras to churn Amrita, the nectar of immortality, from the ocean of milk. During this exercise, the ocean spewed out many wonderful gifts that were claimed by the Devas and Asuras and Vishnu. Finally the ocean spat out vast quantities of poison known as Halahal. No one wanted this. So everyone prayed to Shiva, the gullible hermit, and begged him to receive it. Shiva did it with no qualms as he did not find any difference between Amrita and Halahal. As the lord of yoga, only he had the power to digest this dreadful poison.

Shakti, however, was angry at how Shiva was being treated by everyone. Like a protective and concerned wife, she squeezed Shiva's neck and did not let the poison go beyond his neck. The poison turned Shiva's neck blue, which is why he came to be known as Nila-kantha.

Shiva once told Parvati, 'It is not what I am offered. It is the emotion that accompanies it that matters to me.' The Tamil epic *Periyar Puranam* tells the story of a tribal youth called Tinnan who, every evening after the day's hunt, offered forest flowers to a Shiva-linga that he carried in his hair, water from a mountain stream that he carried in his mouth and meat of the day's hunt, after deboning it with his own hands. The same Shiva-linga was offered flowers and incense and ashes and milk and fruits in the manner prescribed in the scriptures. To test whose devotion was genuine, Shiva caused the Shiva-linga to sprout a pair of eyes. One of the eyes started to bleed. The priest ran away, believing this was a bad omen. Tinnan,

Poster art of the Nath Yogis

Mendicants of Shiva who live outside mainstream society

however, tried his best to control the bleeding. When he failed to control it, he cut his own eye and offered it to the linga. 'Now, that is genuine emotion,' said Shiva, welcoming Tinnan to Kailasa.

In her role as wife, Shakti asks Shiva many questions. She forces him to break his silence and reveal his wisdom. Many Hindu scriptures take the form of conversations between Shakti and Shiva. It is said that the Ramayana, written by the sage Valmiki, was narrated to Valmiki first by the sage Narada, who heard it from the bull Nandi, who overheard a conversation between Shakti and Shiva. The Yakshas overheard the conversations between Shakti and Shiva and transmitted it in the form of the *Brihad-Katha-Sagar*, the ocean of stories, the fountainhead of all fables that entertain children through the ages, throughout the world.

Once a fish overheard a conversation between Shiva and Parvati. The wisdom enabled him to break free from his animal form and be reborn as a human. He became known as Matsyendra-nath. He taught the Tantras to his students, the Naths and the Siddhas. That is why the Tantras are often written in the form of Shiva-Shakti conversations.

The Tantras are sometimes known as Agamas to differentiate them from the Vedas, which are known as Nigamas. The difference between Agamas and Nigamas is that Agamas focus on the worship of a deity with form, i.e. saguna brahman, while Nigamas focus on the worship of a formless deity, nirguna brahman. Agamas tend to be more exoteric and celebrate the tangible while Nigamas are esoteric and celebrate the intangible. Agamas give greater value to the emotions that are provoked by

North Indian miniature showing Shiva and Parvati playing dice

Dolls displayed in a south Indian household during Navaratri

the ritual while Nigamas give greater value to the intellectual decoding of the ritual. Agamas approach Prakriti first and then Purusha, while Nigamas approach Purusha first and then Prakriti. In Tantras, Goddess is Shakti or power, to be sought, while in Vedas, Goddess is Maya, delusion, to be transcended.

But often Shiva does not appreciate the inadequacies and limitations of humanity; that they do not have the same capacity and capability as he does. It is in human nature to get bored and restless. Humans struggle to keep their attention still and focused. Often Shakti yawns when Shiva is speaking. This makes him angry. He loses his temper and turns away from the Goddess, leaving the icy peaks of Kailasa and hiding in the daruka vana, the deodar forest. The Goddess then has to woo him back, sometimes by taking the form of seductive Kirata, or tribal woman.

Sometimes Shiva curses Shakti when she displays signs of indifference. Once, he curses her to be born on earth as a fisherwoman. He regrets the curse almost immediately. To bring her back, he takes the form of a fisherman and wins her hand by earning her admiration by catching a fish in the sea, a dangerous shark that threatens the livelihood of the fisherfolk.

Shakti teaches Bholenath to be more patient with human beings. Imagination has other uses besides introspection and wisdom. It allows for fun. And so together the divine couple creates games and dolls that help humanity pass the time. This is why the festivals of the Goddess, such as Diwali and Dussera, are associated with board games and dolls. Shiva looks at games and dolls with disdain; he equates it with the rattle-drum that entertains and distracts the monkey-mind. But Shakti sees them as invaluable tools to help humanity cope with life.

Elephant cave wall carving showing Shiva impaling Andhaka

One day, Parvati covers Shiva's eyes with her palms. The world is plunged in darkness. To get the sun to shine again, Shiva opens his third eye. So fiery is the glance of this eye that it causes Parvati's palms, placed over the left and right eye, to sweat. From this sweat is born a child called Andhaka, the one born in darkness. This child is given to a childless Asura. When Andhaka grows up he invokes Brahma and secures a boon, that he should not be defeated in battle unless he looks upon his own mother with eyes of lust. Andhaka, who does not know how he was created, goes about conquering the world. No one can defeat him in battle. He finally reaches Mount Kailasa and challenges Shiva to a duel. However, Shiva is lost in meditation and does not pay heed to the challenge. Andhaka climbs the mountain and sees Parvati sitting beside Shiva. He is filled with lust, little realising that he desires his own mother. Parvati begs Shiva to open his eyes and stop their son from doing the unthinkable. Shiva opens his eyes; with his trident he impales Andhaka and keeps him alive and impaled for a thousand years, draining him of blood until he is reduced to a bag of bones. Thus tortured, Andhaka realises that the woman he lusted for is actually his mother and that Shiva is his father. He apologises to the divine couple and is allowed to live as a Gana in Kailasa.

It is significant that Andhaka is born when the third eye is opened. The story draws attention to the limitations of the transcendental gaze. The left and right eyes represent a gaze that distinguishes between appropriate and inappropriate conduct. The third eye is indifferent to such distinctions. This eye of wisdom cannot be

Poster art showing Shiva ready to receive the descent of the celestial Ganga

accommodated within culture because culture, by definition, is based on distinctions, demarcations and hierarchies, where some aspects of nature are included and others excluded. In culture, rules transform a woman into a wife, and a man into a husband. The transcendental gaze looks at all rules as artificial and hence delusions. Such a gaze is unable to distinguish between woman and wife. That is why Shiva does not feel awkward offering his wife to Ravana. That is why the child born of the third eye is unable to recognise his mother and overpower his incestuous designs.

Shiva, they say, is so innocent that he does not know the difference not only between woman and wife, but also between man and woman. And so when Vishnu takes the form of Mohini, he intimately hugs Mohini right in front of his wife. Both Vishnu and Parvati do not know how to tell Bholenath that such a display of affection is inappropriate in culture. At the same time, Bholenath forces them to question cultural norms itself: why is certain behaviour acceptable and other behaviour not, what is the basis of appropriateness, why should culture stay static, why should any human construction not change as the human gaze changes?

One day, Bhagirath invokes Brahma and begs him to allow the river Ganga, which flows in the sky as the Milky Way, to flow on earth. This was to enable Bhagirath's dead ancestors to be reborn. 'Everyone, even the vilest of human beings, deserves another chance,' he says. Brahma agrees and orders Ganga, a river-nymph, to descend from the starry skies. But the force of the falling river can destroy the earth. A frightened Bhagirath requests Shiva to break the fall of Ganga. Shiva agrees and stands under the falling Ganga. The proud and arrogant Ganga suddenly finds herself getting entangled in Shiva's mighty dreadlocks. The force of her

Temple wall images showing Shiva as Hara-Hari, merged with Vishnu, and as Ardha-nari, merged with Shakti

waters are contained by Shiva's hair. Shiva becomes Gangadhara, bearer of Ganga. The mighty river then springs out of Shiva's top knot as a gentle stream ready to water the earth, cleanse the living and enable the dead to be reborn.

If Shiva's thick locks represent the power of spiritual reality, then Ganga's force represents the strength of material reality. Shiva contains Ganga's force and controls her flow so that she does not overwhelm the earth. Thus, Shiva's power is contained in his body and is transmitted to the world through the Ganga. In Shiva temples, therefore, water and milk are poured on the Shiva-linga, in the hope that they will absorb tapa from within Shiva and make it available to the world around him. Only when Shiva's tapa leaves his body will the snow around him melt, and the river flow. Shiva, who lived alone in snowy Kailasa, therefore sits as Shankara along with Gauri on the banks of the river Ganga in the city of Kashi.

# 5. Ganesha's Secret

*Food alone does not satisfy hunger*

South Indian bronze sculpture of Shiva as Gajantaka, the elephant-killer

As long as the lion is hungry, the deer is afraid. As soon as the lion is fed, it forgets its fear of scarcity and the deer no longer has to fear the predator. Food thus plays a fundamental role in allaying fear.

The elephant has access to a lot of food, thanks to its great size. And thanks to its size, it has no natural enemies. This makes the elephant the least frightened of all animals in the jungle. This makes the elephant a symbol of power. Its presence points to a rich ecosystem that is fertile and green and full of water, capable of supporting many human settlements. This makes the elephant a symbol of prosperity. Naturally, it is associated with Indra, king of the Devas, ruler of the sky and Lakshmi, goddess of wealth.

Shiva however kills the elephant. He is Gajantaka, slayer of the elephant, who flays the elephant alive, dances on its head, and wraps its skin around his body. Elephant skin is not easy to cure and tan; it is full of fat and blood and rots easily. Shiva drapes around his body this Gaja-charma or elephant-skin. This reinforces Shiva's desire to stay away from all things material. He wants to break free from nature. He does not want to even depend on Prakriti for food.

When Parvati goes about setting up her kitchen in Kailasa, Shiva does not see the point. He watches her collect fruits and vegetables and grain and spices in baskets. He watches her domesticate fire in the stove. He watches her collect water in a pot. He watches her get her pots and pans and spoons ready. Then he sneers, 'What is the point of food? Everything will one day die anyway.' In response, the Goddess instantly disappears along with her kitchen. Now there is no food in Kailasa. Shiva's Ganas weep. Food, they say, keeps

Calendar art of Shakti as Annapurna of Kashi offering Shiva food

the hunger pangs away. Food, they say, with its many flavours and textures, excites the senses, and helps them experience the variety of nature. Food, they say, provides contentment and allows the mind to move away from fear. Shiva feels the pain of his Ganas. He experiences what they experience. He yearns for what they yearn. He realises that these needs and cravings of the body force him to think about mortality. From fear of death stems the yearning for immortality and this yearning for immortality eventually paves the path towards spirituality. If there is no food, there is no body, no engagement with Prakriti, no encounter with Kama or Yama, no feeling whatsoever. Shiva realises how food plays a key role in the human journey from Prakriti to Purusha. He sets forth in search of his wife. He finds her on the banks of the river Ganga, in the city of Kashi, as the Goddess Annapurna, providing food to all those who come to her. Shiva extends his begging bowl. The Goddess, with great affection, fills it with hot, flavoursome food.

As a reminder of the value of the Goddess and her kitchen, uncooked food in the form of nuts and raw milk is offered to the hermit Shiva of Kailasa, while the householder Shankara of Kashi is offered cooked food.

Hindus believe that when a person dies, Yama claims his physical body, or sthula sharira, and his mental body, or sukshma sharira, which animates the physical body. But there is a third body — the body of subconscious memories, full of fears and resulting prejudices, known as karana sharira, which outlives death. This body envelops the Purusha and prevents it from observing the true nature of Prakriti, and hence realising its true self. That is

Bronze of Shiva holding the trident

why, when a person dies, the karana sharira travels across the river Vaitarni and reaches the land of the dead where it resides as a Pitr. As long as the karana sharira exists, fear still exists and the Pitr is not able to reach Shiva's Kailasa where there is bliss forever. In order to reach Shiva's abode, one has to purge the karana sharira of all fears and prejudices. This can only be done in the land of the living. For this, one needs a human body that offers the wherewithal to imagine and reflect and choose. To obtain the human body, the Pitr have to be reborn. Once reborn, to sustain the flesh, they need food.

The scriptures state that every living creature is obligated to produce children to repay the debt they owe to their ancestors who gave them life. This is Pitr-rin. During funeral ceremonies, the Pitrs are offered balls of mashed rice. The balls represent the human body because, ultimately, food forms the building block of the flesh. By offering these balls to ancestors, the living assure the dead that they will produce children, enable the dead to regain sthula and sukshma sharira, and thus repay their debt.

The concept of debt is a cultural thought that forces the human male to produce children. This cultural thought is needed because, of all creatures on this planet, only human couples can choose whether to have children or not. In case of all other animals, procreation is fettered by natural rhythms, not free will. Even amongst humans, the male of the species has greater choice. The female of the human species can be forced to conceive a child, but the human male cannot be forced to make a woman pregnant. Even if aroused, he need not spill the seed in the womb. Thus he can take pleasure but not father a child. The concept of debt to ancestors or Pitr-rin is an integral part of culture aimed at preventing men from

Temple wall image from Belur, Karnataka, showing Shiva and Shakti on a bull

North Indian miniature showing Shiva and Shakti atop Mount Kailasa

becoming indifferent, self-absorbed hermits and forcing them to become householders, responsible for others.

When Parvati expresses her desire to be a mother, Shankara argues, 'I owe no debt to any ancestors, as I have no ancestors; I was never born, and I will not die, so I need no children who will help me be reborn.' When Parvati persists, Shankara walks away from her to meditate in serene isolation in the dense daruka vana, the deodar forest.

Here, children are a powerful metaphor for true involvement with the material world. Through marriage, the Goddess has managed to open the eye of Shiva. Shankara observes nature, but does not feel responsible for nature. The only way he will feel empathy for the world, is when he creates something in it. A child is therefore necessary.

Since Shiva refuses to give her a child, Parvati decides to create a child on her own. She anoints her body with a paste of turmeric and oil, then scrapes it off, collects the rubbings which have mingled with her sweat, and moulds out of it a doll into which she breathes life. This is her son, whom she calls Vinayaka, the one born without (vina) a man (nayaka). She tells her son to guard the gate of her house and not let anyone in.

Shiva, who had withdrawn from the Goddess following her repeated demands for a child, returns only to find his path to Kailasa blocked by a stranger. He asks the stranger to step aside. The stranger refuses. Shiva gets jealous as he wonders about the beautiful boy who blocks his path. He gets angry because the boy is strong enough to block his path. The boy reminds him of the

Calendar art showing the creation of Ganesha

territorial Brahma and Daksha. He decides to get rid of the obstacle that blocks his path to the Goddess.

So Shiva raises his trident and beheads the boy. The head of Vinayaka is destroyed. Shiva marches in triumphantly, covered with the boy's blood. When Parvati sees this, she screams and runs to the threshold of her house, where she finds the headless body of her son. She wails and unties her hair and beats her chest in agony. 'My son, my son. You killed my son.' She transforms from the gentle, demure Gauri into the dark and fearsome Kali. She becomes wild in her fury. Shiva trembles.

Shiva realises his insensitivity. In satisfying his own need for solitude, he did not consider Parvati's loneliness atop the snow-capped peaks of the Himalayas. He did not look at her; he did not do her darshan. Had he known her needs, he could have satisfied them or helped her outgrow them. But he did neither. Unless the self-contained engage with the needy, the needy will never learn how to become self-contained. Parvati's temper, her transformation from Gauri to Kali, served as a darpan or mirror, reflecting Shiva's indifference. What use is imagination, if it simply ignores and invalidates the other?

Vinayaka does not recognise Shiva. Shiva does not like this. The Goddess thus turns the table on Shiva through Vinayaka. All this time, Shiva had shut his eyes to Shakti. Through Vinayaka, Shakti shuts her eyes to Shiva. When humanity ignores imagination, there is no growth, no quest to outgrow fear, no desire for spiritual reality. Evolution does not happen. Spiritual reality remains undiscovered. Only the self matters; others remain invisible. In other words, humans stay animals.

Realising the value of Prakriti and of the head that has been

Calendar art showing Shiva and Parvati with their son, Ganesha

destroyed, a considerate and caring Shankara decides to resurrect the boy. He orders his Ganas to fetch him the head of the first creature they encounter in the northern direction. The Ganas find an elephant. The *Brahmavaivarta Purana* says this elephant was Airavat, the mount of Indra. Others say it was one of the elephants that flanks Lakshmi. The head is placed on the severed neck of Vinayaka and he is brought back to life.

Shiva declares him to be his son and names him Ganesha, first amongst Ganas, and Ganapati, master of the Ganas. Until this moment, the Ganas followed Shiva, but Shiva was indifferent to their presence. But now, thanks to his tryst with Parvati and Vinayaka, he looks at the Ganas, becomes sensitive to them, understands their inadequacies, includes them in his vision, and provides them with a leader, his own son. Ganapati thus embodies Shiva's empathy for the trials and tribulations of humanity.

Most scholars agree that the cult of Ganesha had an independent origin and that it merged with the cult of Shiva later in history. In early Vedic scriptures, there are references to multiple malevolent beings called Vinayakas, some of whom have elephant heads. In later Puranic scriptures, there is one gentle elephant-headed being who becomes the child of Shiva and Shakti.

There are many stories of Ganesha's birth besides the one in which Shiva beheads Vinayaka. In one story, Ganesha is born when Shiva and Shakti make love taking the form of elephants. In another, Shiva creates a child of his own image for the pleasure of Shakti, but since he looks too much like the father, Shakti replaces his head with that of an elephant.

Patta painting of Ganesha from Odisha

The cult of Ganesha was the most popular in Maharashtra, especially under the patronage of Maratha kings. Scriptures such as *Ganesha Purana* and *Ganesha Upanishad* were written in the 18th century in adoration of Ganesha, describing him as self-created. He is associated with the earth's fertility as well as the arts and wisdom. He is also described as a warrior who kills demons. One of the demons he killed was resurrected and turned into a rat, or Mooshika, which is Ganesha's vehicle.

Though the son of a hermit, Ganesha's corpulent belly indicates great affluence. He is surrounded by abundance. He is often worshipped with Lakshmi, the goddess of wealth. He is associated with several fertility symbols such as rats, serpents and blades of grass. The population of rats rises rapidly soon after its numbers have been exterminated, indicating their fertility. Serpents also slough old skin for new, and are thus able to regenerate themselves. Grass grows back as soon as it is plucked. Regeneration is critical to survival. Regeneration compensates for losses incurred by death. A shepherd who loses sheep to a wolf depends on the ability of the other sheep to reproduce to make good his numbers. A farmer who has harvested the crop depends on the regeneration of earth's fertility to ensure he does not starve the next season. Ganesha's association with fertility symbols is an acknowledgment of the cycle of life that sustains material reality. In the material world, everything dies and is reborn. Rats, serpents and grass are very visible and potent symbols of this principle.

In rituals, Ganesha is often worshipped with two mothers. They are identified as the elder mother and the younger mother. In

Photograph showing Ganesha being worshipped with his two mothers

Photograph showing Ganesha being immersed in water

Goddess tradition, Shakti is often worshipped with a female companion, her sakhi, who is identified as her sister or her servant. Some identify the younger mother as Lakshmi, and others as Ganga. The identification of two women as mothers draws attention to the greater role played by the Goddess in the creation of Ganesha. She initiates his creation; Shiva completes it. Ganesha draws attention towards the value of nature, of food and of worldly life.

Ganesha is worshipped twice a year, before the spring and autumn harvest. The more popular of the two Ganesha festivals is the one that takes place after the rains, in autumn, when the earth is green. Ganesha is worshiped with his mother, Gauri. She is the earth and he is the vegetation born of her that sustains life on earth. Both festivals of Ganesha involve making of clay statues of Ganesha. These are worshipped with blades of grass for ten days and then immersed in water. Ganesha's image thus comes and goes in a cyclical way, a reminder of nature's cycles, of the seasons of sowing and harvest, of life and death.

In many parts of India, Ganesha is considered a bachelor god. They say he did not marry as no woman was as good as his mother. So he stands in the shade of the banana tree who is his mother. There is another story for Ganesha's association with the banana tree. No one wanted to marry a man with the head of an elephant. So, his mother draped a sari around a banana plant and gave it to Ganesha as his wife. This is the reason a banana plant with a sari is found next to Ganesha during Durga Puja, celebrated in autumn. She is called Kola-Bau, the matriarch of the clan.

The banana plant is a valuable source of nutrition, demanding

Image of Kola-Bau and Ganesha from a Durga pandal in Bengal

Image of Vyasa and Ganesha

hardly any maintenance, constantly regenerating itself to provide more fruit. The pith of the banana plant is also edible. And the leaves of the banana plant serve as disposable dishes on which food is served. The banana is thus the Goddess taking care of food so that Ganesha can focus on wisdom. Ganesha therefore serves as a scribe to help the sage Vyasa write down the epic, the Mahabharata. This story captures the essence of life's truth, balancing Shakti's kitchen and Shiva's meditation.

Ganesha broke one of his two tusks to use it as a stylus with which he could write the epic that Vyasa narrated. In another story, he broke the tusk to strike the moon when it made fun of his huge size. In still another story, this tusk is broken when he is fighting either Parashurama or Balarama, both forms of Vishnu. By breaking one of the tusks, Ganesha's masculinity is toned down. Though son of Shiva and Shakti, he is closer to his mother, hence nature, and worldly life.

In folklore, tusks are associated with pretension: elephants show one set of teeth while they eat with another set of teeth. By breaking off one of the tusks, Ganesha is breaking pretension. The tusks are symbols of aggressive power. Ganesha is breaking it so that strength is used only to defend and nourish, not dominate and exploit.

Ganesha's association with wisdom is endorsed by his association with the Muladhara Chakra in Tantra. Tantra is the technology for the finite Brahma to reach the infinite Shiva with the help of Shakti. This is visualised as the rise of a serpent, Kundalini, representing our wisdom. Tantra visualises this serpent as resting at the base of the spine and rising up through the spine to the brain. As the serpent rises, lotus flowers bloom in the form of chakras. The final chakra

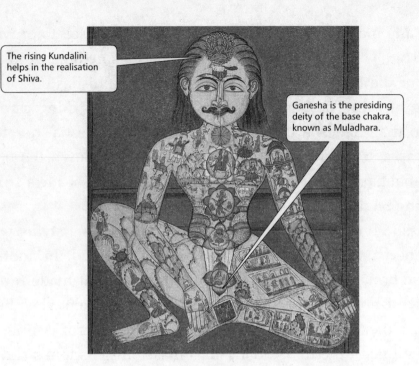

The rising Kundalini helps in the realisation of Shiva.

Ganesha is the presiding deity of the base chakra, known as Muladhara.

Seven chakras of Tantra

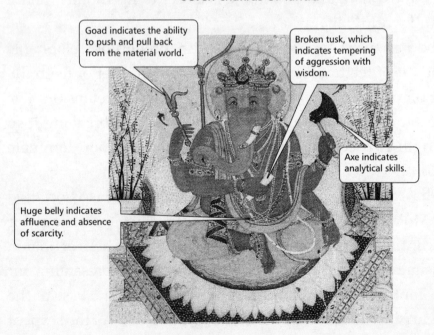

Goad indicates the ability to push and pull back from the material world.

Broken tusk, which indicates tempering of aggression with wisdom.

Axe indicates analytical skills.

Huge belly indicates affluence and absence of scarcity.

North Indian miniature of Ganesha

to bloom is the thousand-petalled lotus on top of the head. The first chakra that blooms is the Muladhara Chakra, located at the base of the spine near the anus. It marks the most basic instinct of man — the craving for food stemming from our fear of scarcity, and hence, death. Unless one outgrows this fear, the rise of the Kundalini and the journey to realisation of Shiva will not even begin. Only when Ganesha is realised will the journey begin.

Ganesha's wisdom manifests in the two symbols he carries in his hands. In one hand he holds an axe, and in the other hand he holds a noose. The axe represents analytical skills that enable one to separate objective from subjective reality, thought and form, animal instincts from human conditionings, sense of self from the sense of other, me from mine. The noose represents the ability to outgrow these divides, to unite the opposites, synthesise solutions, to recognise that ultimately, in nirguna brahman, Shiva and Shakti are not separate but one.

In some images, Ganesha holds a sugar cane in one hand and the elephant goad or ankush in the other. Sugar cane represents Kama, the god of desire and freedom. The elephant goad represents Yama, the god of death and bondage. Ganesha thus acknowledges the life-giving aspect of nature as well as the life-taking aspect of nature.

The lore of Shiva constantly refers to beheadings by Shiva. Shiva beheads Brahma. Shiva beheads Daksha. Shiva beheads Vinayaka. Each time the beheading is prompted by territorial behaviour resulting from amplified fear. But in Vinayaka's case, Shiva makes an error. Vinayaka is not being territorial. He is ignorant. He does

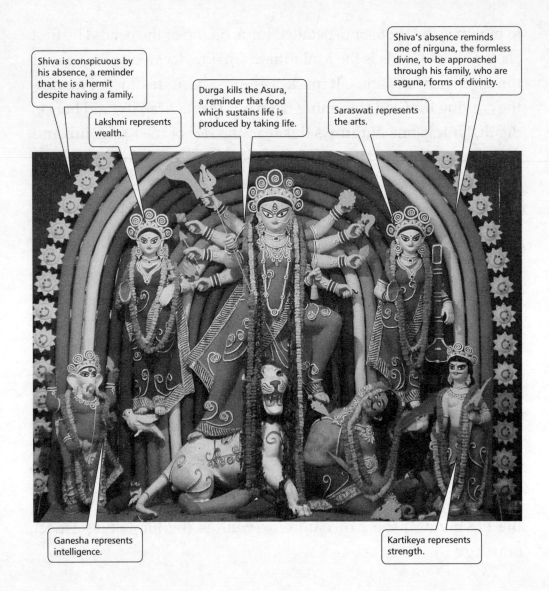

Bengali image of Parvati as Durga and her children

not know about Shiva, because Shiva has not contributed to his birth. Shiva is thus responsible for creating Vinayaka who ends up becoming his own obstacle. A restless Goddess may dance to arouse Shiva, but Shiva also has to dance to calm the Goddess. It is not a one-way street. It is in the human imagination that Purusha and Prakriti can move towards each other and finally meet. Ganesha embodies that possibility.

The Goddess can provide food to allay hunger. But Shiva has to give meaning to both food and hunger. Humans are the only creatures on earth, who can reflect on life. Humans wonder what is the purpose of life, why do we live, why do we eat. Nature offers no answer. Humans are able to domesticate the earth, establish fields and orchards and gardens and grow abundant food. Surrounded by great wealth, only humans wonder why do they have such power over nature. Humans can build great walls and establish rules and make themselves secure. But the heaviest of security does not take away death. Humans feel invalidated, weak and helpless, and wonder what is the point of human life. When no answer is forthcoming, a frightened man starts hoarding things, not just to secure his future, but to create the delusion of immortality. Our wealth and family, our possessions become an extension of our bodies. It is the fourth body — property that outlives the death of the other three. We hoard more and more property and thereby give ourselves meaning.

Yakshas are hoarders. They are visualised as enormously fat creatures who hoard wealth. They are closely associated with another race, also described as Rakshasas. Both share a common grandfather, Pulatsya, son of Brahma. It was Kubera, the leader of Yakshas, who built the golden city of Lanka. Ravana, leader

Both have a pot-belly.

Both have a rodent: Kubera has a mongoose and Ganesha, a rat.

Kubera holds a purse containing money.

The rat is eaten by the serpent, which is eaten by the mongoose.

Ganesha holds a sweetmeat.

**Stone images of Kubera and Ganesha**

of Rakshasas, became jealous of Kubera. He drove Kubera out of Lanka and usurped the kingdom of Yakshas. Yakshas are thus creatures who have lost their home. No one gives them refuge, as everyone hates them. Everyone wants their treasures, not them. Abandoned and excluded by everyone they find refuge with Shiva. They become his Ganas.

Kubera keeps talking about all his wealth. So Parvati, who sits on Shiva's lap, reaches out, plucks out his left eye and eats it. Kubera howls in agony. 'Surely you can replace that eye with all your wealth,' says the Goddess. Kubera realises he cannot. He becomes aware of his mortality. He realises how wealth cannot compensate for his fear of death. Wealth cannot give meaning to existence. To remind himself of this, he replaces his lost eye with an eye of gold, which is why Kubera is called Pingalaksha, he with a golden eye. Shiva makes him the guardian of the northern direction, so that he will guide people towards wisdom.

Once, Kubera felt sorry for Ganesha. 'Let me feed you,' said Kubera, 'as clearly your father cannot afford to do so. You clearly look like someone who enjoys food.' Ganesha accepted Kubera's invitation, went to his house, and ate all that was offered. 'I am still hungry,' said the elephant-headed god. Kubera had to procure more food using the money in his treasury. Ganesha ate all that was served and kept asking for more. Finally Kubera fell at his feet and begged him to stop eating. 'You are draining my treasury dry,' he cried. Ganesha then said with a smile, 'You seek food to conquer hunger and end up hoarding food. My father shows how to outgrow hunger, and hence is happy even in the absence of food.'

Kubera and Ganesha are very similar to each other, yet very different. Kubera is a Gana but Ganesha is their leader. Kubera

Poster art of Ganesha with his father

Image of the sweetmeat modaka with dhurva grass

is Shiva's follower but Ganesha is Shiva's son. Kubera holds a money bag in his hand while Ganesha holds a moneybag-shaped sweetmeat called modaka in his hand. All living creatures need food to survive; humans hoard food to allay imaginary fears of future starvation. From this desire to hoard comes the notion of wealth and the craving for property and gold. Kubera indulges this hunger of man. Ganesha focuses on what really matters — food!

In nature, rats eat grain, snakes eat rats and mongooses eat snakes. Thus the mongoose is on top of the food chain. Kubera has the mongoose as his pet. Ganesha has the serpent around his belly and the rat at his feet. The predator and the prey are thus in harmony. This represents the idea of heaven — a perfect world without fear. Kubera thus seeks a world where he is the dominant overlord, while Ganesha symbolises a world where there is no need for a pecking order.

Kubera, the Gana, is trapped in the fear of scarcity and predation despite having wealth. That is why he hoards treasures but loses it all to the Rakshasas. Shiva makes Ganesha the leader of Ganas to help outgrow all fears. Only when fear is outgrown will the habit of hoarding be overcome. Only then will the Yakshas who came to Kailasa from Lanka truly discover the north, the land of the Pole Star, which represents a state of mind where there is no dependence on nature, no fear of death, no fear of scarcity or predation, only bliss.

The Rakshasas, like the Yakshas, are consumed by fear. That is why Ravana grabs what the Yakshas create. But that is not enough

Ravana handing over the Shiva-linga to the cowherd, who is Ganesha in disguise.

Statue of Ravana and the cowherd

Ganesha placing the Shiva-linga on the ground, preventing it from going to the south, to Lanka, the land of Rakshasas.

Poster art of Ganesha and Shiva

for Ravana. When he learns Kubera has now earned the affection of Shiva, he starts craving it as well. But rather than moving north towards Shiva, he seeks to bring Shiva south.

Shiva gives Ravana a Shiva-linga, instructing him not to place it on the ground before he reaches Lanka. The gods know that once the Shiva-linga reaches Lanka, the Rakshasa-king will never share him with the world. They beg Ganesha to stop Ravana. So Ganesha causes Ravana to experience an intense desire to answer the call of nature. He then takes the form of a boy and offers to hold the Shiva-linga while Ravana relieves himself. As soon as Ravana gives Ganesha the Shiva-linga and turns his back, Ganesha places the Shiva-linga on the ground. There it stands steadfast. No matter how much Ravana tries, it remains rooted to the spot. This Shiva-linga that Ganesha prevented from reaching Lanka is located at Gokarna, along the Konkan coast. Ganesha thus prevents the hoarding of Shiva by the Rakshasa-king.

In a similar story, Ravana's brother Vibhishana tries to take the image of Vishnu to Lanka. Once again, Ganesha foils this plan by placing the image of Vishnu on the ground while Vibhishana is performing his ablutions. This image of Vishnu known as Ranganatha is found on the banks of the river Kaveri. Ganesha is thus the obstacle to the hoarding of all things.

Ravana and Vibhishana look at divinity as commodities to be hoarded, which is why they seek to take Shiva and Vishnu to the south. They want divinity all for themselves. Like the hoarding Yakshas, they are not concerned about the other. This self-absorption is the consequence of fear. They want to secure themselves at the cost of the other. They are still pashu despite being surrounded by immense wealth and despite being in the presence of Shiva.

Calendar art showing Ganesha with his two wives, Riddhi and Siddhi

Ganesha therefore stops their journey south and forces them to look north, towards his father, towards wisdom.

That Shiva gives his son an elephant head is significant. Animals never overeat. Humans, because of imagined and amplified fears, end up spending their lives gathering food like the Yakshas and forget to reflect on the meaning of food. By replacing the human head with an elephant head, Shiva draws attention to human greed that is rooted in fear and that prevents humanity from discovering bliss. With the head of an animal that knows neither scarcity nor predator, Ganesha becomes the symbol of contentment and wisdom. His corpulent form evokes not just power and abundance but also satisfaction.

The elephant whose head is given to Ganesha is no ordinary elephant — it is found by Shiva's Ganas when they move in the northern direction as directed by Shiva. North is the direction associated with the Pole Star, with stillness, hence spiritual wisdom. The elephant is a symbol of material abundance. The elephant found in the north combines both ideas, and so is a befitting head for the son of Shiva and Shakti.

All the Ganas, including the Yakshas, accept Vinayaka as Ganesha, their leader. He makes them reflect on hoarding and inspires them towards contentment. The wives of Kubera, Riddhi and Nidhi, are associated with material growth and wealth accumulation, whereas Ganesha's two wives, Riddhi and Siddhi (sometimes called Buddhi), balance wealth with wisdom. Siddhi means emotional and intellectual maturity.

In calendar art, Ganesha is shown with Lakshmi instead of

Calendar art showing Ganesha with Lakshmi and Saraswati

Riddhi, and Saraswati instead of Siddhi. The two goddesses, draped in red and white, are associated with wealth and knowledge. If Lakshmi brings wealth, then Saraswati brings peace. The two are rarely seen together. Only Ganesha is able to bring them together. He removes the obstacle to wisdom.

Ganesha is said to have two sons, Shubh and Labh, which means 'auspiciousness' and 'profit'. His daughter is called Santoshi, goddess of satisfaction. These are metaphors to indicate that when Ganesha is brought into the house, he removes all obstacles to wealth, peace, auspiciousness, growth and happiness. He does so by enabling the potbellied Ganas to outgrow fear of scarcity. That is why he is their leader. That is why he is Ganapati.

# 6. Murugan's Secret

## Face fear to outgrow it

Mysore painting of the boyish Murugan

Mysore painting of the six-headed Murugan

The Devas are not afraid of dying. They have Amrita, nectar of immortality. But fear of predation envelops them. Asuras are the predators, eyeing the good life of the Devas with hunger. It is for protection from the predatory Asura that the Devas wanted Shiva to marry. This story comes to us from the *Shiva Purana*, the *Skanda Purana* and the famous Sanskrit work *Kumara-Sambhava*, or the conception of Kumara, by the acclaimed poet, Kalidasa.

Kumara is the name of Shiva's other son. In some texts, Kumara is the elder son of Shiva and Parvati, while in other texts, he is younger, and Ganesha is the elder son. This difference is attributed to the fact that both Ganesha and Kumara are deities who became part of mainstream Hinduism much later in history.

While the worship of Ganesha received maximum attention in Maharashtra, the worship of Kumara is most popular in Tamil Nadu where he is known as Murugan. In all probability, he was originally a deity of southern hill tribes. While in the north, Kumara was feared and revered as a warrior-god, in the south Murugan was much admired and adored as a child, lover and guardian.

The story goes that there was an Asura called Taraka who had defeated the Devas and overrun their paradise. The only way to restore cosmic balance was by killing him. But Taraka had a boon: only a little baby who led an army could kill him. The Devas wondered how they could produce a warrior who was strong and mature enough to fight a battle even though he was a baby. They approached their father, Brahma, who informed them that such

Clay dolls of Shiva's two sons

a child that defies the law of nature can be produced by Purusha alone. In other words, Shiva.

In Tantrik physiology, a child is born when the white seed of man merges with the red seed of woman. From the father, a child gets the nervous tissue, including the brain, which enables humans to imagine and access spiritual reality. From the mother, the child gets flesh and blood. In other words, the father is the source of Purusha and the mother, the source of Prakriti. Ganesha is the mother's child, a child of Prakriti. Now the gods want the father's child, a child of Purusha.

In mythology, a man can produce a child outside a woman's womb if the white seed is adequately energised by the spiritual fire, tapas. That is why Tapasvins are able to create children without the intervention of women. Rishi Bharadvaja is able to father Drona when, on seeing a nymph, he sheds his semen in a pot. Rishi Vyasa is able to father Suka when, on catching sight of a nymph, he sheds his semen on fire sticks. Rishi Vibhandak is able to father Rishyashringa through a doe that eats his semen, shed at the sight of a beautiful woman. Devas realise that to kill Taraka they need semen that has not been shed for eons. It must be so powerful that it can germinate into a child without needing any womb to incubate it. Such white seed, they learn from Brahma, exists only in the body of Shiva.

To get Shiva to release the seed, the gods first sent Kama, the god of lust. But he fails miserably, and is reduced to ashes by a glance of Shiva's third eye. So the gods appeal to Shakti, the Goddess herself, to do the needful.

As Parvati, daughter of the mountains, Shakti prays to Shiva, appeals to his compassion, and secures him as a husband. She

Chola bronze of Shiva, Parvati and Kartikeya

forces him to acknowledge her. In Tantrik narratives, she sits on top of him and serves as his teacher and guide. But despite this, Shiva refuses to shed his seed. Metaphorically speaking, he is engaged with the world through his lovemaking but is still detached. The world stimulates him but he is not ensnared by it.

In the Puranas, when Indra, king of the Devas, feels that a Tapasvin will use his tapa to dethrone him, he sends an Apsara to seduce the Tapasvin. Tapasvins are fire-ascetics (tapa = fire) and Apsaras are water-nymphs (apsa = water). They compete. She tries to enchant him while he resists her charms. Sometimes, the Tapasvin succeeds and the Apsara leaves him alone. Sometimes, the Apsara succeeds and the Tapasvin sheds his semen, fathers a child, and loses all the power he gained through tapasya, much to Indra's satisfaction. Shiva, however, refuses to shed his seed, despite the intervention of Kama. So on behalf of the Devas, the Goddess appeals to Shiva to shed his seed.

The Devas have another problem. They cannot let Shiva's semen enter Shakti's womb and have a child produced the normal way. For Shakti's red seed is equal in power to Shiva's white seed. They will neutralise each other and create a powerful, but normal, child. They want the child to be hyper-masculine, capable of fighting battle even when he is barely six days old. They do not want him to possess anything feminine in him. Once again, this is a metaphor.

The Devas do not want a child of nature, who like all living creatures, suffers from the fear of scarcity and predators. They want a child who suffers no such fears. Shiva has no such fears, but is totally detached from the world. The Devas want a child who is like Shiva in all respects, except that he actively engages with the world, protects against all predators and provides sanctuary to the

Kumara was highly revered as the divine warlord by ancient kings of India.

North Indian warrior-god Kumara

Kumara is identified with Mars, the Roman god of war.

Kumara is identified with the planet Mars, associated with aggression.

Temple wall image showing Kartikeya ready to launch an assault

prey. He will be celibate but not innocent, ignorant or gullible. He will be Kumara, the wise and capable boy-god.

Early narratives describe how the Devas enter the caves of Kailasa, interrupt the lovemaking of Shiva, embarrass Shakti who moves away, enabling Agni, the fire-god, to claim Shiva's semen, which is why Kumara is also called Skanda, the spurt of life. In later narratives, on the request of Shakti and the Devas, Shiva releases his power in the form of six fiery sparks and hands them over to Agni.

Seed or sparks, they are so hot and potent, that even the fire-god cannot withstand their heat. He gives them to Vayu, the wind-god. Even Vayu is unable to cool them down. Vayu gives them to Ganga. The water of the river-goddess starts to boil. The Sara-vana, or forest of reeds, on the banks of the Ganga bursts into flames because of the heat. When the fire dies out, in the embers are found six children. They cry for their mother. The six Pleiades, or the stars of the Kritika constellation, nurse the six babies. Finally Shakti holds the six children in her arms and turns them into a single child with six heads, and finally a child with one head. The first thing the child asks for is a weapon. Shakti gives him the vel, or spear. Thus is born Vel Murugan, the spear-bearing warrior god, ready to do battle on the seventh day of his life.

The Kritikas, or the six stars of the Pleiades constellation, play a key role in the story of Murugan. The Great Bear Constellation is composed of seven stars associated with seven sages known as the Sapta Rishis. Each of them had a wife. One day the seven women were bathing in a pond in which the Devas had placed the

Festival idol of Kartikeya in Bengal

Festival idol of Kartikeshwara in Odisha

six sparks of Shiva, and this made six of the seven wives pregnant. The Rishis accused them of adultery and threw them out of the house. The six wives rejected the children in their wombs and became the Pleiades constellation, or the Kritika Nakshatra. The six discarded foetuses set the forest of reeds aflame, and from the fire emerged Murugan. The sight of Murugan angers the Kritikas who try to harm him at first, but the child's cherubic charm calms them down. Murugan understands their plight and declares that whosoever does not worship them and acknowledge them as his mothers would suffer greatly. Murugan transforms the Kritika maids into wild, fearsome goddesses known as the Matrikas, who live in the forest, and can cause children to suffer fatal fevers with pox and rashes, unless they are venerated. Murugan, the son of the Kritikas, is known as Kartikeya.

As the son of Agni, Murugan is known as Agneya. As the son of Vayu, he is known as Guha, the mysterious one. As the son of the forest of reeds, he is known as Saravana. As the six-headed one, he is known as Shanmughan or Aramughan. As the wild red-coloured warrior, he is Senthil. As the warrior who looks like a baby, he is called Kumara.

On the seventh day of his life, Murugan stepped into battle. He fought and killed Taraka with the spear his mother gave him.

In the *Skanda Purana*, which is a Tamil scripture extolling the tales of Murugan, the story does not end with the death of Taraka. Taraka's two brothers, Simhamukhan and Surpadman, continue the battle. After a fierce battle, Murugan defeats Simhamukhan. Simhamukhan begs for mercy and promises to serve him in any way if his life is spared. Murugan then tells Simhamukhan to serve his mother, Shakti, as her vahana, or mount. Simhamukhan turns

Stone carving of Shakti with her two sons, Ganesha and Kartikeya

into the lion that Shakti rides when she transforms into Durga.

The battle with Surpadman is the fiercest of all. Finally Surpadman turns into a gigantic mountain in an attempt to withstand Murugan's onslaught. Murugan hurls his spear and splits the mountain in two. One half turns into a rooster. The other half turns into a peacock. The rooster becomes Murugan's emblem and the peacock becomes his vehicle.

Murugan thus defeats the enemies of the Devas and is declared the commander of all celestial armies. Through him, Shiva becomes the guardian of the Devas.

Murugan is visualised as a muscular god surrounded by symbols of martial power and authority such as a spear, a peacock and a rooster. Ganesha, in contrast, has a corpulent body and a potbelly and is associated with symbols of fertility such as grass, rat and serpent. Murugan is the warrior son of the Goddess, while Ganesha is the scholar son. Murugan is renowned for killing demons, while Ganesha is renowned for his cleverness.

Of course, this is not entirely true. In Maharashtra, where Ganesha is the most popular deity, there are legends of how he killed many demons. And in Tamil Nadu, where Murugan is most worshipped, there are stories of how he revealed the secret of the sacred sound, Om, to his father, Shiva. Thus the two brothers compete with each other in matters of brain and brawn. Through them, the distant Shiva reaches out to the common man, much like how Vishnu reaches out through his many avatars.

Narada, the wily, trouble-making sage, once wanted to know which of Shiva's two sons could go fastest around the world

Poster art of Ganesha and Kartikeya on a race

three times. Murugan leapt onto his peacock and flew around the world three times but was declared the loser because his brother, Ganesha, had simply gone around his parents three times and said, 'I went around my emotional world, which matters more than the external world that my brother went around.' Murugan argued his case but the decision had been taken. Furious, Murugan left his father's house and went south of the Vindhyas.

Murugan's movement to the south is metaphorical as well as real. North is the realm of Shiva; the realm of stillness and wisdom. South is the realm of Shakti; the realm of movement and fear. The Goddess moves north to turn Shiva into Shankara. Their son now returns to the south, to help humanity outgrow every fear.

In the geographical north, Murugan is the ascetic-warrior who fights wars where men die and women become widows. But in the south, Murugan is the wise and responsible householder-guardian with many wives, who fights demons while his mother, Kotravai, a local name for Kali, drinks the blood of the fallen.

Murugan embodies Shiva's wisdom expressed when Shiva takes the form of Dakshinamurti, the teacher who faces south. Knowing Shiva to be Adi-nath, or the primal teacher, all the sages rushed north towards the Himalayas to hear Shiva's discourse. This rush to the north created a cosmic imbalance. The earth began to tilt north. Sensing trouble, Shiva asked his foremost disciple and devotee, the Rishi Agastya, to move south with his students, until the end of the discourse.

As Agastya moved south, the sun-god, Surya, sought his help. He said that the Vindhya mountain that separated the north from

Stone image of Agastya

Poster art of the Siddhas

the south was growing in size and blocking his path. 'Please stop his growth so that I can travel the sky without any obstacle.' Agastya promised to help. On seeing Agastya, the Vindhya mountain bowed in reverence. 'If you truly respect me,' said the Rishi, 'then stay in this bent position until I return north.' Vindhya agreed. To ensure that the mountain never rose again, Agastya remained in the south. There, he spread his wisdom through students who were known as the Siddhas, because Agastya taught them the siddhis or the secrets of alchemy. Agastya also composed the Tamil language.

Agastya is said to have brought the river Kaveri to the south. Ganesha, in the form of a crow, toppled Agastya's water pot, which contained the water of the Ganga, and so was born the river Kaveri, on whose banks flourished the Tamil culture.

Agastya missed the northern Himalayas so much that Shiva asked one of his Ganas, Idumba, to carry two mountain peaks south. The names of the two peaks were Shiva-giri and Shakti-giri. Idumba carried the two mountain peaks in a kavadi, a bamboo pole slung over the shoulder, with each peak hanging on either end in baskets. It was a long and tiring journey. At one point, after crossing the Vindhyas, Idumba placed the mountains on the ground and rested. When he tried picking up the kavadi again, he could not. One of the peaks had become too heavy. He noticed a young boy seated on it, pushing the mountain down. He realised this was no ordinary boy; it had to be a son of Shiva. Idumba bowed to the lad, who identified himself as Murugan and made the hill his home. Today, that hill is known as Palani and is one of the sacred spots for devotees of Murugan.

In Tamil Nadu, devotees of Murugan often carry a kavadi which is decorated with peacock feathers. A similar practice is seen in

The sling is a symbol of worldly burdens and responsibilities.

Kavadi carried by Murugan-worshippers in the south

The pots are not placed on the ground till the devotee reaches his village temple.

The pot contains waters of the Ganga meant to cool the fiery Shiva.

Kanwariyas, who carry the holy water of the Ganges on a sling

north India where devotees of Shiva, the Kanwariyas, carry pots of Ganga water. The kavadi is a symbol of worldly responsibilities that entrap humans in the material world. Murugan moves to the metaphorical south to help his devotees fulfil their responsibilities and to remind them that they have not been abandoned by Shiva.

Across India there are many ascetics who shun the householder's life but are guardians of village communities. Murugan is the most famous one. And like Murugan, other guardian gods are identified either as local manifestations of Shiva or his sons.

In Tulsidas's *Ram Charit Manas*, which is a retelling of the Ramayana written in the 15th century in north India, Hanuman, the monkey-god who helps Ram defeat the Rakshasa-king Ravana, is called an avatar of Shiva.

In Tamil Nadu is another village god known as Aiyanar, who is born when the seed of Shiva is incubated in the womb of six Matrikas. He is shown riding an elephant or a horse. Sometimes, he has a dog next to him. He is a village guardian god, to whom villagers offer votive terracotta horses.

There are stories of how Shiva shed semen when he saw Mohini, the female form of Vishnu. From the shed semen were born the various warrior-gods who protect the villages of India, Hanuman included.

In Kerala, the son of Shiva and Mohini is called Ayyappa or Manikantha. He is Hari-Hara-Suta, the son of Hari (Vishnu) and Hara (Shiva). He is raised by the local king who has no children of his own. When the queen bears a son of her own, she becomes insecure and tries to harm Ayyappa. She asks him to fetch for her

Poster art of Hanuman

Poster art of Ayyappa

Aiyanar, the village god of Tamil Nadu with his companions

the milk of a tigress, hoping that the quest will result in his death. Instead, the boy goes to the forest, encounters and kills a demoness called Mahishi, finds a tigress, milks her, and returns to the city riding a tiger. This reveals his divinity, and the queen realises her mistake. She begs for forgiveness. Ayyappa declares that he will never marry; he gives the kingdom to the queen's son and promises to be the guardian of the kingdom from atop a nearby hill.

Like Murugan, Ayyappa stands on a hill. He is a very masculine god who shuns female company. So does Hanuman, who serves Ram. Celibacy and ascetic practices are closely associated with Shiva. It indicates nivritti-marga, withdrawal from the world. Serving as a warrior, however, indicates participation in worldly affairs. It indicates interest in worldly matters. Celibate warrior sons of Shiva thus embody that aspect of Shiva which is more connected with culture. Through these forms, Shiva acknowledges the human yearning for sanctuary and security.

The city of Kashi is associated with Kotwals, or policemen, who are called Bhairavas. In this form, Shiva protects the town like a guard dog. He is feared and appeased by travellers who seek entry into the city. Without his permission, no one can enter. This role of doorkeeper and guardian is often performed by gods who are both celibate and warriors. Goddess temples are flanked by images of two Bhairavas, the white Bhairava and the black Bhairava, locally known as Gora Bhairo and Kala Bhairo. Shiva here plays a very mundane, earthy role. There is nothing transcendent in this function. In Ram temples, Hanuman plays the role of guardian and doorkeeper.

In the Deccan region, there is Khandoba, or Mallana, a warrior-god who rides a white stallion and goes into battle with his

Poster art of Khandoba, the guardian-god from Maharashtra

dog. He fights the demons Mani and Malla, and secures the land for the local villagers. He is visualised with a thick moustache and glaring eyes, visuals that are aimed to enhance his machismo. He was the patron god of the Maratha warriors who controlled India in the 17th century. Like a warlord, he is associated with horses and dogs. He came to be identified with the more aggressive and martial forms of Shiva: Virabhadra, the righteous warrior, and Bhairava, the fearsome warrior.

Khandoba is, however, married. He has many wives. And these wives are daughters of local village communities. One of his wives belongs to the shepherd community. Another belongs to the trading community. Another is the daughter of a tailor and a fourth is the daughter of a gardener. Other wives belong to communities of oil pressers, even Muslims. Thus through marriage, Khandoba, the guardian god of the village, is anchored to the village community. He protects them and they give him wives for pleasure.

There is great dispute in the scriptures about whether Murugan is married or single. In north India, he is typically seen as a lone bachelor god who is obsessed with war; women shun his shrine. In south India, he is typically seen with two wives, Valli and Sena. Marriage is a metaphor for worldliness.

According to one tale, after killing Taraka, Kartikeya was so filled with energy and passion that he yearned the company of women. But the women did not want his company as he was the god of war and full of bloodlust. Wherever he went he brought destruction and death. Every time Kartikeya approached a woman, they appeared to him either as his mother or as mourning

Poster art of Murugan, the boy-god

widows. This is why Kartikeya never got married and that is why in the few north Indian temples of Kartikeya, women choose to stay out.

In Haryana, in Pahowa, Kurukshetra district, is a temple dedicated to Kartikeya. No woman is allowed to enter this temple as the deity here is a bachelor and because the deity is the god of war and death. The deity, identified with Kartikeya, has no skin. He gave it to his mother so that no woman would find him attractive and so not marry him and risk becoming a war widow. Oil is poured on the body of this war-mongering deity to calm him down and to please all soldiers who have died in battle. It is said that Yudhishtira was advised by Krishna to visit this shrine and pour oil on the image of Kartikeya after the Mahabharata war, in which eighteen million warriors were killed, so as to seek the forgiveness of the dead.

According to another tale, Kartikeya was upset when his parents chose to give Ganesha wives first. Feeling that his mother favoured Ganesha over him, Kartikeya left his northern abode and moved south.

The southern direction is associated with Yama, with death, with change, with fear. Shakti came from the south. In the south lives Daksha, her father, who through yagna domesticates nature and creates culture. Shiva holds culture in disdain, but his son goes south and assimilates his father's ascetic wisdom with the ways of culture. This is metaphorically expressed through marriage.

Murugan marries twice. The first marriage is an arranged marriage, an expression of social obligation. This wife is Devasena,

Gigantic image of the bachelor
Murugan from the Batu caves, Malaysia

Rare temple of Kartikeya in north India
at Pahowa, Kurukshetra, Haryana

Image of Murugan with two wives from a Tamil temple shrine

or Sena. She is the daughter of Indra given to Murugan in gratitude for defeating Taraka. Devasena means 'army of the gods', and so can also be seen as the embodiment of a thought: Murugan is married to his army.

The second marriage is the result of romance and passion. The woman who wins Murugan's ascetic heart with her raw tribal energy is Valli. She was found by her father, Nampi, a tribal chief, in a hole dug by women looking for wild forest yams (valli), hence her name. She is thus a child of the forest. When she comes of age, she is asked to guard her father's millet field. And that is when Murugan hears of her from the sage Narada, who is instrumental in bringing him to the south.

Murugan comes down from his hill and is smitten by this young girl. He takes the form of a young warrior and woos her. She hesitates. She is not sure how to respond. Suddenly a wild elephant appears and a frightened Valli seeks refuge in Murugan's arms. The elephant turns out to be Ganesha who removes all obstacles. Valli succumbs to Murugan's charm. She is besotted by his power. She surrenders to his will.

Songs and stories describe the love of Murugan and Valli. How she keeps it a secret from her father, how everyone in the village notices the sorrow of the girl when she is not in the millet field, the secret trysts a female companion orchestrates between the lovers. The mood is passionate, romantic and clandestine. At first Murugan is unable to understand Valli's apprehension. As the son of a hermit and as the warlord of the gods, he is not familiar with the ways of culture and the concerns of a father for a daughter. Finally, he understands and presents himself in full splendour to Nampi. Nampi realises that his daughter's secret

Murugan with Valli and Sena

lover is none other than the patron deity of his tribe, the warrior-god who lives atop a hill. He bows to Murugan and welcomes him home as son-in-law.

Thus while Ganesha helps devotees move from south to north, Kartikeya himself moves from north to south for the benefit of devotees. While Ganesha tempers materialistic cravings with spiritual insight, Murugan tempers his martial attitude with divine grace and romantic emotions. Thus the Goddess helps Shiva connect with humanity through her two sons.

# 7. Nataraja's Secret

*Destruction is deconstruction*

Modern sculpture of Shiva as the lone ascetic

Image from Maharashtra showing Shiva as Shankara, the householder

*B*rahma creates. Shiva destroys. Brahma is <u>not</u> worshipped. Shiva is worshipped. This is because Brahma creates Kama, Yama, and Tripura — desire, death and three worlds. Shiva is Kamantaka, Yamantaka and Tripurantaka — destroyer of desire, death and the three worlds.

Humans desire life, fear death and construct three worlds because humans fear death more than any other living creature on earth. Our fear is greater because we can imagine. We imagine what happens after death, we imagine a world without death, we imagine a world without us and wonder what is the point of life. Unable to make sense of things, we try to control life — we get attached to things, we resist change and we create property. Human civilisation is thus rooted in fear. It is a delusion. Brahmanda or culture is maya.

The first people who brought the word 'maya' into English were 18th-century scholars who lived when Europe was in the throes of the scientific revolution. They used the word 'illusion' to translate the word 'maya', and the word 'destroyer' to describe Shiva. Since Hindus describe the world as maya and worship Shiva, Europeans concluded that Hindus were a people who held worldly life in disdain. This romantic, exotic, world-denying perception of India, in general, and Hinduism, in particular, still persists as tourist brochures are full of images of the Kumbha Mela at Allahabad, where naked mendicants smeared with ash and holding tridents, just like Shiva, line up to bathe at the confluence of the Ganga and Yamuna every twelve years.

The European gaze was assumed to be scientific, objective, free of bias and hence modern. However, in the 1970s, scholars realised

Though hermit, Shiva is the only deity in the Hindu pantheon to be visualised with a wife and children. Neither Vishnu nor Ram nor Krishna are depicted thus.

Poster art of Shiva as the householder

The animals associated with the members of the family are sworn enemies as they are predators and prey, yet they live in harmony, representing ideal family values.

Every member of the family has his or her own vehicle.

Miniature painting of Shiva as the householder

that 'modern' thought was actually not as logical and free of bias as it was claimed to be; it was informed by cultural prejudices. The translations of European scholars were clearly based on the one-life framework. Since the God of the Bible is described as creator and hence worthy of worship, they were bewildered as to why Hindus worship Shiva, not Brahma, a conundrum that still persists in modern academia. This was postmodern thinking. Hindu ideas need to be seen in the Hindu context, not using the one-life framework of Europeans, but the rebirth framework of Indians. When this is done, a more appropriate translation of maya is 'construction'. Shiva then does not destroy; he deconstructs!

The word 'construction' emerged as part of the postmodern vocabulary; it was not part of the modern (or rather pre postmodern) vocabulary of the 18th century. Thus 18th century scholars were ill-equipped to explain Indian thoughts.

Construction means a perception of the world shaped by a measuring scale that depends on cultural norms and personal prejudices. This perception changes every time there is a change in cultural norms and/or personal prejudices. What is considered right or good or beautiful today may not be considered so tomorrow, all sensory inputs remaining the same. Thus the perception can be 'de-constructed' and 're-constructed'. The word 'illusion' came from typical scientific arrogance that logic can decipher the truth free of all bias. The word 'construction' admits that all understanding is rooted in bias.

For Hindus, maya is a constructed reality. More accurately, maya is the measuring scale that values and devalues all things in Prakriti, and by doing so gives rise to Brahmanda, an individual's perception of the world. It is neither a bad thing nor is it a good

Image of Shiva as the formless linga

thing. It is just the way the human mind perceives reality. Animals do not live in maya, because they do not possess imagination. Human beings do. Humans are therefore subject to maya.

The intention of tapasya is to reflect on and deconstruct and be liberated from it. Tapa or spiritual fire burns maya and destroys Brahmanda. Shiva, the lord of Tapasvins, is therefore the destroyer of maya. Maya nurtures aham, the ego, that imagines itself to be master of the world. Shiva destroys aham so that atma or soul can be realised. When this happens, human life is validated. Pashu, or animal, becomes Purusha.

When there is no construction, when there is no maya, when there is no perceived reality, no aham, what remains is the linga, the pillar of Shiva. This is possible only when the human imagination has no fear. The absence of fear fills the mind with bliss. This is ananda. This is the linga, the erect phallus of Shiva. It is Swayambhu, self-created and self-contained, as it does not depend on external stimuli for its existence. This can only happen when there is wisdom. But wisdom for whom?

Humans are the only creatures who can imagine other people's fear. Humans can empathise. The Shiva-linga therefore does not stand alone; encasing it is the Shakti-yoni, the womb of the Goddess. She is the temple in which the linga is enshrined. She is the world around the temple. She is the water pot hanging above the Shiva-linga, dripping water on him, making sure he does not shut his eyes, but opens them to look at the other. Shakti thus ensures Shiva looks at jiva, humanity that has succumbed to aham, maya and Brahmanda out of fear.

The banyan tree represents immortality.

Shiva, as Dakshinamurti, faces south.

The Siddhas who seek wisdom from the teacher.

The Vedas or books containing wisdom.

The demon of fear and forgetfulness and ignorance.

Shiva as Dakshinamurti, the teacher

It is ironical that Shiva, the hermit-god of Hinduism, is the only Hindu god to be visualised as a householder with a wife and children. All gods have a consort by their side — Vishnu has Lakshmi, Ram has Sita, Krishna has Radha — but no one is visualised with their children apart from Shiva.

Shakti is nature. In nature, all creatures fear death. That is why they hunt for food and are wary of predators. Through Ganesha, Shakti makes Shiva take away fear of scarcity. Through Kartikeya, Shakti makes Shiva take away fear of the predator. With these two fears gone, humanity can focus on its greatest fear — the fear of meaninglessness, the fear of invalidation. It can resist the creation of aham, and realise the atma.

To facilitate this deconstruction, Shiva becomes the primal teacher, Adi-nath. Adi-nath teaches the world in two forms, either as Dakshinamurti or as Nataraja.

Dakshinamurti means the one who sits facing south. In this form, Shiva sits under the still Pole Star in the shade of the banyan tree. Nothing moves here, nothing grows here, except wisdom. Here, sages sit at Shiva's feet in rapt attention.

The direction that Shiva faces is the direction of Yama, of death, of change. Shiva helps his students face this change with wisdom. He draws attention to the three forms of change: natural, social and personal. Animals experience only one kind of change — the natural, the change of seasons and tides. Communities experience changing values of society. Social values change as one moves from place to place; and social values in one place invariably change over time. In addition, individuals experience personal change,

Shiva's dance is the symbol of change; dance can only be created when the dancer keeps moving. What is created in a moment is destroyed in the next.

Dance occupies three dimensions of space: length, width and depth.

Dance traverses three dimensions of time: past, present and future.

Stone carving of dancing Shiva from Badami, Karnataka

The three blades of a trident and three leaves of a bilva sprig

change that happens when context changes. We behave differently in times of prosperity and differently in times of crisis. Our own understanding of the world changes as we experience fortune and misfortune.

The linga is offered the sprig of the bel or bilva, which has three leaves joined at the stem. The three leaves represent the three changes: of nature or Prakriti, of society or Sanskriti and of individual perception of Brahmanda. The stem is wisdom that we seek from the teacher, the wisdom that will help us recognise maya, and appreciate the various constructions that shape our notions of reality.

The blades of Shiva's trident symbolise Tripura, the three constructions we occupy because of maya. It means the natural world, the cultural world and the personal world. It also means the world of 'me' (our physical and mental body), 'mine' (the wealth and knowledge and relationships we claim ownership over and control) and 'not mine' (all things we do not claim ownership over and are unable to control). It also means the three bodies: sthula sharira (physical body), sukshma sharira (conscious mind full of opinions) and karana sharira (unconscious mind full of impressions). The staff that Shiva holds is the staff of wisdom, the linga beyond the maya.

Shiva's sacred mark, the Tripundra, is made of three horizontal lines of ash. Ash means that which survives when matter is destroyed. Ash represents the atma that never dies. The three lines represent the three worlds that are deconstructed and destroyed by Shiva's third eye of wisdom.

Miniature of Shiva emerging from light

As Dakshinamurti, Shiva sits atop Kailasa, the heat of tapa locked in his body turning the world around him into a desolate snow-clad landscape. This Shiva is the impatient and angry Rudra who beheads Brahma and transforms into Kapalika. This Shiva is Bhairava with the dogs and Virabhadra with the sword. This Shiva is alone.

Shakti draws the heat out, causes the snow to melt and turn into the Ganga that flows down to fertilise the plains and sustain human settlements. On the banks of the Ganga, she invites Shiva to settle in her city, Kashi, as Shankar-Shambho, the kind, benevolent, understanding form of God.

Kashi is the city of Ganga and Gauri, known locally as Annapurna, the kitchen goddess. Ganga and Gauri are two aspects of Shakti, one representing the bubbly river and the other the patient mountain. The two goddesses make Shiva understand and empathise with human fears and frailties in Kashi. Here, the head of Brahma, which clings to Shiva's fingers and sears into his palm after being severed, is washed away at the Kapala-mochan-ghat, because Ganga forgives all crimes, even the vile, incestuous gaze of Brahma. Here, Shiva becomes the lovable Shambhu who is both the dog-riding Kala Bhairava, remover of malevolent spirits, and the bhang-drinking Gora Bhairava, who enjoys the company of ghosts. Here, he is Vishwa-nath, master of the world. Only in Kashi does the Ganga flow northward, drawn by the wisdom of Dakshinamurti.

Further south, in Chidambaram, he is the dancer, Nataraja. He teaches through dance because words are too literal to capture the essence of the intangible nirguna. One needs symbols that dance is best able to communicate. A book occupies space but not

South Indian painting of Shiva as Nataraja

Poster art of Shiva as Nataraja

time, a discourse occupies time but not space, a dance occupies both space and time. It can be seen and heard and read. It is a performance that appeals to the senses, stirs the emotions and demands intellectual analysis. In the process, tools to deconstruct maya are passed on.

The story goes that a group of Mimansikas was performing yagna in a forest when Shiva walked past naked. Shiva was totally oblivious to them for he was in a state of bliss. The Mimansikas, however, were distracted by him and held him responsible for the distraction.

Mimamsa means investigation or inquiry. Mimansikas are those who yearn to understand the meaning of life. Mimamsa is divided into two schools: the early school or Purva Mimamsa and later school or Uttar Mimamsa. This division emerged as the former school paid too much attention to form and failed to realise that thought had shaped the form. The later school paid great attention to the thought of the form.

Those who were performing the yagna saw Shiva's form and did not see the thought. What they saw frightened them. They saw a man who was so content and blissful, he did not need all the things the Mimansikas aspired for. He did not seek wealth, he did not seek knowledge, he did not seek power. He was self-assured, self-contained and self-fulfilled. The sight of the naked Shiva made them feel inadequate and insecure. He possessed what they did not possess. And they felt their wives would leave their sides and chase Shiva.

In fear, they saw Shiva as a predator and decided to destroy

South Indian bronze sculpture of Shiva as Urdhva-Nataraja

PLEASE WRITE 1 parag

him. Using their knowledge of yagna, they invoked creatures from the fire and unleashed them against Shiva. First came the tiger, then a serpent, and finally a demon.

Shiva showed no signs of fear. He simply caught the tiger by its jaw, skinned it alive and wrapped its hide, dripping with blood, around his body. Shiva then picked up the snake and put it around his neck; there it sat, still, with upraised hood. Finally, Shiva jumped on the back of the demon, breaking his back, and started to dance, the only music being provided by his rattle-drum.

At first the Mimansikas were terrified. They realised this naked man was no ordinary man. Fear turned to awe as the performance continued; it was mesmerising! Shiva's hands, feet and body moved gracefully, in perfect coordination. His whole form seemed to expand. The ends of his hair rose up to touch the skies; the stars and the planets stopped to gaze. The tips of his fingers grazed the horizons where the gods assembled, spellbound. The thud of footsteps forced the demons and serpents to rise from their subterranean kingdoms. Such a performance had never been seen before. No nymph had danced like this. Shiva's consort, Shakti, smiled from afar as she fell in love once again.

The Rishi Bharata made a note of all that he saw: the change in expressions or abhinayas, the twists of the body known as angikas, the hand gestures known as mudras, the mood evoked known as bhavas, the feelings stirred known as rasas. All this he put down in the Natya-shastra, the treatise on the performing arts.

The Mimansikas realised this was no ordinary performance. Unlike a gentle, seductive dance which is meant to enchant, known as lasya, this was tandava, forceful, as if demanding attention and evoking thought. Shiva was communicating. This was not

Shiva dancing on one foot

entertainment. This was enlightenment. This was the Ananda-Tandava, the dance of bliss.

Shiva struck a whole series of poses in order to stir the imagination. He finally froze. This final pose contained the wisdom of the Vedas. What had not been realised by the Mimansikas after performing hundreds of rituals was realised by that one dance pose.

Shiva's right palm was upraised. This is the a-bhaya mudra or the gesture that communicates 'do not fear'. Shiva sensed the fear of the Mimansikas. Why were they so obsessed with the yagna? Because the ritual made them feel less afraid as it granted them control of the world around them.

To feel safe, the Mimansikas had created the Jyotisha-shastra, that enabled them to study the stars and planets and predict the future. They had created the Vastu-shastra that enabled them to control the movement of energies across eight directions, so that positive forces moved their way. They had put together Dhanur-vidya, that enabled them to create weapons and secure themselves. They even had Ayur-veda, the science of health and healing that offered the promise of immortality. But despite all this, fear still remained. Because the source of the fear had not been understood.

The upraised right palm is strategically placed on the left hand that is pointing to the left foot that swings across the right leg and is poised midair. Attention is thus being drawn to the moving left leg.

This raising of the left foot leaves the body imbalanced. Yet Shiva is balanced, calm and composed. He holds this position without

South Indian painting of Shiva Ekapada

thoughts of falling down. He is comfortable. He is Shiva Ekapada, the one who stands on one leg.

The left leg is in fact in motion; it moves round and round creating a ring. It represents the precariousness of existence, the endless change of nature, and the transformations of the world. The left leg thus mimics nature that is the source of fear.

That the left hand and the left leg are moving towards the right, makes one wonder what is so special about the right side. In mythic vocabulary, the left side of the body is associated with the rhythm of the material world because it is where the heart is located. Just as the heart beats at regular intervals, the material world goes through rhythmic changes in the form of tides and seasons. The right half then becomes the side of spiritual reality; it is still and silent. The left side represents Prakriti, nature's constant change. The right side is Purusha, the human potential to stay still. To exist, one needs both sides, left and right, Prakriti and Purusha.

The Mimansikas are unable to still their mind. Faced with the whirling material world, their mind goes into a spin. They use rituals to fight change, and fail. But still, they continue to fight back with more rituals as they know no better. Shiva presents an option, a way out from fear, not by controlling nature but by recognising the truth of nature.

The tiger killed fearlessly by Shiva represents nature that frightens Brahma. Shiva refuses to let nature intimidate him. At the same time, he does not seek to control or domesticate nature. He observes nature like the serpent coiled around his neck. The hooded cobra is

Stone sculpture from Belur, Karnataka, of dancing Shiva

the symbol of the alert and still Tapasvin who sits unmoving and watches with full attention the world around it.

Unlike the Mimansikas who were busy conducting rituals to tame nature, the Tapasvin observed the rhythms of Nature — manifesting as breath, heartbeat, tides and seasons. He also observed the rhythms of culture and the rhythms of thoughts and emotions in every human being. He saw how fortune follows misfortune, joy follows sorrow, excitement follows boredom, pain follows pleasure. On careful, focused attention, he realised that everything changes over time — some things change by the second, some by centuries, but all things material and tangible have to change form. The body has to age and die. Ideas come and go. Societies rise and fall. But new life is always being created. Thus nothing ends forever. There is always a new beginning.

This cyclical view of things is represented by the wheel of fire in which Shiva dances. It is the wheel known as samsara or the wheel of rebirth. All living creatures die and are reborn. All thoughts and dreams rise and fall. At each birth a different form is taken, sometimes human and sometimes animal. At death this body is discarded. Shiva advises the Mimansikas to sit back, sit still and observe this. Awareness will take away anxiety and fear. It will bring repose and faith.

Although nature's truth is timeless, we often forget it. Shiva dances on the back of a demon called Apasmara, which means the demon of forgetfulness. We forget that what goes around comes around. As we suffer the winter cold, we forget that the previous year it was cold too but it did pass. As we suffer, we imagine the suffering will never end. Apasmara makes Brahma forget who he really is, who he was before he chased Shatarupa, before he

Chola bronze of Shiva as Nataraja

sprouted five heads, before Shiva severed one of them. We humans forget what our mind was before it was contaminated by imagined, amplified fear. We forget that we construct Brahmanda, subjective reality, to cope with objective reality. We forget that only we can destroy this Brahmanda, with its three constituent worlds of 'me', 'mine' and 'not mine'. Because we have the third eye of wisdom.

When two people meet, initially fear governs the relationship. This fear goes away when each one is convinced the other is no threat. This fear is amplified when one dominates the other. Shiva offers the third way, one where fear is outgrown. This happens when one empathises with the other, when there is love for the other, when one recognises the autonomy of the other and neither seeks to dominate or be dominated or dependent in any way. But to empathise with the other, we have to look at the other, not in fear, but with genuine affection and sensitivity. This is darshan, the gaze of understanding.

Nataraja's two upper arms hold up the options that we have as we go through life. In one hand he holds the damaru, or rattle-drum, while in the other he holds tapa, the spiritual fire that burns without fuel.

One option is to spend our lives ignoring the reality of life, like monkeys spellbound by the rattle-drum. We can focus on meaningless activities that keep us busy, help us pass the time, and prevent us from getting bored or distract us from introspecting and reflecting on life.

The other option is to introspect and reflect on life. We can ask ourselves what shapes our decisions and where does our self-

Miniature of Shiva with five heads

image come from. Why are we in certain situations like the petrified deer, and in other situations like the dominant lion? We will realise that notions such as victim and villain and hero are all imaginary constructions, stories within our heads and stories that we receive from society. In other words, they are maya, constructions to fortify ourselves from fear, subjective realities that make us feel powerful.

Maya gives us meaning to survive this world until Shiva, the destroyer, gives us the strength to outgrow fear and hence outgrow dependence on constructed realities. Shiva helps us realise that heroes, villains and victims are creations of fear. When fear is destroyed, there is no hero or villain or victim. Shiva, the destroyer, thus offers wisdom to outgrow fear. This is liberation. This is moksha.

# 7 Secrets of the Goddess

*As nature, she is mother*
*As culture, she is daughter*
*Creator of humanity*
*Creation of humanity*
*She is wealth, power, language*
*Lakshmi, Durga, Saraswati*
*She is Devi*
*Answer to that masculine anxiety*
*Which keeps resisting enquiry*

Locked in her stories, symbols and rituals are the secrets of our ancestors. *7 Secrets of the Goddess* attempts to unlock seven.

# Author's Note

## On Reality and Representation

*L*akshmi massages Vishnu's feet. Is this male domination? Kali stands on Shiva's chest. Is this female domination? Shiva is half a woman. Is this gender equality? Why then is Shakti never half a man?

Taken literally, stories, symbols and rituals of Hindu mythology have much to say about gender relationships. Taken symbolically, they reveal many more things about humanity and nature. Which is the correct reading? Who knows?

*Within infinite myths lies an eternal truth*
*Who knows it all?*
*Varuna has but a thousand eyes*
*Indra, a hundred*
*You and I, only two.*

# On Capitalisation

*C*apitalisation is found in the English script but not in Indic scripts. So we need to clarify the difference between shakti and Shakti, maya and Maya, devi and Devi, goddess and Goddess. We may not always be successful.

Shakti is a proper noun, the name of the Goddess. It is also a common noun, shakti, meaning power. Likewise, maya means delusion, and Maya is another name of the Goddess. The word devi, spelt without capitalisation, refers to any goddess, while Devi, spelt with capitalisation, refers to the supreme Goddess. Often Mahadevi is used for the proper noun instead of Devi. Shiva may be Mahadeva, who is maha-deva, greater than all devas; similarly Shakti is Mahadevi, who is maha-devi, greater than all devis.

Without capitalisation, devi/goddess may also refer to limited forms of the female divine, while limitless ideas are referred to as Goddess/Devi using capitalisation. Ganga is devi, goddess of a river, while Gauri is Devi, Goddess embodying domesticated nature.

Context needs always to be considered. Kali is goddess in early Puranas, where she is one of the divine feminine collective; later she is Goddess embodying untamed nature. Saraswati seen alone is Goddess, but when visualised next to Durga, who is Devi, she becomes the daughter, hence goddess.

# 1. Gaia's Secret

### Male anxiety is outdated

Greek mythology: Gaia, the earth-mother

$G$aia is the earth-mother in Greek mythology. Her mate Uranus, the starry-sky, clung to her intimately and gave her no space. The only way her son, Cronus, could leave Gaia's womb was by castrating his father. From the blood drops arose Aphrodite, goddess of love, and the Erinyes, the goddesses of retribution, who were fiercely protective of the mother. Cronus then declared himself king and, to the horror of the Gaia, ate his own children to prevent them from overpowering him as he overpowered his father. Gaia saves one son, Zeus, from the brutality of Cronus, raises him in secret, and eventually Zeus attacks and kills Cronus. In triumph, Zeus declares himself the father of gods of men, takes residence atop Mount Olympus that reaches into the sky. Gaia remains the earth-mother, respected but distant.

This idea of a primal female deity, first adored, then brutally side-lined by a male deity is a consistent theme in mythologies around the world.

The Inuit (eskimo) tribes of the Arctic region tell the story of one Sedna, who, unhappy with her marriage to a seagull, begs her father to take her back home in his boat. But, as they make their way, they are attacked by a flock of seagulls. To save himself, Sedna's father casts her overboard. When she tries to climb back, he cuts off her fingers. As she struggles to get back in with her mutilated hands, he cuts her arms too. So she sinks to the bottom of the ocean, her dismembered limbs transforming into fish, seals, whales, and all of the other sea mammals. Those who wish to hunt her children for food need to appease her through shamans who speak soothing words.

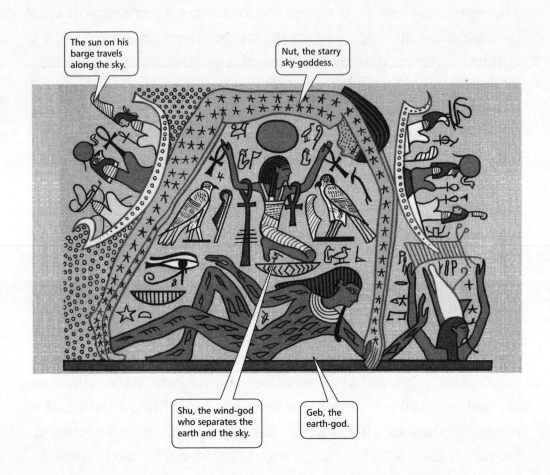

Egyptian mythology: Nut, the sky-mother

The Tantrik tradition of India speaks of the primal one, Adya, who took the form of a bird and laid three unfertilised eggs from which were born Brahma, Vishnu and Shiva. Adya then sought to unite with the three male gods. Brahma refused as he saw Adya as his mother; Adya cursed him that there will be no temples in his honour. Adya found Vishnu too shifty and shrewd, so she turned to the rather stern Shiva who, advised by Vishnu, agreed to be her lover provided she gave him her third eye. She did, and he used it to release a missile of fire that set her aflame and turned her into ash. From the ash came three goddesses, Saraswati, Lakshmi and Gauri who became wives of Brahma, Vishnu and Shiva. Also from the ash came the grama-devis, goddesses of every human settlement.

Egyptian mythology acknowledges a time before gender. Then there was Atum, 'the Great He-She', who brought forth the god of air Shu and the goddess of dew Tefnut who separated Geb, the earth-god, from Nut, the sky-goddess, who gave birth to Isis and Osiris, the first queen and king of human civilisation. Then Seth killed Osiris and declared himself king, until Isis gave birth to Horus and contested his claim.

In these stories from around the world, the male deities compete for the female prize. This can be traced to nature, where all wombs are precious but not all sperms. So the males have to compete for the female. In many bird species, the female chooses the male with the most colourful feathers, the best voice or the best song, or with the capability of building the best nest. In many animal species, such as the walrus and the lion, the alpha male keeps all the females for himself; thus there are always 'remainder' males who do not get the female. This selection of only the best males creates anxiety amongst the not-so-good males and translates into

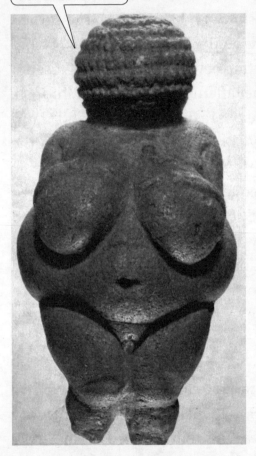

The corpulent female form indicates fertility and access to abundance of food, making this image sacred.

The ram is a symbol of male virility and autonomy.

Stone Age Venus from Europe          Sacred ram from Mesopotamia

the fear of invalidation in the human species. To cope with this fear of invalidation, social structures such as marriage laws and inheritance rights come into being, often at the cost of the female.

As human society learnt to domesticate animals and plants, trade and build cities, we saw a gradual shift in social laws, deterioration in the status of women, and rejection of Goddess-worship in favour of God-worship.

After thousands of years as hunter-gatherers, humans learned to tame and breed animals. These pastoral communities valued all the cows but realised they did not need all the bulls to maintain numbers. Many bulls could be castrated and turned into beasts of burden, pulling carts and ploughs.

Could this apply to human society too? Not all males were necessary for reproduction. This is reinforced in the story of Nari-kavacha, whose name means 'he who used women as a shield', found in Hindu Puranas. When Parashuram slaughtered all the Kshatriya men, only one man survived by hiding in the women's quarters. From this 'cunning coward' sprang all the future Kshatriya clans.

That a tribe needed women, not men, for its survival manifests in Stone Age art where we find an obsession with fat, fertile female forms, or images of bejewelled women with their genitals exposed, while men are either reduced to the phallus or worshipped as the alpha bull, ram or goat.

This is the same reason why, in the Bronze Age, we find images of groups of women worshipped alongside a single male. Similar thoughts gave rise to the Yogini shrines found across India with

Indus seal showing goddess worship

Poster art showing self-sacrifice

Poster art of Hinglaj Mata of Balochistan

just one male, the Bhairava, and the practice of Kanya Puja, which involves worshipping a group of young girls accompanied by a single boy in north India during vasant navaratri or spring festival of the Goddess. A few anthropologists even argue that Krishna's raas-leela may have its roots in old matriarchal tribes where the women valued only one male of the village.

To get access to the women, men had to fight each other or simply submit to the woman's choice. This explains the origin of the 'swayam-vara' ceremonies described in the Hindu Puranas, designed to get the best male for the woman.

In such female-dominated cultures, the male could not refuse the woman: in the Mahabharata, when Arjuna refuses her advances, Urvashi curses him to turn into a eunuch. Any man who forced himself upon a woman was killed: in Greek mythology, Artemis turns Actaeon, the man who seeks to ravish her, into a stag that is ripped to pieces by his own hunting dogs. Anyone who attacked the man the woman chose would be put to death by other males: in Greek mythology, all the Greek warlords swear to protect the man Helen chooses as her husband. But there were always men eager to kill rivals and take their place as lovers: Greek mythology tells the story of Adonis, the boy-lover of Aphrodite, goddess of love, who is killed by the more virile and jealous Mars, god of war. These tales hark back to a pre-patriarchal, matriarchal, society.

To ensure that the dominant males did not have exclusive and eternal rights to women, the ritual of killing the chosen males at regular intervals emerged. The chosen one came to her during the sowing season and he was sacrificed at harvest season. The woman had no say in the matter. She could choose her lover, but her choice was fatal. The triumph of the dominant male was in fact a march

Diana of Ephesus

Ishtar of Babylon

Greek mythology: Adonis and Aphrodite

to death. So we find in Sumerian mythology, Innana mourning for her lover Dumuzi who comes to her every spring but departs in winter. In the *Rig Veda*, there is a hymn where Urvashi's husband, Pururava, pines for her while she leaves him for the realm of the gandharvas.

The only way to survive being killed at the end of the term as king and consort of the Goddess was by castrating oneself. And so in the Near East, the priests of Cybele, called the Galli, ritually castrated themselves emulating Attis, the castrated son/lover of the goddess. Some anthropologists trace similar thoughts to the practice of male priests dressing up as women and carrying pots during the worship of many grama-devis, the village goddesses of India.

We can speculate if the male heads around Kali's neck are the heads of men who were killed after they gave a child to the goddess of the tribe: an indicator of the price paid by the male sexual gaze. In Vaishno-devi, the Goddess is a virgin who kills the Bhairava for approaching her sexually, but then, after beheading him, she asks her devotees to worship him too. We can only speculate if this can be traced to the ancient rejection, or subjugation of the male sexual gaze.

It was perhaps at this phase of human culture that the Goddess came to be addressed as virgin mother, an ironical phrase it seems today, for how can a virgin bear a child? Today a virgin is a woman who has never had sex. But earlier it meant a woman who was ready to bear a child. Every woman then was a virgin between menstruations at the time of ovulation. This virginity was restored after childbirth. This thought informs a detail in the epic Mahabharata, where the heroine Draupadi walks through fire to restore her virginity before she goes to the next husband.

**Polynesian mythology: Maui and Hine**

We also find the virgin being referred to as a whore, which means a prostitute. This is a pejorative term today but long ago, before the idea of property became the cornerstone of human culture, it simply meant a woman who was free to go to any man. She was like the earth that accepts seeds from all plants freely; she was no field where the farmer controls the sowing and claims the harvest.

Over time, meanings changed and 'virgin' became a word of praise while 'whore' became an insult. The shift in meaning reflects a shift from an older time when women were free to a later time when women were bound to men.

The close association of women with sexual pleasure and childbirth on one hand and death on the other is made explicit in the stories of Yama and Yami, the first living creatures in the *Rig Veda*. Yami, the sister, approaches Yama, the brother. He rejects her advances on moral grounds and eventually dies and finds himself trapped in the land of the dead as he has left no offspring behind in the land of the living. Thus, rejection of sex turns him into the god of death. Yami mourns for him, turning into the goddess of the night, Yamini, as well as the mournful dark river, Yamuna.

Similarly, in Polynesian mythology, Maui tries to get immortality for humanity by entering the vagina of Hine, goddess of death and the netherworld, traversing her body and leaving it by her mouth. But just when he enters, she wakes up and, realising what Maui is trying to do, bites him with the teeth she has lining her vaginal lips. Even in Greek mythology, humanity is at the mercy of goddesses known as Graces or Fates who spun the thread that determined the quality and length of everyone's lives.

Biblical mythology: Samson and Delilah

This connection of death with sex, sex with pleasure and pleasure with women resulted in men associating women with immorality, misery and vulnerability. Rejecting women through celibacy offered physical strength. In the Bible, Samson loses his hair and his strength when he succumbs to the charms of Delilah; he regains it when he rejects her and turns to God. Rejecting women granted freedom from suffering. In Buddhism, the daughters of Mara, god of desire, are associated with decay, disease and death; in rejecting them, Gautama Siddhartha of the Sakya clan finds freedom from suffering, and comes to be known as Buddha, the enlightened one. Rejection of women even granted liberation from death. In the Tantra we hear how semen shed into a womb creates the son but weakens the father; however, if one is able to achieve urdhva-retas, reverse movement of semen up the spine towards the head, one can get siddhi, magical powers to control nature, even outsmart death. These ideas led to the rise of monastic and mystical cults that sought to either control nature or escape from it.

To get celibate ascetics to marry, or at least produce children, the idea of ancestors arose, in China and India, obligation to whom forces a man to have children before he renounces the world. In the Puranas, these 'pitr', who hang upside down like bats in the land of the dead, goad sages like Kardama and Agastya to look for wives and father children.

But getting a wife was not easy. The Puranas refer to Gandharva-vivah, where women chose their lovers, alongside Asura-vivah, where women were bought, Rakshasa-vivah, where women were abducted, and Pisacha-vivah, where women were made pregnant while they slept.

These stories suggest the rise of trading communities, where

Kalamkari print of archery contest for the hand of Draupadi in marriage

Poster of Krishna abducting Rukmini

women became popular commodities with high demand and low supply, forcing men who did not have the qualities to attract or the wealth to buy, to turn to abduction, even rape, to secure wives. In the *Bhagavata Purana*, Krishna has to tame wild bulls to marry Satya, daughter of Nagnajit. In the Mahabharata, Bhisma abducts Amba, Ambika and Ambalika in order to procure wives for his brother, Vichitravirya. They were embodiments of wealth and power, mediums to create the next generation.

If pastoral society gave greater value to the stud bull while castrating the rest, if trading society started valuing the female as a commodity in great demand, then agricultural society introduced the idea of ownership.

At first, both men and women owned their bodies and so traded it freely. We hear of sacred prostitutes in Levant (Near East) and Babylon (Mesopotamia) dedicated to love-goddesses such as Astarte and Mytilla. The prostitutes were mostly women, but included a few men who were described as effeminate, or even castrated, known as catamites, who existed for the pleasure of men.

One reason given for the rise of sacred prostitution is that men took over all the economic activities of society, from animal husbandry to farming to trading, leaving women with no choice but to trade their bodies for pleasure and their wombs for procreation. Prostitute became a pejorative term as only the rich could afford the most beautiful of women. Gradually the word was used for all women who freely chose and discarded her lovers for a price. Eventually it came to be associated with exploitation, as women were denied ownership of their bodies. The woman's body, like

Roman mythology: Rape of the Sabine

the land, belonged to the father, brother, husband and even son. She was reduced to being just the field; man was the farmer, owner, customer and abuser. Her child now belonged to a man, either her brother in matrilineal communities or to her husband in patrilineal communities.

With fathers claiming ownership over daughters and deciding who she should marry, the practice known in Sanskrit texts as 'swayam-vara', where women chose their own husbands, came to an end. We find, in the *Bhagavata Purana*, Rukmini choosing to elope with Krishna rather than marrying the man, Shihupala, chosen by her father and brother. Likewise, in the Mahabharata, Subhadra chooses to elope with Arjuna, the man she loves, rather than marry the man chosen by her brother Balarama.

The Puranas speak of a Prajapati-vivah, where a man approaches the girl's father for her hand in marriage on grounds of merit. A Brahma-vivah is one where the girl's father offers her hand to a worthy man with the promise of dowry. In Deva-vivah, she is payment for services rendered by a man. In Rishi-vivah, a sage is given the daughter as a charitable gift, along with a cow (source of food and fuel) and an ox (beast of burden) so that he can become a householder. In the Mahabharata, Yayati gives his daughter Mamata to a priest who passes her on to four kings because it has been foretold she will be the mother of four kings. In exchange, each king gives the priest horses. Thus the priest is able to fulfil his promise to his teacher with the help of Yayati. No one asks what Mamata wants. But she forgives her father and retires to the forest.

In Nepal, until recently, women were dedicated as 'deukis' in temples. They had to take recourse to prostitution in order to survive. Many believed sex with deukis would cure them of many

The fierce and independent Bhagavati of Kerala

Devadasis who were dedicated to the temple deity

ailments. Children born to them have neither caste nor inheritance, as everything comes through the father. Similar practices have been traced to many parts of India, such as the mahari in Odisha and kalavant or deoli in Goa. These women were also associated with art and entertainment as they used song and dance to attract potential customers, and the relationship was not always sexual. The Sanskrit word 'devadasi' came into prominence only in the 19th century, when reform movements sought to outlaw these 'sacred prostitutes'.

Men wanted to 'own' their wives as they owned fields to ensure the child she bore was their child and not someone else's. Kunti states in the Mahabharata that at one time women were free to go to any man they pleased. Gradually their movements were restricted after Shvetaketu found his mother in the arms of another man and realised he may not be his father's son. Shvetaketu created marriage laws, limiting the number of men a woman could go to, and those only with her husband's permission. The Mahabharata limits the number of men a woman can go to as four, which is why Draupadi, who has five, is called a whore in the gambling hall by the men of the time. Significantly, in Vedic marriage rites, a woman is given to the moon, then to Gandharva Vishvavasu, then fire, and eventually her husband, thus forfeiting her rights to have more husbands.

In the Mahabharata, when Vichitravirya dies, his widows go to Vyasa in order to bear sons. Though biologically the children are Vyasa's, legally they belong to Vichitravirya. Thus the crop belongs to the owner of the field and not to the landless labourer who ploughed the field and sowed the seeds. Likewise, the five Pandavas are called children of Pandu even though he never makes his wives pregnant.

Greek mythology: Leda and the swan

Restricting the number of men a woman had access to ensured even the 'remainder' men of the tribe could get wives. But there was always the fear of being cuckolded by the wife, and of 'lesser' men ending up fostering the children of the dominant males. In Greek mythology, Zeus, king of Olympian gods, often seduces the wives and daughters of kings in secret. He takes the form of a swan and makes love to Leda. He takes the form of a beam of sunlight and makes love to Danae. He makes love to Alcmene by impersonating her husband, Amphitryon. In Hindu mythology, Indra makes love to Ahalya by impersonating her husband, Gautama. In the Ramayana, the sexual prowess of Ravana is constantly described leading to street gossip in Ayodhya as to whether Sita was truly chaste while held captive in the rakshasa's palace.

Further, there was great fear of a woman's 'excessive' sexual appetite. The Mahabharata tells the story of one Bhangashwana who was cursed by Indra to live half his life as a man and half his life as a woman. When asked what he preferred, he said a woman's life because the sound of 'mother' is sweeter, and because a woman has greater pleasure during sex. A similar story is found in Greek mythology where the seer Tieresias has lived life both as a man and a woman, and when Zeus asks him who gets greater pleasure during sex, he answers woman, angering Hera, wife of Zeus, who takes away his eyesight.

Fear that they would never be good enough to satisfy their wives, and that their wives would therefore find any excuse to seek another, more worthy lover, led to the imposition of strict laws on fidelity. Thus rose the Hindu concept of 'sati'. A wife's fidelity gave her magical powers, or 'sat', and made her 'sati'. For example, Renuka was so faithful to Jamadagni that she could

Sati shrine in Rajasthan

collect water from the river in unbaked pots made from riverbank clay. Sita proves her fidelity by going through a trial by fire.

A sati's fidelity allegedly offered her protection from widowhood. The Puranas tell the story of one Shilavati who carries her leper husband on her shoulders as he cannot walk. She satisfies all his desires. She even takes him to prostitutes. A sage is so disgusted by the husband that he declares he will die when the sun rises next. Shilavati then uses her power of chastity to prevent the sun from rising.

Belief in sati meant a widow was seen as a woman who could not prevent the death of her husband. To prove her chastity, she was encouraged to burn herself on her husband's funeral pyre, giving rise to the terrible practice of Sati and the worship of women who immolated themselves.

If rural cultures valued fertility, urban cultures valued obedience, for it indicated control and discipline. While fertility was rooted in women, obedience was enforced through men. With urbanisation came more rules and the idea of evil, one who does not submit to the rules. We find women at the receiving end of the rules, suggesting the city was a masculine invention.

This is explicit in Chinese mythology, where two natural forces work in harmony to create life: yang and yin. The masculine yang is like a dragon in the sky. The feminine yin is the earth, which like the phoenix rises from its own ashes, regenerating itself. There is no superior or inferior force in nature, say Taoist traditions, but in Confucian traditions, which favour culture over nature, hierarchy emerges, where the man becomes more important. The Emperor

Mesopotamian mythology: Tiamat and Marduk

is given the Mandate of Heaven to sit on the Dragon throne in the Forbidden City, and asked to domesticate the earth, bring order where there is chaos.

A patriarchal society links women with nature and men with culture. Just as culture domesticates nature, men are asked to domesticate women. This is explicit in the Mesopotamian epic, *Enuma Elish,* where the god-king Marduk defeats the primal female monster Tiamat and brings order to the world. It is also explicit in Greek myths of Zeus chasing and raping nymphs across the land and fathering offspring.

In Japanese mythology, the first man Izanagi and the first woman Izanami stir the oceans to create the islands of Japan. They build a house with a pillar and go around it in opposite directions with the intention of copulating when they meet. When they meet, the woman speaks first and deformed demons are born. They go around once again and this time the man speaks first when they meet, and normal humans are born, thus establishing the need to make women subservient to men.

The battle of sexes found in Japanese mythology continues into the next generation. Izanagi's daughter, Amaterasu, the sun-goddess, born of his right eye, shares the sky with her brother, Tsukuyomi, the moon-god, born of his left eye. But then Tsukuyomi strikes the goddess of earth in disgust for producing food from all her orifices, including nose, rectum and mouth. So Amaterasu refuses to see him, resulting in the division of night and day, with the night belonging to the moon-brother and the day to the sun-sister. Amaterasu also competes with her other brother, Susanoo, the storm-god. He produces five men using her necklace and she produces three women from his sword. He says he won as he produced more offspring, but

Japanese mythology: The primal twins

she says she won as his sword produced women and her necklace produced men, thus inadvertently admitting that male offspring are of superior value to female offspring.

In cities we find the battle of power, the desire to be king, the competition between men, the younger lot seeking to overthrow the elders and the elders always suspicious of the youth. Women are the trophies of this masculine rivalry. They are seen as dangerous forces who seem to value desire over rules. Everyone is told to be wary of them.

In Greek mythology, for example, Zeus, fearful of human heroes, sends a box to Pandora, a woman, with a warning never to open it. She disobeys and out pours all the problems of the world that promise to keep humanity too busy to bother with trying to overthrow the Olympians. From that day, men are advised to be wary of all women; they were deemed the source of all problems in life. Not surprisingly, Greek democracy valued only men, and excluded women.

In biblical mythology, the woman Eve is tempted by the serpent to break the law of God by eating the fruit of the tree of knowledge, and compels Adam to do so too. For this act of transgression, both Adam and Eve are cast out of Paradise and Eve is made subservient to Adam. Before the creation of Eve, God is said to have created Lilith, of hairy legs, but she refused to be subservient to Adam and so was cast out: she became the mother of monsters.

As walls were built around cities, and wealth hoarded, urban centres often found themselves at war and under siege, surrounded by hungry tribes from the countryside who wished to tear down

Greek mythology: Pandora

Greek mythology: Furies chasing Orestes

their walls and claim what was hidden. In this world, a man was valued by what he had, women included. The raiders were keen not just to possess the wealth of those who lived behind the walls, but also their women. This led to increased isolation of women 'for their own good'. They were restricted to inner courtyards, and forced to go under the veil. Higher the social status, greater the isolation. Greater the isolation, the more valuable and desirable a woman became. Thus we find the concept of the virginal Snow White in European folklore, and a-surya-sparsha or 'untouched by the rays of the sun' in Indian folklore.

Society located its honour in a woman's body. And so a thousand Greek ships sailed to bring back Helen, wife of Menelaus, king of Sparta, who eloped with Paris, prince of Troy. Her action, say the epics, brought shame to all of Greece. After Troy was torn to the ground, the wives of Trojan warriors were brought back to Greece as concubines. Agamemnon, the leader of the Greeks, who had sacrificed his daughter, Ipigeniah, to ensure good winds as they sailed to battle, returned with the Trojan princess Cassandra by his side. Agamemnon's wife, Clytemnestra, was so angry that she murdered her husband and his concubine.

Orestes, son of Agamemnon, avenged his father's death by killing his mother, and her lover, Aegisthus. For the crime of killing his mother, Orestes was pursued by the dreaded female spirits known as Erinyes (also known as Furies) until Athena, goddess of good sense, intervened. She defends Orestes, and appeases the Erinyes by declaring them as goddesses of justice. This story reveals a shift from matriarchy (when the lover of the queen was ritually murdered and killing the mother was the greatest crime) to patriarchy (when killing women who challenged male authority

Biblical mythology: The rape of Dinah

 Devdutt Pattanaik

and dishonoured the family was justified).

The Hebrew Bible tells the story of Dinah, daughter of Jacob, leader of nomads, who was abducted and violated by a Cannanite prince, who so wanted to marry her that he was even willing to circumcise himself so as to be an acceptable groom. This suggests the abduction was perhaps elopement and violation was perhaps intimacy by mutual consent. The brothers of Dinah did not think so. They killed the Cannanite prince while he was sore following the circumcision, and then they go on to plunder his lands, to the horror of their father, Jacob, who does not desire this enmity with the city folk. But the brothers argue, 'How can we let him treat our sister as a harlot?'

This assigning of honour to women plays out elaborately in the Indian epics. In the Ramayana, after Ram rescues Sita from the clutches of Ravana, he says, 'I rescued you not because you are my wife but to protect the honour of my family into which you married.' In the Mahabharata, the Kauravas publicly denigrate Draupadi by seeking to disrobe her only to humiliate her five husbands, the Pandavas. In these stories, the woman stops being a person; she is dehumanised and turned into a symbol of masculine honour. This transformation from prized possession to venerated object marks the triumph of patriarchy.

Excessive urbanisation also resulted in disgust for all things material. Meaning was sought beyond the city walls: in the untamed earth below and the open sky above.

Those who looked at the earth below saw it as the Goddess, manifesting in pairs and triads, embodying the paradoxes of the

Greek goddess triad of the Fates

Shift from earth to sky

world. There was Ishtar, the fertile, and Ereshkigal, the barren, in Sumerian mythology; Kali, the wild, and Gauri, the domestic, in Hindu mythology; the cow Hathor and the lioness Sekhmet of Egyptian mythology. In Greek mythology, there are the Fates triad who spin thread, the length of which determines the duration of human life, and the Grace triad who constitute the three seasons of spring, summer, and winter. Thus, the world is seen in feminine terms.

But gradually, the gaze turned upwards towards the sky. Gravity became a fetter, the earth a trap, and women bondage. Escape was sought. The serpent, messenger of the goddess, was rejected in favour of winged beings or angels who take humanity to 'higher' realms, above the earth.

In biblical mythology, the serpent becomes the symbol of the Devil, he who disobeys and tempts others to disobey. God, who makes all the rules, becomes male and resides in the sky. Prophets carry his word to earth. They are mostly male: Abraham, Moses, Jesus, Muhammad. They overshadow the few female prophets: Miriam, Deborah and Anna.

For Christians, Jesus is the son of God. There is no mention of a daughter of God. Mary was voted, only in the Catholic tradition, as the Mother of God, an eternal virgin celebrated as she conceives immaculately; but she is no Goddess. There is talk of Shekinah, the female spirit of God, in occult Judaic traditions, but she is never given form. There are many Marys in the Bible but none of them become apostles, not even the three Marys who witness Jesus' crucifixion and are the first to know of his resurrection.

In Arthurian legends that became popular in medieval Christian Europe, woman is the damsel, symbol of purity, who has to be

Lilith, who was born before Eve.

Ishtar of Mesopotamia.

In all probability a Mesopotamian goddess turned into mother of Christian demons.

Mother Mary and Jesus.

Adam and Eve as they break the rule of God and eat of the fruit of knowledge.

Hand of Fatima, daughter of the Prophet Muhammad.

**Biblical mythology**

constantly rescued by the knight in shining armour. She is also the dangerous witch. In fairly tales, she is the Sleeping Beauty who can be awoken only by the kiss of a Prince Charming. Monastic orders around the world sought liberation from this burden of taking care of women and the children they bore.

In Islam, there is a folk tradition of how the Devil tries unsuccessfully, to include in the Koran through Muhammad, a verse that makes the three goddesses of Mecca — Urs, Mannat, Lat — mediums to Allah. These were the infamous Satanic verses. Still the feminine makes her presence felt as the hand of the prophet's daughter, Fatima, which is a common talisman used for protection and warding off the 'evil eye'.

In Jainism, all the Tirthankaras who establish the bridge out of ignorance to wisdom are male. In some traditions, one of the Tirthankaras, Malli-nath, is female. His female body is the result of a demerit: in his former life he fasted more than his companions in illness, and he did not inform his companions about it. He rejects his female body, viewing it as a vessel of putrefaction.

In the early days of Buddhism, Buddha refused to include women in his monastic order until he saw his step-mother cry at the death of his father and realised women suffer as much as men. Early Buddhist traditions saw wisdom in intellectual terms only. But later Buddhism made room for the emotional. Compassion was seen to be as important as knowledge. And compassion took the form of a goddess called Tara. She appeared as a tear shed when Buddha heard the cries of the suffering. Buddha decided not to accept nirvana but work tirelessly as Bodhisattva to help other suffering souls. All Bodhisattvas are male. But then we do hear of Guanyin, the female Bodhisattva of China, whose presence gave

Older Buddhism did not acknowledge the feminine.

Later Buddhism acknowledged the feminine as Tara who gets Bodhisattva to engage with the world out of compassion.

Guan-yin, the female problem-solving boon-bestowing Bodhisattva, who became popular in China.

Buddhist mythology

solace to all the suffering souls in the land of the living and in the land of the dead.

Four thousand years ago, before the rise of Buddhism, Vedic Hinduism paid greater attention to devas or gods like Agni (fire), Indra (rain), Vayu (wind) and Surya (sun), over devis or goddesses like Ushas (dawn), Vak (speech) and Aranyani (forest).

Since two thousand years, after the rise of Buddhism, in Puranic Hinduism, the gods gave way to God (bhagavan, ishwar). But God could not be explained without the Goddess (bhagavati, ishwari). She was no supplement; she was an intimately inextricably linked complement. This value placed on the feminine has been attributed to the popularity and influence of village goddesses or grama-devis, who have been revered in settlements across India since the dawn of time, long before the Vedas or the cities of the Indus Valley civilisation.

Three sects emerged in this later Puranic Hinduism: two masculine, focused on Shiva and Vishnu, and one feminine, focused on Devi.

Shiva is the ascetic who attacks Brahma for coveting and trying to control Devi; he shuns worldly life until Devi transforms into Gauri and makes him a householder and father.

Vishnu is the householder who looks upon Devi as Lakshmi, goddess of auspiciousness and abundance; taking various avatars to enable Brahma and his sons to cope with Kali.

But Devi is divinity in her own right, independent as the earth, responding to the gaze of Brahma who seeks to control her, Vishnu who enjoys her and Shiva who withdraws from her. She is their

Tantrik mythology: Adya, mother of Brahma, Vishnu and Shiva

mother, daughter, sister and wife. She allows them to dominate but never lets them have dominion over her. She enables everyone to outgrow the anxiety that creates patriarchy as well as the anxiety created by patriarchy.

# 2. Kali's Secret

*Nature is indifferent to human gaze*

Kali of Kolkata's Kalighat temple

$\mathcal{K}$ali is perhaps the most dramatic form of Devi in Hindu mythology. She is naked, with hair unbound, standing or sitting on top of Shiva, sickle in hand, with a garland of male heads around her neck, her blood-stained tongue stretching out.

Is that tongue directed at us? Or are we just witnesses? Does she give that tongue meaning, or do we?

To understand Kali, it makes sense to appreciate the rise of Devi worship in India. And for that we have to appreciate the transformation of Hinduism over four thousand years from the pre-Buddhist Vedic phase of Hinduism where rituals were more important than gods (devas), through the post-Buddhist Puranic phase of Hinduism when devotion to God (bhagavan) gained paramount importance, to the rise of colonial gaze and the native reaction to it.

During this journey we shall see how the idea of Kali is more ancient than the name and form that we today associate with her. We shall also see how Kali's tongue transformed from being a weapon, to the symbol of wisdom, to the symbol of shame.

Around 2500 BCE (Before Common Era, formerly known as BC, or Before Christ), a city-based civilisation thrived along the Indus and Saraswati rivers (the latter dried out by 2000 BCE). Here we find clay figures of naked but bejewelled women alongside images of clay bulls. The bulls represent untamed male virility. The women, with their jewels, are representations of nature that has been domesticated. Together they represent nature's fertility

Indus valley Goddess images

over which humans seek control for their material welfare. We do not find any Kali-like images, but we do find an appreciation of the conflict between the wild and the tame. These cities ceased to exist by 2000 BCE but their cultural practices continued to thrive and spread in the Indian subcontinent.

Around 1500 BCE, a cattle-herding people migrated from the Indus-Saraswati river basins to the Gangetic river basin. Their relationship with the Indus cities has yet to be resolved. Their hymns, known as the Vedas, reveal a great yearning for cows, horses, grain, gold and sons. With fire (Agni) as their medium, they invoke virile warrior gods like Indra, and other masculine denizens who reside in the sky, more frequently than earth-bound goddesses. But there is reference to one Nirriti, who is acknowledged but asked to stay away for the sake of health and prosperity. Her name means one who disrupts 'riti', or the regular rhythms of nature.

Around 1000 BCE, Brahmana literature that links hymns to ritual elaborates on the nature of Nirriti. She is described as dark and dishevelled, associated with the southern regions, which is traditionally linked with death. This Nirriti is often identified as a proto-Kali especially since Kali is often addressed in later literature as Dakshina-Kali, she who comes from the south, south being the land of Yama, god of death. Nirriti embodies the human discomfort with the dark side of nature.

In Jaiminya Brahmana, there is the story of one Dirgha-Jihvi, she-of-the-long-tongue, who licked away the soma created during a yagna, much to Indra's irritation. This soma gave everyone, the devas included, long lives, happiness and health. Indra sends a young man called Sumitra to overpower her. But Dirgha-Jihvi rejects the man as he has just one manhood, while she has

Chola bronze image of Kali

many vulvas seeking satisfaction. So Indra gives that man many manhoods. Seeing Sumitra transformed thus, Dirgha-Jihvi is much pleased. They make love. Pinned down during the act of sex, Dirgha-Jihvi is momentarily immobilised, giving Sumitra the opportunity to kill her. This is also identified as a proto-Kali due to the references to the tongue and unbridled sexuality. It reveals male anxiety before female sexual and reproductive prowess.

Around 500 BCE, Buddhism and other sharmana (ascetic) traditions — which rejected the materialistic obsessions of society — grew. Words like karma and moksha gained popularity. There was talk of meditation, and bondage, and freedom. The yagna gradually went out of favour.

It is at this time that the name Kali appears for the first time, in early Upanishad literature, but it is the name given to one of the many tongues of Agni, the fire-god. In later iconography, we do find images of Kali with flames for hair. One can only speculate if the flame called Kali is in any way linked to the Kali with flames for hair.

The post-Buddhist period saw the gradual rise of Puranic literature. This literature spoke of a single, all-powerful divine entity, or God, who came to the rescue of devotees. Different people visualised God differently. For some, the Supreme Being was Shiva, the hermit. For others it was Vishnu, the householder. And for still others, it was the Goddess, Devi. Each school of thought vied for supremacy. Accordingly, stories came into being of how Devi vanquished asuras that neither Shiva nor Vishnu could defeat. Amongst Devi's many manifestations were Kali and Kali-like goddesses.

Poster of birth of Kali from Durga's brow

Shiva, Vishnu and Devi, and their many forms, can be traced to Vedic literature, while others to grama-devas or village-gods of India, where oral traditions perhaps pre-date the oldest Vedic hymns. Appropriation of grama-devas into more mainstream codified religions was common in this period, and so it is not uncommon to find similar gods and goddesses in Buddhist, Jain and Hindu mythology that became more elaborate during this period.

The earliest stories of the Puranas are found in the epics, the Ramayana and the Mahabharata, dated between 300 BCE and 300 CE. In them, we find a goddess called Kalaratri appearing on the final night of the battle at Kurukshetra when Ashwatthama ruthlessly murders the sons of the Pandavas at night when they are asleep. In Tamil Sangam literature, composed around this time, we come across the Goddess Korravai with flames for hair, associated with battlefields. Both Kalaratri and Korravai are Kali-like goddesses associated with rage and violence.

From around 300 CE, when the early Puranas were put together, Kali appears as a discrete goddess. She is born from the locks of Shiva's hair along with her brother, Virabhadra, and together they attack and destroy Daksha's yagna. In the *Devi Mahatmya,* which is a part of the *Markandeya Purana,* she is born from Durga's forehead to kill the demons Chanda and Munda. The *Devi Mahatmya* also retells Kali's most famous tale involving her tongue.

An asura called Raktabeeja had obtained a boon from Brahma that if a drop of his blood (rakta, in Sanskrit) fell on the ground it would transform into a seed (beeja) and sprout a duplicate of himself. No deva was able to defeat Raktabeeja. Any attempt to strike him with weapons only made matters worse. So the devas

Miniature painting of Durga and Kali combating Raktabeeja

   Devdutt Pattanaik

led by Indra went to Brahma, who expressed his helplessness and directed them to Vishnu. Vishnu also expressed helplessness and directed them to Shiva. Shiva also expressed helplessness and appealed to the Goddess. And the Goddess rode into battle in two forms. The first form was of the multi-armed Chandi on a tiger ready to do battle. The second was Kali of outstretched tongue. Chandi struck the many Raktabeejas with her weapons, beheading them. Kali drank each Raktabeeja's blood before it fell on the ground. Thus, no duplicate Raktabeeja was created and the asura was killed. The Goddess made a garland of the asura's many heads and wore them as adornment.

Around 500 CE, Tantrik literature began to be composed. Unlike the Puranas, which seemed more interested in the external world, and in matters such as devotion and pilgrimages, the Tantras were more interested in the occult and alchemy. Here we find Kali and Kali-like goddesses such as Tara, Chamunda or Chinnamastika appearing with increasing frequency as part of a collective of three, seven, nine, ten, sixty-four goddesses variously known as Tri-devi, Tri-ambika, Matrikas, Maha-vidyas and Yoginis. These collectives include benevolent and fecund goddesses alongside malevolent and morbid goddesses. While these goddesses are also mentioned in the Puranas, their nature is elaborated on in the Tantras, which reveals a deeper appreciation of nature, sex and violence.

These goddesses embody folk deities associated with wild and domesticated spaces, and were gradually incorporated into Puranic and Tantrik, even Buddhist, literature. In the Mahabharata, we hear of Shiva's son Skanda informing a group of such wild female deities that if they are not worshipped and respected they have the freedom to harm pregnant women and children. In Buddhist

Poster image of Kali with the Maha-vidyas

literature, we hear of a child-devouring female demon called Hariti who is transformed into a child-protecting female demon by the Buddha.

By 1000 BCE, Kali emerges out of the collective and starts being seen as an independent goddess. In the *Kalika Purana,* she is the perfect, most primal representation of the Goddess. Some addressed this Kali as Maha-Kali to distinguish her from other Kalis. What distinguished her from all other goddesses was her nakedness, her unbound hair, her thirst for blood, her unbridled lust, her outstretched tongue and her domination of a male form, identified as Shiva or Bhairava. She either had one foot on him, stood on him or sat on him. But he is not a demon she has defeated. He is identified as her husband, one whom she awakens. She is the Goddess who makes him God.

By this time, when Hinduism is marked by the rise of vast temple complexes, Devi is identified with nature, and Kali with the most primal form of nature, before culture and outside culture, unaffected by rules and opinions of humanity. She is power, raw and elemental, both venerable and frightening. Human society is created within her; she ultimately consumes human society.

It often becomes difficult to distinguish Kali from Kali-like goddesses in Puranic and Tantrik literature. They seem to belong to a single continuum.

Bhairavi is often linked to Kali. But while Kali is shown standing or sitting on Shiva, Bhairavi and Shiva are seen as a pair, either located in crematoriums or wandering in the wilderness. Shiva is called Bhairava. As a pair they invoke violence, sexuality and

Miniature painting of Chinna-mastika

Devdutt Pattanaik

an indifference to social disapproval. Their images are also found on Jain temple walls indicating their popularity. Down south, Bhairava is often shown holding a human head. It is said to be the head of Brahma who dared seek to sexually dominate Bhairavi. In some tales this head cannot be placed on the ground and so Bhairava and Bhairavi take turns holding it; when they grow tired and place it on the ground, the world comes to an end.

Chinna-mastika means one whose head has been severed. She severs her own neck and her detached head drinks the blood spurting out of the neck. Thus she kills and nourishes herself, embodying that aspect of nature where the prey is killed to feed the predator. Thus in nature, violence becomes nourishment and contributes to survival. She also sits on Kama and Rati, god and goddess of desire, as they are copulating. Here, the woman is always on top of the man, indicating she is not the passive partner but the active one, initiating the sexual act, not simply the recipient of male passion. Here the sexual act is about procreation, not so much about pleasure, to keep rotating the cycle of life. Thus in nature, sex becomes procreative and contributes to survival.

Tara is indistinguishable from Kali, though they are named separately in Tantrik literature. She is both a Buddhist and a Brahmin goddess. Tara of Buddhism invokes compassion in Buddha and transforms him into Bodhisattva who delays his own liberation to help people out of the ocean of suffering. Likewise, Tara of Hinduism invokes compassion in Shiva and transforms him into a caring householder. In Bengal and Odisha, some distinguish Tara as the milder, more approachable form of Kali, one who need not be feared, one who can be invoked not only by hermits but also by householders.

Gaunt features.

Scorpion in the navel.

Riding a ghost (preta).

**Stone image of Chamunda**

Chamunda is distinguished from Kali by her gaunt form. She is emaciated, sits on a corpse or a pile of corpses, and has a scorpion for her belly-button. This form seems to embody decay and drought. She is associated with dogs feeding on corpses either in the aftermath of a battle or an epidemic. She evokes despair and suffering.

As temples were built to enshrine Shiva, Vishnu and Devi, it became crucial to establish relationships between the three major deities of Hinduism. Shiva's ascetic nature connected him to to the wild forms of Kali. If she was nature that is indifferent to the mind (prakriti), he embodied the mind that is independent of nature (purusha).

In the more masculine Shaiva literature, nature is seen as passive, even subservient. Shiva enables the domestication of Kali on the request of Brahma and the other devas. Thus we have stories of how Shiva competes with Kali in a dance competition only to triumph over her by taking up positions that Kali is too embarrassed to assume. There are also stories where, by taking the form of a beautiful man or a cute child, Shiva is able to bind Kali by evoking marital and maternal desires in her. In this literature, the other does not exist. Nature, in particular, and all other living creatures in general, are but objects around the subject. Everybody and everything needs to be controlled.

But in the more feminine Shakta literatures, nature is active. Kali wants Shiva to pay attention to her for the benefit of humanity. Indifferent, he is no different from a corpse, or shava. In the less subtle Tantrik imagery, Kali does not merely step on Shiva, she sits

Position of upraised leg taken by Shiva that Kali refuses to emulate.

Bronze image of Shiva dancing

The Goddess covers her face with a lotus flower out of embarrassment.

This image is not associated with any textual material and so evokes many speculations related to fertility and the Goddess.

Stone image of Lajja-gauri

on top of him, intent on copulating with him. Only by engaging with her does he turn into Shiva, the auspicious one. Kali sits on top of Shiva, and gently coaxes him to make love to her, acknowledge her desires and satisfy her. She refuses to be invisible. This literature evokes the consciousness of man, the human ability to be sensitive and caring, the human ability to pay attention to the other. Here, nature is also a subject, as are others around the subject. Everybody and everything has a soul that needs to be respected.

Both Shaiva and Shakta literature tell the tale of how sages stumble upon Shiva and Shakti when they are making love. There are two versions of what follows.

In one version, the Goddess is shy. So she covers her face with a lotus flower. Shiva does not stop and so the rishis declare that Shiva would be worshipped only as a symbol, never in human form. This story explains the name Lajja-gauri, or shy consort of Shiva, given by male archaeologists to the clay image of the Goddess found in fields across India, where she is spread-eagled as if ready to receive a lover or deliver a child, and with a lotus for a face. It also explains why Shiva is worshipped as an erect stone (linga, or phallus) in a leaf-shaped trough (yoni, or womb) and rarely in human form.

In the other version, the Goddess is not shy. She simply sticks out her tongue, either in defiance of their disapproval, or in jest, amused that they seek to judge nature, for she is nature, unaffected by human opinions. Here Kali's tongue is a symbol that mocks the limitations, as well as the assumptions, of the human gaze. It reminds us that nature is sovereign. In nature, sex and violence ensure survival of the fittest. Human gaze judges sex and violence in ethical, moral and aesthetic terms. Be that as it may, humans have

Bhadra Kali, whose right foot is on Shiva

Smashan Kali, whose left foot is on Shiva

no choice but to submit to sex and violence in order to survive.

These two versions depict the conflicting attitudes towards sexuality that emerged in the post-Buddhist period, which saw the rising influence of monastic orders. In a similar vein, one finds, especially in Bengal, two forms of Kali. One in which she steps on Shiva with her left foot and raises a sickle in her right hand, and another where she steps on him with her right foot and raises her sickle with her left hand. The first one is seen as more fearsome and is called Smashan Kali, Kali of the crematorium. The second one is seen as more considerate of cultural norms and is called Bhadra Kali, Kali who is modest. The latter Kali was also called Tara, linking her to the compassionate Buddhist goddess. Smashan Kali is nature that ultimately consumes humanity. Bhadra Kali is nature that is understanding of human shortcomings. Smashan Kali is wild and free, beyond domestication. Bhadra Kali offers the strength to cope with the limitations of a domesticated life.

In Kali-kula Tantra, or Tantrik worship revolving around Kali, the point of eroticism was not indulgence or subversion, but a desire to confront one's deepest fears. It demanded that the aspirant break free from the social structures, customs and beliefs that offered him security. If he succeeded in doing so, he became vira, a hero. Confrontation with fears jolted the vira into wisdom. An encounter with Kali transformed a fool into one of India's greatest poets: Kalidasa, servant of Kali, who lived around the 5th century AD at the time of the Gupta kings, wrote extensively on unfettered love and longing in a world restrained by rules and hierarchies. Such a confrontation could also transform the vira into a rasa-siddha, he who knows the mysteries of alchemy. That is why Kali was also a venerated deity in the nath-sampradaya, a monastic

Poster art of Tarini, a local form of the Goddess in Keonjhar, Odisha

order which originated around the 10th century, and was made up of wandering jogis who revered wise and powerful gurus such as Matsyendra-nath and Gorakh-nath. Similarly, legend has it that Krishnadevaraya, of the 16th century Vijayanagara empire, had a court jester called Tenali Raman who acquired his wisdom because he was amused rather than intimidated by the vision of Kali.

Since Kali was connected with Shiva, she could not be associated with Shiva's rival deity, Vishnu. The *Bhagavata Purana* tells the story where Vishnu in the form of Krishna fights a Kali-like goddess while she is defending Shiva's devotee, Bana, whose daughter, Usha, falls in love with, and abducts, Krishna's handsome grandson, Aniruddha.

And yet, the character most intimately associated with Vishnu's most popular avatar, Krishna, has all the characteristics of Kali, not in form though, but in thought. Her name was Radha.

From the 12th century onwards, Radha makes her appearance in the Hindu imagination in Prakrit works. But her popularity is traced to the 13th-century Sanskrit work, *Gita Govinda,* which describes in intimate detail her nocturnal and clandestine erotic dalliance with Krishna. The idea of gopis or milkmaids swooning over Krishna, leaving their homes in the dead of night and dancing around him to the tune of his music in the middle of the woods on the banks of the river, was known before the arrival of Radha. In the *Bhagavata Purana,* dated to the 12th century, there is no mention of Radha, but the rasa-leela is described to evoke various moods such as bhakti or devotion, shringara or eroticism, madhurya or tenderness, and viraha or longing created by separation. When

Miniature painting of Radha and Krishna intertwined

Radha appears, a new flavour emerges.

Unlike the gopis who are subservient and even admonished for being possessive, Radha is demanding. She quarrels with Krishna, and Krishna tries hard to appease her, even wearing her clothes sometimes, or falling at her feet. Unlike the self-contained hero of earlier works, he is distraught in Radha's absence. When duty beckons, and Krishna has to leave the village of Vrindavan and go to the city of Mathura, the gopis weep, but not Radha. Krishna promises that he will return but Radha knows he will not. When Krishna does not return and sends Uddhava to pacify the heartbroken milkmaids, Radha admonishes him for offering intellectual remedies for their emotional despair: she demands the right to feel frustrated and angry, but she does not begrudge her Krishna. She does not expect him to return. She describes him as a honey bee whose nature it is to go from flower to flower, but she, the flower attached to the branch of the tree, has nowhere to go but yearn for him and languish in memories and unfulfilled dreams and find validation therein. Thus she becomes the embodiment of true, unconditional, immersive love.

Later poets such as Vidyapati and Chandidas highlighted the scandalous nature of Radha's relationship with Krishna. She is described as a married woman in some songs, a woman who is older than Krishna in others, and in some oral traditions, his aunt, wife of Yashoda's brother. This makes the relationship extramarital, inter-generational and incestuous, breaking all boundaries imposed by society. This grants the nature of the relationship a very Tantrik theme.

Not everyone was pleased with such breaking of boundaries. There were fierce arguments about whether Radha was parakiya,

Miniature painting of Radha and Krishna in Madhuvan

belonging to another, or svakiya, belonging to Krishna. The folk traditions and regional literature were comfortable with the idea that Radha was married to another man, but in later Puranas such as *Brahmavaivarta,* concerted efforts are made to show how Radha and Krishna are two halves of the primal being, married in heaven but separated on earth. It reveals the discomfort with all things Tantrik commonly seen in mainstream society, and points to Radha alluding to Kali, despite being fully clothed.

It is interesting to note that Radha as an idea emerges after the arrival of Islam, which has been identified as the reason why Indian women, especially in the northern part of the subcontinent, started using the veil. Temples depicting Tantrik iconography were torn down to cater to the increasingly conservative mindset. Yet, Radha emerges, defying convention from behind the veil, leaving the inner courtyard to be with Krishna in the forest located beyond the influence of structures and hierarchies of the village.

The idea of Radha flourished primarily in the Gangetic plains. But it arose in the eastern areas of Odisha, Bengal and Assam, which were prominent centres of Tantra and Kali worship. Jayadeva, who wrote the *Gita Govinda,* lived near the Jagannath temple in Puri, Odisha, renowned for its temple dancers who were unattached to any man and were dedicated to the temple.

Later Radha's fierce love for Krishna would feature prominently in the devotional movement of Chaitanya to the extent that even men started identifying themselves with Radha, considering Krishna to be the only true, complete and perfect man. The psychological intensity of the romance was not mirrored physically; in fact, both the Chaitanya of Bengal and Shankardeb of Assam would celebrate continence and celibacy arising from true love for Krishna. Thus

Miniature painting depicting the rise of the Shakta cult

the overtly Tantrik traditions were tempered; yet, the idea of Kali who is indifferent to social conventions survived in the mind.

By the 15th century, the Ramayanas and Mahabharatas written in regional languages start associating their wronged heroines, Sita and Draupadi, with Kali. In the Adbhuta Ramayana, while Ram kills Ravana who has ten heads, Sita is able to kill a Ravana who has a hundred heads. In the Tamil Mahabharata, Draupadi transforms into Kali at night, running naked in the forest, eating elephants and buffaloes, as she is disappointed with her husbands, the five Pandavas. It is this Kali-side of Draupadi that makes her take the vow that she will wash her blood with the hair of the men who abused her. In fact, in these traditions, the story goes that Vishnu takes his various avatars such as Parashuram, Ram and Krishna only to satisfy the bloodlust of Kali, who wants to drink the blood of men who treat her with disrespect.

While Tantrik rituals, where Kali played a central role, were known to many people, and Tantrik symbols could be found in villages across India, the meaning of the rituals and symbols remained esoteric. They were only known to those very few people who were steeped in Tantrik mysteries, people who were unwilling or unable to share their understanding in any coherent way with the masses, and who preferred to pass them on only to serious students and fellow practitioners. So it was only a question of time before Kali's association with Tantra resulted in her being situated outside cultural norms, where normal codes of ethics and morality did not apply. From a forbidding force she became a forbidden force.

There are stories, such as those in the *Katha-sarit-sagar*, which

Image of the mother of God that Europeans were exposed to.

Tantrik image of Kali decapitating herself while she copulates with Shiva; these kind of images shocked the sensibilities of Europeans who were unfamiliar with the occult symbolism and eager to believe the worst about the native 'savages'.

Clash of two worlds

dates to the 11th century, where sorcerers and thieves seek to invoke Kali and get powers from her by offering blood sacrifices at night in crematoriums. In medieval regional Ramayanas, such as the Adbhuta Ramayana written in the 15th century, we find the story of Mahiravan, king of the netherworld, a great magician, who, goaded by Ravana, tries to sacrifice Ram to violent and sexual Kali, but is outsmarted by the serene, celibate Hanuman.

When the Europeans came to India in the 16th century, they could not appreciate Kali's image, especially her nakedness and violence, so far removed from the images of the docile, virginal Mary and her son, Jesus, which they associated with God. In fact, Kali terrified them, endorsed their presumptions about the natives being savages. They became convinced Hindus were worshippers of the Devil, and indulged in human sacrifice. This was reinforced by medieval Sanskrit stories and plays where sorcerers sacrifice men, even women, to Kali in order to get magical powers. In the 19th century, army reports spoke of a band of highway robbers known as Thugees in north India, who worshipped Kali and offered her their victims as sacrifice in exchange for protection. Novels such as *Around the World in Eighty Days* reinforced this image of Kali, savage goddess of savage natives. It justified colonisation as the White Man's Burden to civilise.

Today scholars doubt whether this 'cult of murderous thieves' really existed or were the invention of a hyperactive colonial imagination eager to think the worst of those they were determined to subjugate. In all probability, the 'thuggee' were notorious thieves, driven by poverty not religious dogma, who worshipped Kali like everyone else around them. But the image of a murderous tribe inspired by Kali had such an impact that even today they inspire

Murderous highway robbers known as Thugees were accused of sacrificing their victims to quench the thirst of Kali.

Kali in the Hollywood film *Golden Voyage of Sinbad*.

How the West saw Kali in colonial and post-colonial times

tales not just in Hollywood (*Indiana Jones and the Temple of Doom*, 1984) but also in Bollywood (*Sunghursh*, 1968).

This colonial gaze embarrassed the natives of India, especially the young men of Bengal's privileged classes who were now being educated in English schools and exposed to European ideas. They re-imagined Kali's image differently.

In the 18th century Kali started becoming the object of devotion. She inspired poets like Ramprasad Sen and this created a new musical genre called Shyama Sangeet. Shyama means the dark-one, and is one of Kali's many names. Here, Kali was seen less in terms of power and more in terms of love. Despite her fierce form, which evokes fear and disgust, she was addressed as an affectionate mother who grants supreme wisdom to her helpless children in the most unconventional way: by denying them material pleasures and exposing them to the terror of existence. It is this Kali to which Vivekananda and his guru, Ramakrishna Paramhansa, allude. This devotion to Kali was clearly an extension of the larger bhakti movement that swept India from the 13th century onwards, but this was mostly focused around Shiva and Vishnu. Kali's transformation into loving mother in Bengali devotional literature, which seems to be in denial of her terrifying form, does indicate at one level an attempt to pacify the disapproving gaze of the colonial masters. At another level, it was perhaps born of the desire to explain human suffering: like the Bengal famine of 1770 resulting from the East India Company's excessive taxation policies that claimed the lives of ten million people.

In the tradition of Shyama Sangeet arose a very different story to explain Kali's tongue. It speaks of how Kali, after killing asuras, goes on a killing frenzy, intoxicated by the demon's blood. Terrified,

The mystic Ramakrishna Paramhansa with Mother Kali.

Mother India in chains as depicted in the work of Bankim Chandra.

How Indians saw Kali in colonial times

all the creatures of the world beg Shiva to stop her. So Shiva throws himself to the ground in her path. She steps on him, realises she has stepped on her own husband, and is so embarrassed by her action that she bites her tongue. This makes Kali's outstretched tongue a symbol of embarrassment, even shame, as touching anyone with one's feet is a mark of disrespect in traditional Hindu households, especially the husband who was identified as pati-parameshwar, or the husband-God. This story is steeped in patriarchy. It views Kali's form as transgressive behaviour inappropriate for cultured women. It appealed to the sensibilities of those newly educated in European ways.

With the rise of the freedom struggle, many nationalists accepted the Western discomfort with Kali's image. But they gave it a different spin. Authors such as Bankim Chandra visualised Kali as Mother India, gaunt and naked and dishevelled because she has been reduced to poverty by the British rulers who oppress and exploit her.

In post-colonial times, with the rise of the feminist movement, Kali became an image of revolution and subversion. In her nakedness and refusal to submit to the male gaze, she became a symbol of women's freedom, both in India and abroad. She was seen to embody raw female energy before it was forced to conform to patriarchal norms. She was also seen as female energy that will ultimately triumph over masculine hegemony.

Increasingly Kali is becoming part of global neo-paganism and neo-feminism that seeks not to confront masculinity but embrace it in its fold. She is being seen as the embodiment of a woman's completeness and autonomy, which does not seek a man's gaze to define herself in anyway. In these movements, both men and

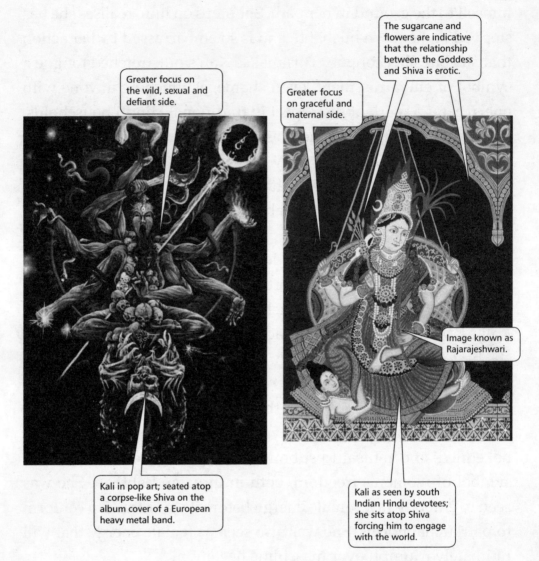

Greater focus on the wild, sexual and defiant side.

Greater focus on graceful and maternal side.

The sugarcane and flowers are indicative that the relationship between the Goddess and Shiva is erotic.

Image known as Rajarajeshwari.

Kali in pop art; seated atop a corpse-like Shiva on the album cover of a European heavy metal band.

Kali as seen by south Indian Hindu devotees; she sits atop Shiva forcing him to engage with the world.

Two ways of seeing Kali

women are encouraged to break free from cultural conditioning, outgrow masculine anxieties related to hierarchy and validation, rediscover the elemental feminine energy of nature, and love life for what it truly is.

# 3. Gauri's Secret

*Culture is dependent on human gaze*

Calendar print of Jagadamba, the mother of the universe

*B*efore humanity, there was only nature. After humanity came culture. In nature, only the fit survive and there are no favourites. In culture, even the unfit can thrive, but there are also favourites. Kali is nature, the mother: naked with hair unbound. Gauri is culture, the daughter, the sister, or the wife: demure and dressed with hair bound.

The characteristic feature of Hindu mythology is the great emphasis on the mind, hence perceived realities.

In the Vedas, the poet or kavi wonders: What came first? Who came first? Was it water? Was it air? Was it the sky? Who witnessed their creation? Who can testify they came first? The gods? But are even the gods creations of the mind? What existed before the mind? Who created the mind? Can we ever know?

Later Vedic texts clearly distinguish between prakriti (nature), sanskriti (culture) and brahmanda (imagined reality of every individual). These are the three worlds we inhabit. The question persists: what came first?

Evolutionary biologists are clear that nature came first, then came the mind and only after that came culture. Life on earth began a billion years ago, but the human brain evolved only a million years ago; language, hence culture, emerged less than fifty thousand years ago. Thus prakriti came first, then Brahma (humanity), then brahmanda (Brahma's egg of thought), then sanskriti. Humanity however deludes itself that Brahma created prakriti first, then sanskriti.

Calendar print of Balambika, daughter of humanity

These ideas were expressed in narrative form in the Puranas. In these stories, the male form is used for the mind, while the female form is used to explain the material world around. The relationship between man and woman, or rather God and Goddess in the Puranas, serves as an allegory to explain the impact of the mind on the world and the impact of the world on the mind.

We are conditioned to assume that mind is superior to matter, hence the attribution of male form to the mind and female form to matter seems like yet another case of gender prejudice. The attribution, however, has more to do with biology: the male form lends itself best to represent the mind as the mind can express itself and affirm its existence only through matter, just as a man can only produce a child through the woman. Semen then, in mythic vocabulary, is a physical representation of thought that becomes reality (the child) through the woman (matter). When a sage spurts semen in the presence of a nymph, it does not mean a man being seduced by a woman; it means a quiet mind that has been provoked into thought by the events in the world around.

That being said, it is easier to read symbols literally ('Shiva is man and Shakti is woman') rather than symbolically ('Shiva is mind and Shakti is matter'). There is no escaping this.

The narrative in the Puranas begins with pralaya, a time marking the dissolution of the whole cosmos. Nothing exists then but waters that stretched into infinity. On the waters Vishnu sleeps, as on the coils of the serpent Sesha. So deep is his slumber that Vishnu is not aware of himself. This form of Vishnu is called Narayana. That is when the twin asuras, Madhu and Kaitabha, emerge out of Vishnu's earwax and create trouble. They steal the Vedas and create havoc. Who got rid of them? It was the Goddess, Yoga-nidra.

Pahari miniature of Yoga-maya

But how do we know? Was there a witness? Who was the witness?

It was Brahma, born of the lotus that rises from Vishnu's navel. He saw the birth of Madhu and Kaitabha, their theft of the Vedas, their killing at the hands of the Goddess, the dismemberment of their bodies, and finally the transformation of their body parts into continents. Brahma sang songs to Yoga-nidra's glory. Only, he called her Yoga-maya.

Narayana here is our sleeping mind, Vishnu is our awakened mind, while Brahma is our partially awakened mind. Madhu and Kaitabha are our thoughts emerging from the partially awakened mind. These are our negative thoughts, hence asuras, commonly (though incorrectly) identified as demons. Positive thoughts, come to be known as devas, commonly (though incorrectly) identified as gods.

The Goddess in this story is nature, present even when there is no human awareness. She is Yoga-nidra: nature witnessed by no one. She is also Yoga-maya: nature witnessed by an unenlightened mind. Yoga-nidra is reality but Yoga-maya is perceived reality, filtered through the human mind. Eventually, the mind will discover that she does not need him but he surely needs her.

What is the name of this perceived reality? She is called Adya, the primal one. She is called Shakti, the energy from which all things are created. She is called Maya, everything that the human gaze defines and evaluates. She is the mother, Kali. She can also be the daughter, Gauri.

Brahma, Vishnu and Shiva are commonly identified as the creator,

Calendar print of the trinity of the Puranas

preserver and destroyer. But what do they create, sustain and destroy?

The assumption is that they create, sustain and destroy nature. But nature, the Goddess, is swayambhu, self-created and self-contained, sustained by karmic laws. What is being continuously created, sustained and destroyed is perceived reality, the multiple impermanent forms of the Goddess.

That is why God-mind is associated with verbs: creation, sustenance and destruction. The Goddess-matter, by contrast, is associated with nouns: wealth, power and language, as Lakshmi, Durga, Saraswati. The God-mind draws wealth, power and language by organising nature into culture.

When Brahma, our unenlightened mind, perceives nature, he is unhappy as she is indifferent to his gaze and his views and his opinions. He seeks to control her. He creates culture by domesticating nature. For him, Gauri is daughter, who must obey him. By controlling her, he derives pleasure from her. This makes Brahma, the creator, unworthy of worship.

Shiva, by contrast, is indifferent to perceived nature. He is the tapasvin, the ascetic, who withdraws completely from nature. His mind has no notion of what nature is or should be. It is pure, clean, uncontaminated by thoughts. This is what makes him the destroyer of culture. Devi seeks to marry him, make him open his eyes, transform from the tapasvin Shiva who is withdrawn to the yogi Shankara who is willing to engage, so that he protects her from Brahma's bothersome gaze.

Shiva is embedded so deep in our consciousness that even we are not aware of it. The purpose of life is to invoke that hidden, unexplored potential. When Shiva awakens and acknowledges

Poster art showing Kamakhya

Shakti, Vishnu is born.

Vishnu is our wise mind capable of understanding perceived nature. Only he appreciates Kali and Gauri. He understands the insecurities of Brahma and the value of Shiva. He balances the two and so is the preserver of culture. For him, Devi is sister. She can also be mother, wife and daughter.

Symbolic readings of mythology are problematic for many reasons. Modern academic education is based on scientific principles as well as Euro-American bias that are more comfortable with the literal, the measurable, the singular and the objective ('this makes sense to all, so is true'). Indian readings of the Puranas tend to be highly individualistic and subjective ('what is sense for you may be nonsense to another and that is fine, for truth is plural'), hence there is room for multiple readings depending on the reader's intellectual capability. Each reading is valid.

From Brahma comes knowledge or Veda. This knowledge exists in the forms of poems called mantras, which are chanted during rituals called yagnas. Details about these yagnas are compiled in manuals known as brahmanas. The keepers of these brahamana texts were known as brahmins.

Killing these knowledge-carriers or brahmins was considered the greatest of crimes in the Hindu world as it meant the loss of Vedic knowledge that enabled humanity to turn nature into culture. However, every Purana tells the story of brahma-hatya-paap, the crime of killing a brahmin, committed by both Shiva and Vishnu.

The *Shiva Purana* tells us that when Brahma's daughter came into being, she went around her father as a mark of respect. But

Poster art showing the Goddess and her attendants

Brahma desired her. Disgusted by the incestuous cravings of her father, she ran away. He pursued her. Her disgust gave rise to Shiva, who beheaded Brahma and took upon himself the great burden of brahma-hatya-paap.

The *Vishnu Purana* tells us that Ravana, a brahmin, abducts Ram's wife, Sita, not remembering that she is actually his daughter whom he had abandoned long ago. Ram ultimately overpowers Ravana with the aid of a monkey called Hanuman, who chooses to stay celibate in the service of Sita and Ram. In this narrative, Ravana can be seen as Brahma, Ram as Vishnu and Hanuman as Shiva. Sita is the Goddess. While Shiva does not apologise for beheading Brahma, Ram performs austerities to rid himself of the demerit earned for his brahma-hatya-paap. For Vishnu understands the fears that make a Ravana behave as he does.

Images of the Goddess in north India are often flanked by images of Hanuman (also called langur-vir) and a childlike form of Shiva (Bhairav-baba) holding the severed head of a man, alluding to the tale of Brahma's beheading for looking upon Gauri with eyes of desire.

This narration of Brahma's incest can be seen literally as reinforcing a social taboo. It can also be seen historically as a reference to the end of the old Vedic culture of yagna that was eventually replaced by the later Puranic culture of puja. But it is more meaningful when seen symbolically and Brahma is recognised as the human mind that seeks control over perceived reality. This symbolic explanation clarifies why Brahma is not worshipped in any Hindu temple.

Brahma is the human mind that misbehaves. Shiva is the human mind that vehemently rejects this misbehaviour. Vishnu

Miniature painting of Bhairavi, the fearsome goddess

is the human mind that does not condone this misbehaviour, yet understands it.

What is this misbehaviour? It is the assumption of property: that culture and all its creation belongs to humans. This assumption is dependent on another assumption: that human value is dependent on property. Shiva, the hermit, rejects this assumption. Vishnu, the householder, traces the origin of this assumption to the human fear of validation. We do not know who we are and what the purpose of our life is, so we find solace in creating and hoarding property. That is why Brahma seeks dominion over Devi, while Vishnu and Shiva don't. That is why Brahma is unworthy of worship and that is why his ritual of yagna, described in the brahamana texts, that sought to establish human dominion over nature, was abandoned in favour of puja, where humanity is encouraged to adore Vishnu, Shiva and Devi.

Gauri is more commonly known as Parvati, wife of Shiva, daughter of Himavan, who is god of the Himalayan mountain range, also known as Parvateshwar, or lord of the mountains. She is also called Uma. In her previous life, she was Sati, daughter of Daksha, son of Brahma who established the yagna ritual. Parvati/Uma is the mother of Ganesha and Kartikeya. She is associated with the household. In folk tradition, and especially in Tamil temple lore, she is the sister of Vishnu. It is Kali who domesticates the hermit Shiva and in the process gets domesticated herself as Gauri.

The story is elaborated in the *Shiva Purana*, where Brahma, after being beheaded, feels that Shiva needs to get a wife. Yes, he went overboard in his relationship with his daughter but that is

Miniature painting of devas invoking the Goddess

no reason to reject culture and stay away from women. So Brahma consults Vishnu and they evoke the Goddess who promises to help by taking birth as the daughter of Daksha.

Daksha is associated with the yagna, a ritual based on exchange, which is the hallmark of human culture. Animals do not exchange; they grab what they want. Humans are capable of exchange. It forms the cornerstone of human society. During the yagna, Daksha makes offerings to the devas and expects gifts in return. He contributes in order to consume. He offers them his daughter and they, in turn, ensure that nature provides for all his material needs. He demands obedience from all his daughters and his sons-in-law for the sake of stability and predictability. He fears disobedience as he thinks it will herald the collapse of the structure he has created.

More than disobedience, Daksha fears indifference. The tapasvins ignore him and do not care about his yagna. They value tapa, mental fire churned by tapasya, more than agni, physical fire of the yagna. Tapa evokes thoughts that make a man wise; agni transforms things that make a man rich and powerful. Daksha despises the tapasvins.

So it comes as a huge shock for Daksha when his youngest daughter, and his favourite child, Sati, shows a preference for Shiva, the supreme tapasvin. When her father does not grant her permission to marry him, she simply leaves the house and follows the naked hermit. To teach her a lesson, Daksha conducts a grand yagna where he invites all his daughters and his sons-in-law, except Sati and Shiva.

Sati, as stubborn as her father, arrives at Daksha's doorstep anyway, despite Shiva warning her not to go, and demands to be treated as a daughter returning home should be treated. Daksha

Calendar print of Sati immolating herself

Calendar print of Bhadra-kali destroying the yagna

does no such thing. Instead he insults her and her husband explaining why he is not worthy of an invitation to the yagna. 'He follows no rules. He is covered with ash. He drinks poison and narcotics. He has no family or friends. Alone, he wanders naked in crematoriums in the company of dogs and ghosts. He is unfit for civilisation.'

Sati tries to explain to her father that Shiva is no rebel, but a hermit. He simply does not value himself through social structure, rules and property that indulge human hunger and fear. He performs tapasya and ignites tapa to outgrow hunger and fear.

But Daksha does not listen. For Daksha, unquestioning participation in the yagna is the only virtue. So angry is Sati at being unable to get through to her father that she leaps in the pit of fire in the ritual precinct and burns herself to death. Still the yagna continues, for Daksha refuses to be cowed down by his stubborn, defiant daughter.

When Shiva learns of Sati's death, his otherwise tranquil nature gives way to rage. He becomes Rudra, the howler. He tears out the locks of his hair and strikes them to the ground. Out come the sword-wielding Vira-bhadra and Bhadra-kali, manifestations of his outrage. They storm into Daksha's house, disrupt the ceremony, drive away the devas and ultimately behead Daksha.

But when the yagna stops, civilisation ends. Vishnu appeals to Shiva and begs him to restore the yagna by bringing Daksha back to life. Shiva does that, for he has no problem with the ritual itself, his problem is only with the assumptions and attitude of Daksha who seems to repeat Brahma's primal incestuous misbehaviour. Finally, Daksha is given an animal head, that of a goat, a reminder that a more worthy offering in a yagna is his own desire to dominate and

Odisha patta painting of Shiva carrying Sati's corpse.

Naina-devi where the eyes fell.

Kali-ghat where the toe fell.

Jwala-mukhi where the tongue fell.

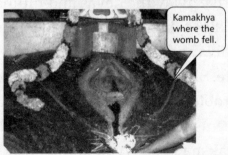

Kamakhya where the womb fell.

The Shakti-peethas

control the world like a dominating alpha goat.

Shiva then picks up the charred lifeless body of Sati and wanders the world, weeping. No more is he the detached hermit. He is now the lover inconsolable in his loss. His pain and suffering disturb the gods who beg Vishnu to put an end to it, for all things have to end, even bereavement. So Vishnu cuts Sati's corpse into tiny pieces. These fall in different parts of the world and became Shakti-pithas, centres of Goddess worship.

With Sati gone, Shiva shuts his eyes and resumes his meditation, withdrawing all attention from the world, generating inner fire and creating a cold, icy, desolate landscape around him.

Eons pass before the devas remember Shiva and want him to open his eyes, marry and father a child. For they are in trouble. Their paradise has been attacked by asuras. The devas need a commander to lead their armies. Their king, Indra, is not capable, for the leader of the asuras can only be killed by a warrior-child. Such a child can only be produced by a man who has been celibate for a long time. In other words, Shiva.

But when the gods send Kama, the god of desire, to strike Shiva with his arrows that arouse the senses, Shiva opens his third eye and lets loose a missile with his glance that sets Kama aflame and reduces him to a pile of ash. So the devas turn to the Goddess once again. And she promises to help, becoming Parvati, the daughter of the mountain-god, Himavan.

Parvati makes Shiva open his eyes and marry, but very differently. Unlike Sati, she does not follow Shiva. Unlike Kama, she does not arouse him sexually. She simply prays to him by

Chola bronze of Tapasvini Parvati

refusing to eat, drink or move, thinking only of him, resisting all temptations, until he is forced to appear before her and give her what she wants. Shiva finally appears and agrees to come to her house as a groom comes to receive his bride.

Shiva, unaware of the ways of the world, comes riding not a mare but a bull, wearing animal skins not silks, decked with ash not sandal paste, serpents not garlands, with ghosts and wild forest spirits instead of family and friends. Parvati's parents are not amused, but Parvati refuses to change her mind. She begs Shiva to temper his form to the satisfaction of her parents, and he, eager to indulge this devotee of his, transforms into the most elegant of beings, Mahadeva, more beautiful than all the devas.

And so Shiva marries Parvati and takes her to Kailas, a mountain peak covered with snow where nothing grows. Here she makes a home even though Shiva does not understand the concept. He is content living in caves during the rains, in crematoriums in winter and on mountain peaks in summer.

Parvati and Shiva make love, but he offers his semen not to her, but the devas. It is so fiery that it burns Agni, the fire-god, and remains resistant to the touch of Vayu, the wind-god. It boils Ganga, the river-goddess, and sets aflame Saravana, the forest of reeds. From the ashes emerge six boys from Shiva's single seed who are nursed by the six star-goddesses who make up the Krittika constellation. Parvati takes the six children in her hand and fuses them into one. Thus is born the six-headed Skanda, warrior-child, who leads the devas into battle and defeats the asuras.

Skanda, or Kartikeya, or Murugan, as he is known in the south, is Shiva's son, born of his seed, incubated in multiple wombs. Parvati now wants a son of her own. Shiva refuses to indulge

Calendar art of Shiva agreeing to marry Parvati

Miniature painting of Shiva's wedding procession

this wish as he says children are needed only by mortal beings who seek rebirth. He is immortal and so has no need for children. Parvati argues that children are also needed to receive and give love.

When Shiva does not grant Parvati what she wants, she anoints her body with turmeric, scrapes it off and from the rubbings creates a child without a man (nayaka), and names him Vinayaka. When Shiva discovers this child, he does not recognise him as Parvati's. In a fit of rage and jealousy, he cuts his head, but when Parvati reveals who the child is, replaces it with an elephant's head to pacify her. Thus is born Ganesha, the god who removes obstacles, associated with affluence and abundance.

The two sons of Shiva, Skanda and Ganesha, take care of the two primal fears of man: fear of being killed by a predator and fear of dying of starvation. Skanda fights the asuras and provides security, while Ganesha removes all obstacles to material prosperity. Thus the sons of the hermit Shiva indulge all the desires of the householder. They would not exist if Parvati had not come into the picture. Parvati thus embodies that aspect of domesticated nature, which evokes the best of the human mind.

Shiva beheads Brahma. Shiva beheads Daksha. Shiva also beheads Vinayaka. With each beheading, a new wisdom emerges. The first marks the destruction of the desire to claim ownership over nature, hence the Goddess. The second marks the destruction of the desire to control culture, hence the Goddess. The third marks the destruction of the desire to block access to nature, hence the Goddess.

Calendar art of Shiva's marriage

Cambodian sculpture of Shiva and Parvati on Nandi

The *Shiva Purana* begins with Shiva's refusal to marry. When married, he is reluctant to make love. When he finally makes loves, he is reluctant to shed semen. When he sheds semen it is not in his wife's womb but outside. He refuses to give Parvati the child she wants. By creating a child on her own, Parvati declares her autonomy. She does not need Shiva. But by then Shiva needs her. He wants to be with her. When Vinayaka blocks his path to her, he removes the obstacle brutally. This violence indicates Shiva, who once loved isolation, now yearns for companionship. Devi thus has successfully domesticated him. She no longer dances on his chest as Kali. She now sits on his lap as Gauri. The hermit (tapasvin) becomes a contributor (yajaman) in the yagna, though he remains a yogi, one who has no desire to be the yagna's beneficiary (bhogi).

Sati exists in the old Vedic way, where yagna was paramount and all that mattered were the rules of exchange that governed the ritual. Sati is destroyed and, when she is reborn, she emerges in a new Puranic order, one where devotion and adoration, expressed trough puja, is preferred. In the yagna-way, there is no clear concept of God; there are only gods or devas. In the puja-way, gods/devas are replaced by God/Mahadeva, the tone is more emotional than technical. Sati rejects Daksha, hence Brahma, but chooses Shiva as husband, and Vishnu as brother, who become focal points of Hindu tradition.

We can say that Sati and Parvati embody the pre-Buddhist and post-Buddhist forms of Hinduism. Pre-Buddhist Vedic Hinduism thrived before 500 BCE. Post-Buddhist Puranic Hinduism thrived after 500 CE. Buddhism, which dominated the subcontinent for nearly a thousand years, was a major transformative force in India, as it questioned the mechanistic and materialistic way

The domestication of Shiva

of the yagna. But the low value given to emotion in Buddhism was addressed by bhakti traditions, which gave rise to temple traditions, stories of the Puranas and the ritual of puja.

The yagna-way valued fire. This fire ultimately consumes Sati. The puja-way values water. Parvati draws out the heat from within Shiva until the ice melts, both metaphorically and literally. She gets Shiva to break the fall of the river Ganga as she descends from the sky and makes its way to earth. In Hindu tradition, the dead are first burned in a funeral pyre and then their ashes are thrown in a river. Fire consumes death but water helps in rebirth. If Sati embraces death, Parvati brings forth life. She rejuvenates and revitalises Shiva, and the world.

Shiva transforms into the dancer Nataraja and the musician Vinapani in the presence of Parvati. She asks him questions on the nature of reality and the world, and their conversations are heard by birds and bulls and fish who transmit this knowledge to the world. The birds transmit the ocean of stories, *Katha-sarit-sagar*. The bull transmits the knowledge of sensory pleasures, Kama-sutra. The fish transforms into Matsyendranath and transmits esoteric knowledge, the Tantras. Thus, with Parvati's presence, the ice melts and water flows in various ways to enrich culture.

Daksha's approach to culture is rather masculine, based on command and control. Parvati's approach is more feminine, based on affection. When Shiva tells Parvati that he does not feel there is any need for a kitchen in Kailas, she disappears. Shortly thereafter the followers of Shiva, the gana, led by Ganapati, go to Shiva and ask him for food. He has none to give. He goes around the world with a begging bowl but finds no food. Finally, he reaches Kashi and finds Parvati's kitchen there. She smiles and says, 'You may

Calendar art of Annapoorna, the kitchen-goddess

Festivals of Gauri in Rajasthan

have outgrown hunger but not others. The kitchen is for them.' As she feeds her children, Shiva declares her to be Annapoorna, goddess of food, the ideal wife for the hermit who has no hunger. While Daksha's masculine gaze is firmly focused on his own needs, Parvati's feminine gaze shifts the focus to others. Culture then becomes an outcome not of domestication but of empathy.

# 4. Durga's Secret

*Everyone lives on the edge in fear*

Poster art showing Yoga-maya protecting Krishna

*O*fferings to Shiva and Vishnu include food, flowers, leaves, lamps and incense. The aim is to invoke God who is otherwise dormant. Offerings to Devi are strikingly different. Besides the standard offerings to God, there is always something more: haldi (turmeric), kunku (red powder), kajal (kohl), and pieces of cloth to serve as her upper garment — the choli (blouse), the chunari (veil) and the chadar (shawl). The aim is to cover up the Goddess so that she is less Kali and more Gauri. Why so?

This makes sense if we associated the male form of divinity with the mind and the female form of divinity with nature. We want to invoke the mind as well as domesticate nature. Only invoking the mind without domesticating nature is the trait of Shiva, the withdrawn hermit. Only domesticating nature without invoking the mind is the trait of Brahma, who manifests as Daksha, the controlling priest. This tension between mind and nature is a key theme of the Puranas.

And so, the preferred form of the Goddess is Durga, riding her lion, defying domestication. Her unbound hair reveals that she is still wild like Kali, but her nose-ring reveals she is domesticated like Gauri. The weapons in her multiple hands reveal a different kind of violence, one that is restrained unlike Kali's, one that offers protection but can also be used to punish. She is Brahma's defiant daughter, Vishnu's protected and protective sister, and Shiva's affectionate wife. Her affection cannot be taken for granted. She will not be exploited. Domestication of the Goddess (nature) must be mirrored with the awakening of God (mind).

Poster art of Kanya-kumari

From the southern tip of India comes a very interesting tale that challenges the very idea of domestication in order to establish culture.

A young girl, Kanya-kumari, meaning one who is a virgin, invokes Shiva and expresses her desire to be his wife. Shiva agrees. But the devas are not pleased with this news. As long as Kanya-kumari is without husband and children, she has the power to kill demons. Her power unused in marriage and motherhood will also prevent the sea from overwhelming the land. So they go out of their way to disrupt this wedding. They tell Kanya-kumari that to ensure the marriage is a happy one she has to marry at sunrise the following day. But Shiva lives far away in the north on Mount Kailas; he must be asked to set forth immediately and travel through the night. Shiva agrees to travel fast, eager to meet his bride, while Kanya-kumari spends the night preparing the wedding feast, adorning herself with cosmetics and jewellery. In the middle of the night, the devas take the form of roosters and start to crow. Shiva thinks the sun is about to rise and that he will not make it to the wedding on time. So he turns around, disappointed. When the sun really does rise, there is no sign of Shiva. A heartbroken Kanya-kumari breaks all the pots containing the wedding feast: the pulses and grains turn into the colourful sand that one finds near the southern tip of India. She washes away her cosmetics in the sea: that is why the sea is multi-coloured there. She stands on the southern tip, killing demons, preventing the sea from overwhelming the land and, like a divine beacon, enabling fishermen to battle tempestuous seas and come home safe to their wives.

This story displays an ambiguous relationship with

Odisha patta painting of the untamed Goddess

domestication. At one level, we want God to be domesticated (he must be a householder, not a hermit), and at another level, we do not want the Goddess to be completely domesticated (she must stay forest, not become field). Typically cultures use rules and laws (niti) and traditional codes of conduct (riti) to stifle freedom for the larger good. But this can destroy creativity and innovation and even introspection. It can amplify our sense of entrapment. So it is important to retain the wildness of nature, which offers the promise of freedom.

This is why in the *Shiva Purana* and in the *Devi Purana,* the devas often prevent Parvati from bearing Shiva's child herself; they would rather that Shiva's seed be germinated in multiple wombs. Parvati, or Gauri, is not mother in the conventional sense of the term. She is foster mother of Kartikeya, and she creates Ganesha using the paste with which she anoints her body. Neither is born through her womb. This may not make literal sense, but it makes a whole lot of symbolic sense.

This rejection of complete domestication is symbolically communicated through the unbound hair of Durga. Traditionally, well-combed and bound hair indicates domestication. But Durga, dressed in bridal finery, sports unbound hair. She thus stands on the edge, between nature and culture, acknowledging our fear of lawless freedom as well as lawful entrapment.

In the last five hundred years, a deliberate attempt has been made in Hinduism to humanise the divine. God is not a lofty concept out there; it is immediate and accessible. And Goddess is not all of nature; she is the village that sustains a human population.

The worship of Durga as the daughter of
households in Bengal, Assam and Odisha

These ideas were not new. Grama-devis or village-goddesses are perhaps the oldest form of religion known in India, predating Buddha, even the Vedas, and the Indus valley cities. She was identified with termite hills, and snake holes, and rock clefts, for she emerged from beneath the earth, the seat of all fertility.

But five hundred years ago, the relationship became extremely intimate and personal. It was articulated using a very emotional vocabulary in songs and ritual ceremonies. As God increasingly became parent, child, master, friend, even lover, the Goddess became a member of the family. This came to be known as the bhakti phase of Hinduism, where simple human emotions were made portals to reach the divine. In keeping with this trend, in eastern India, in Bengal, Assam and Odisha, we find the Goddess, who is normally addressed as mother, being treated as the daughter of the village.

Every year, during the autumn months, she returns from her husband's house in the form of Durga for a few days of rest in the comforting arms of her mother, the village community. Thus the mother of the village transforms into the daughter and is indulged accordingly. She comes with her children, two sons, the strong Kartikeya and the smart Ganesha, and her two daughters, the rich Lakshmi and the talented Saraswati. She complains that her husband, Shiva, does not work and she is left to provide for the family. Her mother empathises with her but reminds her that she chose the man she married; no one forced her to marry a hermit who wanders with dogs and ghosts, lives in crematoriums, and loves narcotics. She is bathed, and clothed, and fed, and entertained with songs and dances. And finally, she is bid farewell, cast into the river, where her image dissolves, as she makes her way back to

White-complexioned Balarama is identified with Shiva.

Black-complexioned Krishna is identified with Vishnu.

Turmeric-faced Subhadra is identified with the Goddess.

Incomplete features point to the primal tribal origin of this shrine.

Images of Subhadra with her brothers in Puri, Odisha

her husband's house in faraway snow-capped Mount Kailas.

This happens year after year. She comes and she goes. They weep in joy on her arrival and weep in sorrow at her departure. Thus the cyclical nature of the world is reinforced to the village community. Nothing lasts forever. Nothing ends forever. Everything comes back. Everything goes back. It grants solace and hope to the villagers who are facing sorrow. It also warns those who are enjoying fortune not to take things for granted.

What strikes the eye when one closely observes the traditional image of Durga in Bengal is her turmeric yellow skin. She is therefore called Haldi-mukhi, she of the turmeric face. Haldi, or turmeric, is an essential feature of Goddess-worship. It is both an antiseptic and a cosmetic that keeps the skin clean and makes it glow like gold.

In the temple of Krishna in Puri, Odisha, there is another Haldi-mukhi, the goddess Subhadra, Krishna's sister, standing between him and his elder brother Balabhadra. The similar complexion of Durga and Subhadra reminds us of temple lore that Devi who is Shiva's wife is also Vishnu's sister.

In his various avatars, Vishnu keeps fighting for his sister. In one of the folk Mahabharatas is the story of a warrior who saw the entire war at Kurukshetra from the top of a mountain; he had been decapitated before the war but Krishna had kept his head alive so that his last wish of witnessing the war could be fulfilled. When asked what he saw, he declared he only saw Krishna's discus cutting the head of unrighteous kings, and Kali drinking their blood by spreading her tongue over the battlefield.

Miniature painting of the birth of Durga

Simultaneously, this sister protected the world from Madhu and Kaitabha when Vishnu was in a dreamless slumber. It was she who offered herself as sacrifice to save baby Krishna from the murderous Kansa. It was she who ensured Shiva no longer shuts his eyes to the world, that he fathered Kartikeya and Ganesha who protect and provide culture. And when an asura emerges, whom neither Indra, nor Vishnu, nor Shiva can defeat, it is she who is once again invoked.

Thus in the *Devi Mahatmya,* when Indra begs Brahma for help and Brahma takes him to Vishnu and Vishnu takes him to Shiva, Shiva advises all the devas to release the Goddess from within their bodies and merge it to create a Goddess who is greater than all of them individually. Flames emerge from the body of each and every deva and these flames merge in a blinding light to create Durga, who is given weapons by each deva, and who then rides a lion to do battle with an asura. Durga thus is the jigsaw puzzle whose parts come from the different devas. They are 'parts' and she is the 'whole'. She is not the daughter of one deva, she is the daughter of all devas; she is ayonija, born without a womb, with no mother of her own. This establishes her as Mahadevi, the goddess of the gods, just as Shiva is Mahadeva, god of the gods. Thus the Puranas acknowledge her sovereignty. She is, like Shiva and Vishnu, swayambhu or self-created.

Who is this asura that Durga has to defeat? Who is this 'demon' who overpowers god (deva) and God (Mahadeva)? He is identified as Mahisha-asura, the buffalo demon, though he takes many forms, that of an elephant, lion and even human, and fights with

Miniature painting of Durga killing Mahisha-asura

numerous types of weapons, before he is finally killed.

Those who prefer to see mythology as proto-history see this as a story that retells the epic conquest of fair-skinned, cow-loving Aryans of the north over dark-skinned, buffalo-loving Dravidians of the south. The problem with this reading is that here the warrior is a woman and it is hard for scholars to reconcile Vedic patriarchy with the obvious female power embedded in the Durga image. Besides, many scholars have long debunked this racial theory popular in the early 20th century.

Those who see mythology as proto-psychology conclude that Durga destroys the slippery, shape-shifting human ego that seeks dominion over nature. But what is ego?

This word comes to us from Freudian and Jungian psychoanalysis of the 20th century. The word used in Upanishads composed 2,500 years ago is aham. We have assumed they mean the same thing. But do they really?

Aham means how humans imagine themselves as against atma, who we really are. Animals do not have any doubt about who they are in terms of location in the food chain and pecking order. All they care about when they see another animal is: is that a predator, a prey, a rival or a mate? Humans are confused. There is no such clear understanding. Imagination wipes out all structures and we are forced into a struggle between our own desires (how we want to imagine ourselves) and social structures imposed upon us by others based on their desires (how others are expected to see us). More often than not we regress to our animal selves: we want to dominate or be dominated, we want to domesticate others with rules or be domesticated by them. This is Mahisha, the asura. A deva then is one who recognises, like Indra, that there are larger

Poster images of Durga

forces at work in the universe, embodied in Brahma, Vishnu, Shiva and of course, Devi. Mahisha acknowledges Brahma but seeks to triumph over others, and in doing so lies his folly. Mahisha-asura's defeat is not viewed as submission but as realisation: he breaks free from his limited self-indulgent view of the world and internalises the bigger picture. This is called uddhar, or upliftment.

But these are lofty ideas. How were these communicated to simple folk who lived in villages? Our question is presumptuous. We assume that great knowledge cannot come from 'simple rural folk'. We assume that wise brahmins came up with these ideas and passed them on. But the more one studies Indian rituals and texts, the more one realises that the wisdom of India comes from 'simple rural folk', simply articulated in Sanskrit. The brahmins are scribes, compilers and organisers, not sources, of Vedic wisdom. This becomes evident when we look at village rituals associated with the worship of grama-devi. Today, these practices are seen more in the southern part of India, but there are traces in the north too. They are usually seen in technologically backward rural communities who communicate deep psychological ideas through symbols and rituals, rather than words.

Unlike Durga, who is associated with the entire universe, the grama-devi is restricted to her neighbourhood. She makes the universal particular. She embodies the settlement: she is Mumba-devi of Mumbai, Chandika of Chandigarh, Kali of Kolkata. Her image is often just a rock that marks either the navel of the village, or the periphery. Eyes are painted on the rock to indicate she is sensitive to the condition of villagers. She is shown wearing a nose-

Photograph of Saptashrungi-devi of Maharashtra

Photograph of Mhasoba in Pune, Maharashtra

ring, indicator of her domestication. Her palms are either raised to indicate she offers protection, or lowered to indicate she offers bounty. Rarely does she have a body: the village is her body. She is sometimes accompanied by a twin-goddess, identified as her sister or as her friend or just a companion who takes care of her devotees when she wants to rest. Her attendants are brave men, the viras, often with moustaches to emphasise their masculinity, and riding horses in the company of hunting dogs. In south India, the vira is often a Muslim cavalry officer indicating close association with village realities. He is the guardian god who forms a complementary pair with the fertility goddess. He protects; she provides.

Three things are striking in the worship of grama-devi. First, the practice of actually sacrificing a buffalo, or a male goat, or even a rooster, to the Goddess, and mixing her blood with rice and throwing this into fields where crops have just been harvested. Second, the practice of keeping images of Mhasoba (the buffalo-lord), or Pothraj (the buffalo-king) alongside Durga, describing him as her attendant, and sometimes even her husband, who is then called Bhairava, a form of Shiva. There is at least one Puranic tale where Durga finds a Shiva-linga in the throat of the asura. Third, the practice of mostly male devotees ritually torturing themselves for her pleasure during her festival. They swing from hooks, pierce their tongue, walk on fire, whip and even bite themselves. In some parts of the Deccan, in Maharashtra, Karnataka and Andhra Pradesh, the priest who serves the Goddess is called Pothraj, and he typically belongs to non-brahmin communities. At times, the priests dress as women and carry the sacred pot on their head. All this reveals an ambiguous relationship between Durga and the buffalo. Is it only demon or also a god? A villain or also a hero? An

The Goddess represented by three rock protrusions that embody Lakshmi, Saraswati and Durga.

Photograph of Vaishno-devi of Jammu

Bhairava, who was beheaded by the Goddess and, after he repented, was turned into a deity.

Photograph of Bhairava

abuser or also a husband? Does the buffalo represent the 'aham' of devotees?

While in most stories Bhairava comes to the rescue of the goddess, in the story of Vaishno-devi, Bhairava is her abuser. Vaishno-devi's temple is located to the north, in Jammu. Unlike other goddesses, she does not demand blood (this is fairly common of grama-devis of the Jammu and Himachal areas). The story goes that she was Vedavati who resisted the charms and attentions of many men as she was determined to marry Vishnu. When Bhairava tried to force himself on her, she ran through the hills, hid in caves, and finally transformed into the fiery goddess who beheaded Bhairava and then forgave him, after he apologised for his presumptuousness. So, today, those who visit the shrine of Vaishno-devi also visit the shrine of Bhairava. Once her abuser, he is now her guardian. The violence of the tale re-links us with the tale of Shiva beheading Brahma. Ultimately, for culture to happen, domestication has to be voluntary, born of love, not the desire to control.

In one of the many stories associated with Bahuchara-mata in Gujarat, a young bride on her way to her husband's house kills herself to save herself from being assaulted by a highway robber. She curses the highway robber that he will only attain liberation from worldly bondage if he castrates himself and serves as her eunuch-priestess. In another story, a young bride discovers that her husband — who never comes to her room at night, instead riding out on his horse — is (depending on various versions of this oral tale) a homosexual, or a transgendered person, or a cross-dresser, locally known as hijra. Furious that he tricked her into a false marriage that will ruin her life, she turns into a goddess, punishes her husband, and offers him salvation from worldly

Poster art of Bahuchara-mata of Gujarat

bondage only if he becomes a hijra and serves her. Members of the hijra community castrate themselves taking her name. Her temple is also popular with women seeking children. Here too we find the tension associated with marriage, fertility, and woman's frustration in marriage. Here, the demon is husband and abuser.

At the heart of the ambiguous relationship of the grama-devi with her male attendants is humanity's relationship with nature. Humans establish culture by domesticating nature. The process of domestication is a violent one: rivers are blocked, forests are burned, and mountains are razed. In mythological terms, the mother is violated to create the daughter. And she strikes back in various ways, demanding appeasement. She will not be taken for granted. The buffalo-demon then is humanity seeking to control nature, who is at once father, brother and son. He needs to be punished when he crosses the line. But he is also venerated, as he has divinity within him which can be evoked. What is the divinity within man? What is the God who can be awakened? It is the ability to empathise with the world around, with nature and with fellow humans, that keeps human cupidity and stupidity in check.

The grama-devi embodies not just the village but also each and every woman in the village. In many ways, she is the goddess. Her house is the temple. And she is her own priestess. Traditionally, it is she who plastered the house and floor with cow dung each day and painted images on and in front of it with rice flour. This ritual painting is called kolam in Tamil Nadu, rangoli in Maharashtra and alpana in Bengal. She invoked the goddess through rituals known as vrata, which did not involve the intervention of priests. It

Women in south India painting kolam outside the house to invite fortune.

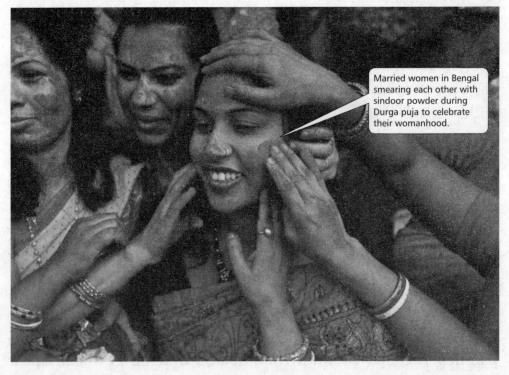

Married women in Bengal smearing each other with sindoor powder during Durga puja to celebrate their womanhood.

Women's rituals

involved her either staying away from a particular form of food or eating a particular form of food. Her rituals brought in good energy into the household, ensured prosperity and peace. Her anger and unhappiness brought in disease. She was the diminutive double of the goddess, dressed as such during the wedding ceremony. Her entry into the house was celebrated as if a goddess were entering the house. For with her entry, the kitchen fire would survive for yet another generation and she would bring forth the next generation of the clan.

In south and west India especially, women hold ceremonies called 'haldi-kunku', during which married women gather and greet each other with turmeric, red powder, flowers and gifts. This is a ritual of women, for women. Widows are not allowed, reaffirming the ritual's links with fertility more than femininity. A similar festival is found in Bengal, where married women smear each other with vermilion powder on the final day of Durga puja.

Domestication of women mirrored domestication of nature. Her freedom was curtailed as she approached puberty. She was not allowed to cook or touch anyone when she was menstruating. She was valued for being fertile and feared when she was not fertile, as during menstruation, or after she became a widow. This created anxiety, depression and frustration in women, which was the common explanation given for 'hysterical trances', a way of letting out repressed emotions. Traditionally this was explained with the phrase 'the devi has come', making women the medium of the goddess who spoke what otherwise could never be spoken.

Stories of goddesses in rural shrines often reflect this tension

Poster art showing Renuka-Yellamma and her story

between the village and nature, as well as the tension between women and men in marriage. The most popular of these stories is that of Renuka-Yellamma. There is a scriptural Sanskrit version of this story in the Puranas, as well as an oral version of the story.

In the Puranic version, Renuka one day sees a handsome gandharva bathing in a river. For a moment she harbours sexual desire for him. Until then she has thought of no one else sexually except her husband, Jamadagni, a great tapasvin. The sage senses her momentary lack of fidelity and demands that she be beheaded. The sons who refuse to do so are cursed to turn into eunuchs. The youngest son, Parashuram, raises his axe and severs his mother's neck.

There are many oral versions of what happens next. In one version, when the father offers his obedient son a boon, Parashuram asks his mother be brought back to life, and she is, thanks to Jamadagni's powers accumulated through tapasya. In another version, a non-brahmin woman tries to stop the matricide and gets decapitated herself; Parashuram replaces his mother's head on the non-brahmin woman's body and the non-brahmin head on his mother's body, creating confusion as to who is his real mother. In still another version, the head and body become deities in their own rights: the head is Yellamma and the body is Huligamma. Here, the tension is not just about fidelity, it is also about caste.

In the oral version of the Renuka-Yellamma story, a young brahmin girl discovers that her husband is no brahmin and in fury beheads him. Some believe this story belongs to a distinctively different grama-devi, often addressed as Ammaveru, whose name means 'the lady', a generic title for the village-goddess.

Photograph of a devadasi of Yellamma

While in the Puranic story it is the woman who is killed, in the folk story it is the man who is killed. In the Puranic story, the brahmin woman is killed because she is 'contaminated' by her adulterous desire as well as by her contact with the non-brahmin woman. In the oral story, the man who is killed is a brahmin-pretender.

Both the body and the head of Renuka are objects of worship, especially in the Deccan region of India. Known variously as Yellamma or Huligamma, she is invoked by women for children, and is commonly associated with the devadasi cult, women who were not bound by limitations of marriage. While this was meant to give these women freedom to choose lovers without losing social standing, it often ended up making them prostitutes as they were denied all sources of wealth.

Chaste women are described in scriptures as Sati and associated with magical powers. Renuka, for example, before she desired another man, had the power to collect water in unbaked pots. In the Ramayana, Sita is able to walk through fire because she is chaste in mind and body. In the Puranas, there is the story of Shilavati, who is able to stop even the sun from rising using the power of chastity. Chastity even makes a wife more powerful than the gods, as we learn from the story of Anasuya.

On the request of their wives, Shiva, Vishnu and Brahma take the form of three young men trying to seduce Anasuya, the chaste wife of Atri. They ask that she let them suckle her breasts so that they can end their vow of fasting. Anasuya agrees, but such is the power of her chastity that no sooner does she bare her breasts than the gods turn into children, and are restored to their normal form

Poster art of Anasuya

only when the wives of the gods apologise.

The belief was that a sati protected her husband with the powers of chastity. When Vrinda's husband, an asura called Jalandhar, was killed by devas, everyone accused her of infidelity. She then learned that Vishnu himself had come to her house taking the form of Jalandhar. A Vishnu devotee, she was furious that he had tricked her so, and she demanded justice. Vishnu was cursed into the shaligrama stone for his overzealous determination to save the devas, while Vrinda was transformed into the tulsi plant and kept in the courtyard of the house — outside yet inside. No worship of Vishnu is complete without offerings of tulsi sprigs. She is present in everyone's house to remind women of the power of chastity.

Belief that a woman's chastity protects her husband led to the popularisation of the infamous 'sati' practices, especially amongst warrior communities like the Rajputs, where women burned themselves on the funeral pyre of their husbands killed in war. This practice was valorised and glamorised, with these women turned into goddesses. It was expected to be voluntary, with everyone believing that the power of Sati would protect these women from the heat of the flames. Rani-sati-mata is still worshipped in Rajasthan and many parts of India, though the practice has been made illegal as this belief has been seen as enabling the oppression and mistreatment of women.

Sita and Draupadi, the female protagonists of the two great epics of Hinduism, the Ramayana and the Mahabharata, are always on the edge between the wild and sovereign Kali and the demure and dependent Gauri. They appear as wives but, when challenged, display their Kali-like form. They are not forced to domesticate

Draupadi is always worshipped alone, without her five husbands, the Pandavas.

The Goddess with her attendants.

Sita is always worshipped beside her husband, Ram.

Worship of epic heroines

themselves; they choose to domesticate themselves out of empathy for humanity. Any attempt to force them to be domestic, as Renuka is, transforms them into fiery goddesses who refuse to be tamed. This is reinforced in the story of Sita who has many reasons to be unfaithful to her husband Ram, who continuously doubts her chastity, but she refuses to turn her back on him.

But Draupadi refuses to take her abuse lying down and demands blood. In the Mahabharata, the Kauravas try to publicly disrobe Draupadi, declaring her a public woman as she has five husbands. A furious Draupadi displays her rage by refusing to tie her hair until she has washed it with the blood of her abusers. She stops being the demure Gauri and evokes Kali. This so frightens the father of the Kauravas that he begs Draupadi to leave the gambling hall with her dignity intact, along with her husbands who had foolishly gambled themselves and her away. Eventually, the war happens, and Draupadi washes her hair with the blood of her abusers. So in south India, Draupadi is worshipped just like other grama-devis as Amman, the mother, who is terrifying and needs appeasement. Amongst grama-devis, Draupadi is much more popular than the silent, stoic Sita, sadly projected as a whimpering, heartbroken doormat even in 20th-century feminist retellings.

In the Mahabharata is the story of the wives of the seven celestial sages who encounter Agni, the fire-god. Six of the seven women approach him without wearing symbols of marriage. As a result, the heat and light of the fire-god makes them pregnant. In later versions, they enter a pond in which Shiva is meditating and so get

Odisha patta painting of Kartikeya with his six mothers, the stars of the Krittika constellation.

The mothers cause miscarriage and childhood fevers if not acknowledged and appeased.

Shitala causes disease but is still worshipped, though her shrine is kept outside the village.

Bengali Kalighat painting of Shitala riding her donkey and wielding a broom.

Images of disease goddesses

pregnant because of Shiva's power that percolates into the water. Their husbands accuse them of infidelity and cast them out of the house. They abort the foetuses in their bodies and go into the forest. The aborted foetuses set the forest afire. When the flames die out, the six foetuses merge into a single child — the warlord Skanda also known as Murugan. The women try to attack him, but he calms them down by acknowledging them as his mothers, and declares that whosoever fails to respect them will suffer. They will have the power to cause miscarriages and kill children with measles, pox and cholera.

Thus, outside the village, often associated with the grama-devi herself, are shrines of goddesses associated with disease and death. They are called Jari-Mari, she who makes the body hot and feverish, or Shitala, she who makes the body cool. From time to time she is offered neem leaves, lemons, and sour curds, along with wedding finery, to make her happy so that she leaves the women and children of the village alone.

The worship of Shitala is an interesting facet of Hinduism. In most cultures, the undesirable is wiped out. But in Hinduism, the undesirable is also considered valid and given due dignity. She who causes fever, pox and skin rashes is worshipped as a goddess: she is considered a part of nature, an undesirable part of nature, but nature nevertheless. She is acknowledged but respectfully asked to stay away from the household. Everyone knows the consequences of ignoring her. She will strike with vengeance, defying every fence and every rule created by man, wiping out all that culture seeks to establish.

The ferocity of this aspect of Devi is evident in the story of Periyachi Amman, found in Tamil Nadu, and even in Singapore

Periyachi, the midwife goddess

and Malaysia where the worship of the Goddess has travelled. There was once a rather nasty king who troubled his subjects. When his wife conceived a child, the oracles foretold that if the child's feet ever touched the ground the world would come to an end. So when the queen went into labour, not a single midwife was willing to offer her services. Finally the Goddess came out of pity for the suffering woman. As soon as the child was delivered, the Goddess held the child in her arms, not wanting to put it on the ground, and asked the king for her payment. He refused to pay knowing that the midwife could do nothing — if she placed the child on the ground, the earth would be destroyed and she would die too. The Goddess was amused. She sprouted several pairs of hands. She ripped open the queen's belly. She crushed the king underfoot. But all the while she kept the child in her hand above the ground to ensure the world did not come to an end.

This story shows the two sides of the Goddess, the malevolent one as well as the benevolent one. Nature can be cruel and kind. We may try to domesticate her in our favour but we have to be wary of her other, darker, side.

The words Durga and Shakti are often used synonymously. But there is a subtle difference. Shakti means power that is natural. Durga evokes 'durg', or the fortress that is artificial. Thus Shakti embodies energy that is natural, while Durga embodies power that is cultural. In culture, power is created through laws. These laws shift power from the strong to provide security to the weak. This makes Durga the defender of the weak, to be invoked at wartime by warriors and kings. She is the protector of the fort,

**Poster art of Durga appearing before Ram**

the patron of kings, and rides into battle on a lion, dressed as a bride, but with unbound hair, her multiple arms bearing a variety of lethal weapons.

In the Ramayana, Ravana and Ram invoke Durga; in Bengali lore, Ram offers her one of his eyes to replace a missing lotus. In the Mahabharata, the Kauravas and Pandavas invoke Durga; in Tamil lore, Arjun sacrifices his son, Aravan. Those who sacrifice end up winners. What do they sacrifice? Ram's eye and Arjun's son embody attachment. Attachment is sacrificed. Attachment to what? Attachment to our delusions, what we assume to be the truth.

In the jungle, there are no heroes, villains or victims. But in culture, there are heroes, villains and victims. We feel we are victimised and seek heroes who will destroy villains. This is humanity's greatest delusion.

One day, a king saw a hawk chase a dove. He decided to save the dove from being killed. 'What will I eat now?' asked the hawk. When the king asked him to eat something else, he said, 'Why should someone else die so that you can save the dove?' When the king asked him to eat something vegetarian, he replied: 'Nature made me a carnivore. Do you think you can improve on nature?'

Human imagination enables us to judge nature and rejects its ways. We reject the way of the jungle, which favours only the fit. We create society where rules ensure even the unfit can survive. By doing so we create victims, villains and heroes. The rules are supposed to save those victimised by nature (the unfit). Those who uphold the law are heroes and those who break it are the villains.

But different communities subscribe to different sets of laws.

Posters depicting complementary aspects of the Goddess

Which is the correct law? Which law works for all? Laws that favour tribal communities (protect the forest) work against laws that favour agricultural communities (create more fields). Laws which favour agricultural communities do not favour urban communities (buildings and office and industrial complexes). What is fair for one is not fair for another (laws that favour heterosexuals and exclude homosexuals). This leads to conflict, war, in which Durga is invoked. More laws, fairer and just laws, are established but they remain laws nevertheless.

In the forest, no animals complain. They accept their place in the food chain and pecking order. They know that nothing is permanent. A predator in one context (snake chasing rat) is a prey in another context (hawk chasing snake). A dominant alpha must give way to a younger, stronger alpha, who invariably emerges eventually. Humans seek rules that establish a permanent world — hence the quest for the elixir of immortality (amrita) in the Puranas which creates Amravati of the devas. But Amravati of the devas is constantly under siege, threatened by asuras who seek to overrun it. The devas fight, seek the help of Shiva, Vishnu and Durga, but forget Shakti, the inner strength, that enables us to appreciate that notions of fairness and justice are human constructs, that different people have different notions of what is fair and just, and hence the conflict.

Inner strength enables us to see that from the point of others, we may be the villains. We are the asuras who are troubling the devas; we are not necessarily the devas who need Durga's help. It is we who have to be beheaded. Our aham is the root cause of the

Shivaji, who created the Maratha nation, in the 17th century.

The Sikh tradition does not recognise the Goddess but the sword was called bhagauti, echoing the idea of Bhagavati.

Tulja-bhavani, the patron goddess of Shivaji and his Maratha soldiers.

Amba-bai became the patron goddess of Maratha royalty when one branch shifted base to Kolhapur.

Goddess of kings

problems around us. Confronting the truth about us is not easy. It needs Shakti. We need to acknowledge that all problems come from fears, our own fears and the fears of those around us. Once we do that, we will be able to evoke the Durga in us, who comforts, protects and empowers the frightened.

# 5. Lakshmi's Secret

## Wealth can liberate

Popular image of eight forms of Lakshmi, all seated on a lotus

The living (sajiva, in Sanskrit) seek food, the lifeless (ajiva) and the dead (nirjiva) don't. This makes food the fundamental target (laksh) of life. From laksh comes Lakshmi. Lakshmi is food (anna) in nature and wealth (dhana) in culture.

Lakshmi is called Kamala, or lotus. Just as the fragrance, colour and nectar of the lotus attracts bees, food attracts all living creatures. Plants go towards sunlight; animals towards pasture and prey. Food never goes to anyone; everyone comes to food.

The quest for Lakshmi establishes the food chain: plants seek sunlight and water for nourishment, herbivorus animals seek plants for nourishment, and carnivorus animals seek other animals for nourishment.

The quest for Lakshmi also creates the pecking order. Herbivores form groups called herds to secure themselves. Carnivores form groups called packs to improve their chances of finding prey. Within the herd and the pack, there is hierarchy based on strength. The strongest is the alpha, who dominates, and gets access to most food and more mates. The omega is the weakest, gets the least amount of food and the fewest mates. Thus the hierarchy ensures only the fittest survive so that the next generation is fitter than the previous one, hence more likely to survive.

The lion is the alpha carnivore, on top of the food chain. But even the lion does not attack the elephant, which is much bigger. The elephant has no natural predator, and unlike the lion, it feeds every day. That is why the elephant is most closely associated with Lakshmi.

Another reason why Lakshmi is closely associated with the

Miniature painting showing Lakshmi with elephants

elephant is because the animal is always associated with water. Where there is water there is life; where there is lots of water, there are usually elephants. Elephants love swimming and they spray water on each other using their trunks. A pair of elephants are often shown spraying Lakshmi with water using their upraised trunks, evoking rain. Dark thunderous monsoon clouds are equated with a herd of trumpeting elephants. In drought, the one animal that always knows where there is water is the old matriarch of the herd who has lived longer than any other animal in the forest.

The Puranas state that there are eight pairs of elephants located at the cardinal and ordinal directions. These are the dig-gajas that hold up the sky in some texts and the earth in others. These are not ordinary elephants; they are special, white as cow's milk, for cow's milk was the much-cherished wealth of the Vedic people who chanted the Shri Sukhta hymn in praise of Lakshmi three thousand years ago.

In the Puranas, Lakshmi has three fathers: Varuna, Puloman and Bhrigu. Varuna is asura in the Vedas, but in the Puranas he becomes a deva, a god of the sea, source of all water. The Puranas describe Puloman as the asura-king and Bhrigu as the asura-guru. This makes Lakshmi the daughter of asuras.

The word 'asura' has been given a moral turn in recent times; they are visualised in children's books as dark-skinned and fat and ugly with horns, the embodiment of evil. It is easy then to assume that Lakshmi's association with asuras stems from the fear of materialism and the corrupting influence of wealth. But equating asuras with evil, and by extension devas with good, is

Temple image from India.

Kubera, guardian of the north, god of treasures, is identified as Lakshmi's husband or brother.

Indra, guardian of the east, god of rain, strives to be Lakshmi's husband.

Image from Konark temple wall in Odisha.

Varuna, guardian of the west, god of the sea, is Lakshmi's father.

Yama, guardian of the south, god of death, and of accounting, is identified as Lakshmi's brother who visits her on the final day of Diwali, Yama-dvitiya or bhai-dooj.

Image from South East Asia.

Image from South East Asia.

Images of Digga-pala, guardians of the directions, who are closely linked to Lakshmi

more a convenient translation than a correct one, the result of a Judeo-Christian-Islamic lens that came to India first via Mughal rulers and then via British rulers.

In the Puranas, devas and asuras are both children of Brahma. Devas live in the sky and asuras below the earth. All wealth exists below the earth, for it is below the earth that seeds sprout, metal is created and water is hidden. To pull this wealth out, we need the sun (Surya), the wind (Vayu), fire (Agni) and rain (Indra); in other words, we need devas, who then become 'gods', as their actions favour humanity. Asuras become 'demons' as they resist sharing Lakshmi with humanity.

Varuna, as god of the sea, gives its wealth of salt and fish and pearls freely, without asking anything in return. That is why perhaps Varuna is not asura, but deva. Varuna is also the symbol of generosity: one is who is truly affluent.

Puloman rules the land below the earth and does not release Lakshmi easily. Humanity has to invent complex agricultural and mining processes to procure wealth from the earth. The wealth obtained is called Pulomi, which means daughter of Puloman, another name for Lakshmi.

Bhrigu, guru of the asuras, is associated with prediction and foresight. His son Shukra is associated with creativity. A man who can predict the future, who has foresight and is creative, is more likely to create wealth. That is why Lakshmi is called Bhargavi, daughter of Bhrigu. That makes her Shukra's sister.

Lakshmi's value comes only when she leaves her father's realm, when she is no longer immersed in water or buried under the earth. The creation of wealth then is a violent process: forests have to be destroyed to make way for fields and human

**Poster art showing Lakshmi with Vishnu**

settlements. Raw materials have to be pulled out of the ground for industries. In other words, 'asuras' have to be killed to obtain Lakshmi. She dazzles only when she leaves her father's realm and is seen seated beside Indra, god of the sky, bringer of rain, lord of Amravati.

Wealth that belongs to humans, which has been acquired from nature, is best represented by the pot. The pot is a human invention that allows people to own water and carry it wherever they go. It is the symbol of cultural intervention, of industry and market, creating value out of natural resources. Water in the forest is available for all animals; but water in a pot belongs to the owner of the pot and whosoever he or she gives it to. The pot that is Lakshmi belongs to Indra, and has been wrenched away from the asuras.

The asuras who are killed by devas are time and again resurrected by Shukra, who has the secret known as Sanjivani-vidya, which brings the dead back to life. This alludes to the fertility of the earth which brings back crops year after year. The act of harvesting the crops is equated with the killing of the asuras by devas, an act of violence that enables Lakshmi to come into the house of the farmer. Thus harvest festivals of India, be it vasant-navaratri (Goddess worship in spring) or sharad-navaratri (Goddess worship in autumn), marking the winter and summer agricultural cycles of India, are invariably associated with the killing of asuras: for example, Durga kills Mahisha-asura in Dassera and Krishna kills Naraka-asura in Diwali. That is why the battle between devas and asuras is cyclical. It will never end as long as humans depend on harvesting nature's bounty and seek the regeneration of nature's fertility.

▽

Miniature painting of Indra, king of the gods

As Indra's wife, Lakshmi is known as Sachi and Indra is known as Sachin. The arrival of Lakshmi turns Amravati into Swarga, or paradise. For she brings with her Kalpataru, the wish-fulfilling tree; Kama-dhenu, the wish-fulfilling cow; Chinta-mani, the wish-fulfilling jewel; the Akshaya-patra, the cornucopia, the pot that is always overflowing with grain and gold. These treasures enable the devas to live a life of luxury. They do not have to work a single day. They simply have to make a wish and their desires come true. It is an enviable lifestyle.

What is never clarified in the Puranas is why Indra is entitled to all the pleasures that Lakshmi has to offer. It is simply assumed that wealth belongs to the devas. No explanation is offered.

Modern retellings often equate asuras with the 'original' forest-dwellers who were displaced by deva 'migrants' who came with superior agricultural and pastoral technology. This is how the eternal battle between asuras and devas is explained sociologically. Marxist anthropologists equate devas as the 'haves' and the asuras as the 'have-nots'. Traditionalists tend to describe devas as 'good' and thus entitled to Lakshmi, but this does not make any sense as Indra in the Puranas is always shown drunk with soma-rasa, immersed in sensory pleasures offered by apsaras, often being indifferent, even rude, to sages.

From the asura point of view, Indra is a thief. But unless the devas 'steal' Lakshmi out of the subterranean realm, Lakshmi cannot have value. The asuras do not see it this way. They simply want their daughter/sister back. So they lay siege to Amravati and constantly fight the devas. This turns paradise into an eternal battleground, or rana-bhoomi, with devas constantly struggling to hold on to their wealth. Indra thus has prosperity but no peace.

Miniature painting of Krishna with Satyabhama

This naturally makes asuras, source of Indra's great displeasure, the villains of the Puranas.

We can equate Indra and the devas with 'wealth-generators' and 'value-creators' who are often at the receiving end of criticism because the process of generating wealth is invariably violent: ecosystems are destroyed and people are compelled to do work so that industries and markets can thrive.

Wealth generation also creates social divides on economic lines, for those who establish industries and markets (devas?) feel entitled to claim the lion's share of the wealth generated, much more than those who actually work in industries and markets (asuras?) who end up feeling deprived and often exploited.

The devas can also be inheritors who have not earned anything but have the benefit of enjoying vast wealth because they were born in a particular family. Indra is unable to see the unfairness of the situation because he is born into privilege. He is unable to see the rage of the asuras. Each one demonises the other. Neither understands the other.

The conflict between devas and asuras is very much like the conflict between capitalists and socialists. For the devas, the battle is between those who create wealth and those who do not create wealth. For the asuras, the battle is between those who steal wealth and those who do not steal wealth. What is 'wealth-creation' for one group is 'wealth-theft' for another group. Neither can agree about who should get the lion's share of the wealth generated. Each one is therefore convinced the other is wrong, resulting in a relentless 'righteous' battle.

Shri on a Buddhist stupa

Padmavati (yakshi) surrounded by Jain sages

As Shri, Lakshmi is part of Buddhist and Jain mythology. Her image is found on Buddhist stupas. She is even worshipped as the guardian goddess Padmavati in Jain temples. She is described as wife of Sakra, or Indra. In that role, she is more commonly addressed as Sachi. But while Indra may be happy with Lakshmi by his side, Lakshmi never seems happy to be beside Indra. She seems restless, always on the lookout for someone worthier.

Lakshmi is sometimes visualised seated next to Kubera, the rich king of the yakshas, who hoards treasure. Kubera is identified as Indra's treasurer in some texts, but other texts identify Kubera's wife as Nidhi, goddess of treasures, another name for Lakshmi.

Sachi is often described as being more faithful to Indra's throne than to Indra the person, for Indra can be easily replaced by one more worthy. This is why Indra is always insecure, never able to enjoy his vast wealth. His throne is always shaky, threatened by rishis, rajas and asuras. That is why Lakshmi is called chanchala or whimsical, even cock-eyed (Lokhi-tera, in Bengali). No one is ever sure who the goddess of wealth and fortune will favour. She can appear suddenly without reason, and leave without warning.

Indra gets nervous when a rishi performs tapasya and seeks to generate tapa, the mental fire that will grant siddhi, powers that will enable the rishi to control devas. So he sends apsaras to seduce the rishis and disrupt their tapasya. He steals horses and disrupts yagnas of rajas so that they are not a threat to his power. And he constantly runs to his father Brahma seeking help to kill asuras who lay siege to his paradise. He knows that he is king because of Lakshmi, and his kingdom is Swarga because of Lakshmi. This narrative reflects the insecurity that comes with wealth. The rich

Poster art showing Ravana abducting Sita

Poster art showing Draupadi being gambled away

are never secure about their possessions; they constantly feel that people around them wish to steal what is theirs. This state of mind is the rana-bhoomi, the eternal battle that consumes Indra's paradise.

The story goes that once Lakshmi left Indra's side and went to the asura-king Prahalad. Brahma advised Indra to disguise himself as a servant and serve Prahalad diligently to find out why Lakshmi favoured him over Indra. Indra did as advised and Prahalad finally revealed his secret, 'Lakshmi is attracted to men of actions that demonstrate strength and smartness. If you display strength and shrewdness, she will come to you. If fail to do that, she will not stay with you for long.' Later, when Prahalad offered the disguised Indra a boon, Indra very shrewdly asked for all the merits that Prahalad had obtained through his strong and shrewd actions. Prahalad, bound by his word, gave his merits away. As soon as merit moved from Prahalad to Indra, Lakshmi also moved from Prahalad's side to Indra's side.

In the epic Ramayana, Ravana, king of the rakhasas, has physical power or strength. He has twenty arms and ten heads. With brute force, he overpowers his brother Kubera and drives him out of the golden island-city of Lanka and lays claim to kingdom and throne. With brute force, he abducts the wife of Ram, prince of Ayodhya. Thus Lakshmi comes to Ravana by force.

In the epic Mahabharata, Duryodhana, eldest of the Kauravas, is shrewd and guileful. He uses cunning to defeat his cousins, the five Pandavas, who are much stronger than him and who he feels are rivals to the throne of Hastinapur which he is convinced is his birthright. First, Duryodhana tries to get rid of the Pandavas by gifting them a palace of lac, which he sets afire while they are asleep. Unfortunately, this plan fails. Later he invites the Pandavas

Jain manuscript showing Lakshmi as Shri

to a gambling match and defeats them by getting his uncle, Shakuni, master of the dice, to play on his behalf. In exchange for their freedom, Pandavas have to forfeit rights over their land for thirteen years. Thus Lakshmi comes to the Kauravas by guile.

But Lakshmi acquired through strength or guile can never be retained. Someone who is stronger or more shrewd always comes along and claims our Lakshmi. Thus Ravana meets his match in Ram, the prince of Ayodhya, who defeats him in battle. And Duryodhana finds his match in Krishna, the wily charioteer, who helps the Pandavas outsmart the cunning Kauravas. Indra is never able to keep Lakshmi by his side for long, as there is always a stronger or smarter asura who comes along.

In the early part of the Vedas indicated by Brahmana texts, we find hymns and rituals about acquiring and celebrating wealth that take the form of cows, horses, grain, gold, children. Wealth is seen as ushering in happiness. In the latter part of the Vedas indicated by the Aranyaka and Upanishad texts, we find a great discomfort with wealth. Wealth is seen as something that also brings with it a great deal of unhappiness: the envy of neighbours, loss of friends, quarrels within family. This shift in thought between early and later Vedic periods on the nature of wealth is reflected in how Indra is positioned. Indra is the great warrior king of the Vedas, but in the Puranas, he is insecure and helpless, constantly seeking the help of Brahma, Vishnu and Shiva.

Giving up wealth simply because its arrival can cause unhappiness is not the answer. What is, then? This enquiry leads us to Vedanta, which explores the relationship between mind and

Stone sculpture of Jyestha, elder sister of Lakshmi

property. Vedanta means philosophy that was milked out of the Vedas. It was communicated to the common man through the stories of the Puranas.

In the Puranas, we learn of Lakshmi's elder sister, Jyestha, also known as Alakshmi, who always accompanies her. She is the goddess of strife. She is the reason why the prosperity of Lakshmi is never accompanied by peace. The only way to get peace into the household is to discover and invoke either Shiva or Vishnu. When Lakshmi accompanies Shiva or Vishnu, then Alakshmi does not accompany Lakshmi, and so wealth is not accompanied by quarrels.

Shiva is a hermit and does not care for wealth. But when he gets married to Parvati, she forces him to pay attention to the needs of his followers, the ganas, and his devotees, the bhaktas. She makes him aware that those around him are not tapasvins like him; they have desires and hungers that need satisfaction. They need food. Shiva satisfies the desires and hungers of his ganas and his bhaktas through his children, Kartikeya and Ganesha. While the mighty Kartikeya provides protection, Ganesha provides prosperity.

Ganesha's form evokes Lakshmi. His head is of a white elephant, like those that raise their trunks and spray water on Lakshmi. His corpulent form evokes Kubera, the god of treasures. He rides a rat, that enemy of farmers, and around his belly is a snake, symbol of regeneration, much desired by farmers. That natural enemies, the rat and snake, are both beside Ganesha reveals a desire to keep away the strife of the jungle and create a culture of peace. In imagery, Lakshmi is often shown beside Ganesha, even though traditionally Lakshmi and Ganesha belong to rival religious sects, the Vaishnavas and the Shaivas. Together, Lakshmi and Ganesha evoke affluence and abundance.

Poster art of Lakshmi with Ganesha

When Ravana drove Kubera out of Lanka, Kubera moved north and sought refuge in Mount Kailas, abode of Shiva. There he built the city of A-Lanka, the opposite of Lanka, which later came to be known as Alaka. It was even more prosperous than Lanka. But Kubera noticed that Shiva was not interested in his wealth. He did not understand how the ascetic Shiva could possibly satisfy the hunger of Ganesha, who clearly looked like one who enjoyed food. So Kubera invited Ganesha to his house to eat 'to his heart's content'. Ganesha accepted the invitation. But Kubera soon realised that Ganesha's appetite was huge: he could eat more than what Kubera could provide. Before long he had consumed all the food in Kubera's house. He even ate all the food that Kubera's wealth could buy. Reduced to poverty, Kubera begged Ganesha to stop, but Ganesha reminded Kubera of his promise to feed him to 'his heart's content'. Kubera realised he had made a huge mistake. Finally, Ganesha said, 'Now you understand why I stay with Shiva and not you. You seek to satisfy my hunger, but Shiva helps me outgrow my hunger. The more food you serve, the more my hunger is fuelled; thus my hunger remains insatiable. The only solution then is to outgrow hunger, for which I need Shiva.'

This story reveals a philosophy very different from the one found in the early Vedas. The point of life is not to satisfy hunger, the point of life is to outgrow hunger. Animals do not eat more than what they need, but humans have an eternal craving for more and more wealth. This craving is insatiable. So rather than trying to satisfy it with food, it is more important to destroy the hunger itself. This does not mean rejecting Lakshmi; it means putting Lakshmi in perspective.

There is a vast difference between real hunger and invented

**Poster art of Lakshmi with Kubera and Nidhi**

hunger. Human imagination blurs the line between need and want. That is why the arrival of Lakshmi is always associated with Alakshmi, goddess of quarrels. If we are able to outgrow our own hunger, without denying her value to the world, then we are able to share Lakshmi with others. When we share, there are fewer quarrels: Lakshmi comes without Alakshmi. To be able to share Lakshmi, we need to discover Shiva and Shakti.

Indra is so focused on Lakshmi, or rather Sachi, his wife, that he is indifferent to Alakshmi. He takes no steps to protect himself from the envy and rage of those around him. Naturally, fortune and happiness are short-lived. Eventually, inevitably, while he is busy with his wine and women and other excesses, his enemies lay siege to Swarga and declare war.

One day, Lakshmi leaves Swarga in a huff when Indra insults her: in a drunken state, he throws a garland of lotus flowers gifted to him to the ground, allowing it to be trampled by elephants. This disrespect shown to wealth and affluence is something Lakshmi does not like, so she dissolves herself in the ocean of milk.

With the disappearance of Lakshmi, the world becomes gloomy, and Indra's paradise loses its affluence. The wish-fulfilling cow stops giving milk, the wish-fulfilling tree stops bearing fruit, the wish-fulfilling gem loses its shine, and the wish-fulfilling pot becomes empty. The only way to get Lakshmi back to Swarga is by churning her out from the ocean of milk. So Indra goes to his father Brahma for help, and Brahma directs him to Vishnu.

Vishnu advises that Indra first make friends with the asuras, as a counter-force is required to churn the ocean. He then forms the

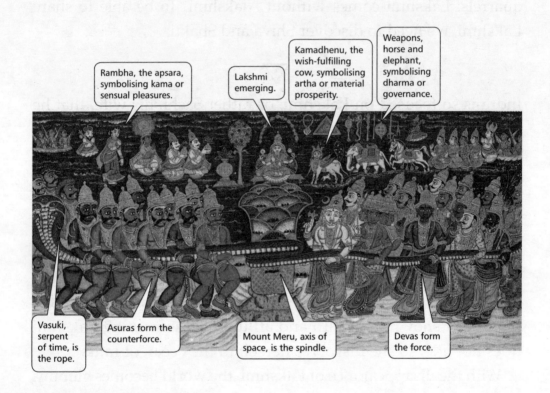

Mysore painting of the churning of the ocean of milk

churning tool by using Meru, the king of mountains, as a spindle, and Vasuki, the king of serpents, as a rope. Akupara, the king of turtles, a form of Vishnu himself, keeps this aloft. The churning begins with the devas holding the tail-end of Vasuki and the asuras holding the neck-end. When the devas pull, the asuras let go. When the asuras pull, the devas let go.

The churning goes on for eons. And finally from the waters arises Lakshmi, along with all the treasures of paradise. Along with her come Kalpataru, Kamadhenu, Chintamani and Akshaya-patra, symbols of wealth. Also with her are the elephant Airavata and the flying horse Ucchaishrava, both white as milk, symbols of royal power. Also with her is Rambha, the most beautiful damsel, who is well-versed in all forms of pleasure, and Soma, the moon-god, the most handsome and romantic of men.

Lakshmi also brings with her a pot of amrita, the nectar of immortality. This is sought by everyone, but Vishnu tricks the asuras and ensures only the devas get to drink the amrita. The devas, rendered immortal, then rise to their heaven with Lakshmi and everything that brings prosperity, power and pleasure.

But there is one change. Lakshmi herself chooses to go to Vishnu. She is drawn to him. This is significant: it establishes Vishnu as superior to Indra. Indra may have defeated the asuras, but it is Vishnu who enabled the victory. And even though Vishnu enabled the victory, he does not claim the much sought-after amrita.

They may seem similar, but there is a vast difference between Indra and Vishnu. This difference is not about form, but thought. Indra's name alludes to 'indriyas', or sense organs. Indra symbolises the mind that enjoys pleasure, hoards wealth, and feels constantly threatened by others. He only wants to satisfy his needs

Poster art showing Lakshmi choosing Vishnu as her groom

and wants. By contrast, Vishnu is concerned about the needs and wants of others.

Like Shiva, Vishnu wants to outgrow the world; but his method is different. While Shiva withdraws from society to outgrow his hunger, Vishnu engages with society to outgrow his hunger. He strives hard to help humans discover their dharma.

Dharma means potential. Every creature has to do what they are supposed to do, what they are capable of. It is the dharma of fire to burn, of water to flow, of trees to grow and bear fruit, of animals to run towards food and mates and away from predators. But what is human potential? Is it to create/hoard/distribute wealth to satisfy one's own hunger like Indra, or is it to outgrow hunger like Shiva? Humans are not clear about what path to take. That is why we need Vishnu.

Vishnu balances the shortcomings of Brahma's sons such as Indra with the possibility offered by Shiva. He knows that humans have the capacity to satisfy their own hunger as well as the hunger of others. They also have the capacity to outgrow — and enable others to outgrow — their own hunger. He works towards enabling people to become aware of this capacity, help themselves by helping others. And he does this in the most counter-intuitive of ways.

Superficially, it seems as though Vishnu favours devas over asuras. But a closer observation reveals it is not as simple as it looks. He is granting devas immortality. Why then is Indra still craving for Lakshmi? Should he not be happy as he no longer has to fear death and hence has no real need for Lakshmi? Should he not be content? But he is not: the hunger for Lakshmi continues.

And ironically, Lakshmi, grabbed from the asuras, rejects the

Stone image of Lakshmi-Varaha from Mammalapuram, Tamil Nadu

devas, and follows Vishnu. Vishnu has that which no one else has.

Yes, Vishnu is stronger than anyone else. When Hiranayaksha drags the earth under the sea, Vishnu descends into the waters as a boar, gores him to death with his mighty tusks, places the earth-goddess on his snout and brings her back to the surface.

Yes, Vishnu can outsmart the over-smart. When Hiranya-kashipu secures a boon that makes it impossible for him to be killed during the day or night, inside a dwelling or outside, on the ground or in the air, by a weapon or a tool, by a human or an animal, Vishnu takes the form of a monster (neither lion nor human), and kills him at twilight (neither day nor night), on the threshold (neither inside nor outside), on his lap (neither on the ground nor in the air), using his claws (neither a weapon nor a tool).

But like Shiva, Vishnu knows that food does not satisfy hunger. It only amplifies hunger. One can never satiate human needs and wants. He demonstrates this in the story of Vaman. When Bali tries to solve the world's problems through charity, Vishnu takes the form of a dwarf, asks for three paces of land, and on obtaining it, transforms into a giant who, with two paces, covers the whole world, and with the third step pushes Bali under the ground. Vishnu demonstrates that the world is infinite and human resources are finite. We cannot solve human problems with things. We need to pay attention to thoughts. Only when humans expand their mind can they recognise their own fears and empathise with the fears of those around them. To do so is human dharma.

This focus on thoughts rather than things is what makes Vishnu attractive to Lakshmi. She sits next to him when he is Varaha, admiring the thought behind his strength. She sits next to him when

Poster art of Lakshmi-Narasimha

he is Narasimha, admiring the thought behind his cleverness. She sits next to him when he is Hayagriva, the horse-headed one, who explains the secret of the scriptures to the sages. And this secret has nothing to do with matter, it has to do with the human mind. While Western philosophy focuses only on science and society, Indian philosophy puts greater emphasis on psychology. In the human mind is the seed of all human problems and all human solutions.

Lakshmi has two forms: Bhu-devi and Sri-devi. Bhu-devi is the earth-goddess and embodies tangible wealth like food. Sri-devi is associated with intangible wealth or glamour. One can say Bhu-devi is natural wealth and Sri-devi is cultural wealth. In south Indian temples these two forms of Lakshmi are seen beside images of Vishnu.

In the Puranas, Bhu-devi is often visualised as a cow. The story goes that a king called Vena plundered the earth so much that the rishis had to intervene and kill this greedy king. They churned his corpse and from the purified remains created a new king, Prithu. Prithu was a form of Vishnu. He discovered that the earth had run away in the form of a cow, so he pursued her with his bow and arrow, threatening to strike her if she did not stop and allow his subjects to milk her. 'If you kill me, the world will cease to exist,' she cried. 'But if you cannot be milked, the world cannot survive,' argued Prithu. So finally, assured that he would protect her and not let anyone plunder her, Bhu-devi let herself be milked by all living creatures under the watchful eye of Prithu.

As Prithu, Vishnu declared that the kings of the earth would

Miniature painting of Prithu chasing the earth-cow

be guardians of Bhu-devi, and that he himself would descend on earth if she was troubled. He becomes the Go-pala, or caretaker of the earth-cow Go-mata.

In the *Bhagavata Purana,* Bhu-devi comes weeping to Vishnu and complains about the weight of greedy kings that she has to bear and begs him to relieve her burden. And so Vishnu descends as Parashuram, Ram and Krishna to kill all the greedy kings of the world. Thus the avatars of Vishnu are meant to secure Lakshmi. She is under Vishnu's protection.

In the stories of his mortal avatars — Parashuram, Ram and Krishna — Vishnu never claims ownership of Lakshmi, even in situations when he is 'entitled' to her.

Parashuram fights brutally to reclaim his mother-cow from the clutches of Kartaviryarjuna, who tries to claim her forcibly. He even enforces his mother's fidelity by beheading her on his father's orders when she has adulterous thoughts. Both actions are done out of obedience for the father, and not for his own benefit.

In the next avatar, the 'rule' of obedience to the father is questioned as it creates crisis in culture, depriving the kingdom of a good king. As Ram, Vishnu is tranquil when his father asks him to give up claims over Ayodhya. He is equally tranquil when the kingdom is returned to him and he is crowned its king. Ram's relationship with Sita reveals the complexity of God's relationship with Goddess in a world that speaks of 'duties' and 'rights'. Ram dutifully accepts Sita as his wife when her father offers him her hand in marriage; he allows her to follow him to the forest during his exile, even though he would be more than happy if she stayed back in the palace; he rescues her from Ravana's captivity but does not reclaim her, letting her choose him over freedom; and when his

Hayagriva is traced to the horse-headed form of Surya who revealed the secret of the Vedas to Yagnavalkya.

Hayagriva is associated with the transmission of Vedic knowledge.

The horse-headed form of Vishnu or Hayagriva is commonly worshipped in south India.

Hayagriva's knowledge grants perspective to humanity and enables them to truly appreciate wealth.

Modern painting of Lakshmi-Hayagriva

subjects gossip about her fidelity, he abandons her in the forest. At one level, Ram's treatment of Sita is disturbing, as he seems almost indifferent to her needs. At another level, he claims no 'rights' over her. And when it comes to 'duties', he chooses his duty as king over duty as husband, unquestioningly following the royal codes of conduct. This demands great sacrifice. When asked to remarry, however, he chooses to stay single, rejecting his 'right to remarry' and his 'duty as king', thereby expressing his affection for the Goddess and his understanding of her: culture needs her, but she does not need culture.

In Krishna's story, the Goddess takes many forms. She is Radha to Krishna before his marriage; she loves him even though she belongs to another, thus defying all cultural norms. She is Rukmini who defies her father and elopes with him to Dwarka. She is Satyabhama who obeys her father and marries him, but constantly reminds him that it is her wealth, not his intelligence alone, that makes him an influential member of the Yadava clan. Krishna treats both the poor Rukmini and the rich Satyabhama with affection, for he is worldly-wise and values both: the love of Rukmini and the wealth of Satyabhama. When Krishna meets Sudama, he wishes to offer all his wealth to his poor friend, but Satyabhama stops him from excessive generosity, reminding him that there are many others in need of charity. Finally, the Goddess takes the form of Draupadi, who is helpless and abused despite having five husbands to protect her. Her husbands, the Pandavas, are described as Indras reborn. She needs Vishnu to help her and he does so as Krishna even though he is not obliged to do so by any social law or custom. He does so out of love.

Unlike Indra, who only sees Lakshmi as pleasure, Vishnu sees

Bhu-devi asks Vishnu to relieve her of the burden of greedy kings and so Vishnu takes the avatars of Parashuram who kills Kartaviryarjuna, Ram who kills Ravana, and Krishna who kills Kansa, Jarasandha and the Kauravas.

Lakshmi as Sri-devi massaging Vishnu's feet.

Indra, king of the devas.

Shiva, the ascetic

Lakshmi as Bhu-devi, the earth-goddess, who is visualised as a cow.

Brahma, the father of all living creatures.

Vishnu lying in repose on coils of Sesha, who is afloat on the ocean of milk.

**Miniature painting of earth-cow approaching Vishnu for help**

Lakshmi as his responsibility. Vishnu seeks to create an ecosystem where Lakshmi is not held captive; instead she is distributed and celebrated by all.

The story goes that humans are in debt because they milk the earth. This debt gets repaid in blood when Parashuram kills Kartaviryarjuna, Ram kills Ravana, and Krishna kills Kansa, Jarasandha and oversees the destruction of the Kauravas. Kali spreads her tongue to quench her thirst resulting from excessive milking of her resources by humanity.

As Hinduism made its journey from Vedic ritualism to Puranic devotion, it became increasingly monastic. This meant that the yogi, one who does not care for wealth, was given more respect in society than a bhogi, one who enjoys wealth. In such a society, Lakshmi was seen as the source of all problems. Rather than taking responsibility for their own inadequacies, human society blamed Lakshmi for the conflicts of society.

This tension between the yogi and the bhogi is a constant theme in the Puranas. The yogi Shiva is turned into the bhogi Shankara when he marries Parvati. The bhogi Indra learns from the yogi Vishnu how to transform rana-bhoomi or battleground into ranga-bhoomi or playground. Similar tensions can be seen in temple lore, where the language is regional, and the themes more practical.

The following is an Odiya story which is part of the temple lore of Puri Jagannath temple where Krishna Jagannath is worshipped along with his brother Balabhadra and his sister Subhadra.

One day, Balabhadra sees Lakshmi entering the house of a sweeper woman. He declares that she has been contaminated and

Lakshmi as she is worshipped in Puri, Odisha

orders his younger brother not to let her into the house. Krishna obeys and shuts the door of the temple. In the days that follow, to the great alarm of the divine siblings, no food is offered to them. On enquiry, they discover there is no food being cooked in the kitchen as all vegetables and fruits and cereals and pulses and spices have disappeared from the pantry and the market. There is not even a drop of water to drink. The siblings trace this catastrophe to their rejection of Lakshmi. Eventually Krishna apologises to his wife and begs her to return to the temple.

In this story, Krishna's ascetic brother, the yogi Balabhadra, learns that notions of contamination and pollution make no sense to the goddess of wealth. These are artificial cultural norms created by humans to satisfy their craving for hierarchy. Food will satisfy without discrimination the hunger of all, be it a sweeper, a king or a god. In other words, food is satya, truth independent of human opinion. Notions of contamination, which is the hallmark of the caste system, is mithya, dependent on human opinion. When we discover that Lakshmi does not discriminate between saint and thief, that all hierarchies are manmade creations, then Lakshmi becomes a tool for liberation.

The following is a Telugu tale from one of the richest temples of India, the temple of Tirupati Balaji that enshrines Vishnu on earth.

The sage Bhrigu, a yogi, decided to pay a visit to Brahma, Shiva and Vishnu. He found Brahma too busy conducting a yagna with Saraswati to pay him attention, so he cursed Brahma that he would not be worshipped at all. He found Shiva too busy being intimate with Shakti to pay him attention. This time, his anger was a little less, and so he said Shiva would be worshipped, but not as he looks — only as an abstract symbol, the linga. He then moved

Vishnu in Vaikuntha enjoying various forms of sensual and material pleasures.

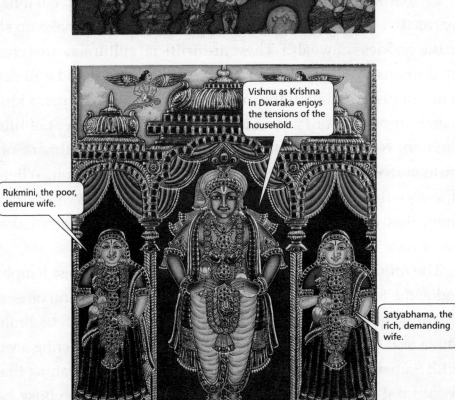

Vishnu as Krishna in Dwaraka enjoys the tensions of the household.

Rukmini, the poor, demure wife.

Satyabhama, the rich, demanding wife.

Images of Vishnu as bhogi

to the ocean of milk, to Vaikuntha, convinced that Vishnu would surely pay him attention. But there he found Vishnu sleeping, his feet being massaged by Lakshmi. Furious that he mattered to none in the trinity, Bhrigu kicked Vishnu on his chest, where is located Srivatsa, the symbol of Lakshmi. Vishnu did not get upset; he understood Bhrigu's frustration and apologised to the sage, and checked if Bhrigu had hurt his foot while kicking his chest. Watching Vishnu touch his feet, Bhrigu was happy. Then realisation dawned as to how foolish he was being: though he claimed to be a yogi, his attention-seeking behaviour revealed he was actually a bhogi.

Lakshmi did not appreciate Vishnu's servility, whatever his reason. She was furious that Vishnu did not punish the sage for insulting the Srivatsa. She walked out of Vaikuntha in a huff and went down to earth. Vishnu followed her, desperate to bring her back, for Vaikuntha cannot remain Vaikuntha without Lakshmi. He decided to stay on earth until Lakshmi agreed to return. But he found no house; devotees would give him shelter until someone richer or more powerful came along. Finally, he saw the seven hills that reminded him of the seven hoods of his serpent Sesha on whose coils he reclined on the ocean of milk. This was Tirumala, the sacred hill. Homesick, he wished to settle here, but for that he had to marry the local princess Padmavati, born of a lotus flower. Her father, the local king, demanded a huge bridal price. Without Lakshmi by his side, Vishnu was the impoverished Daridra-Narayana, and so he had no choice but to take a huge loan from Kubera. This narrative demonstrates the value of wealth in society; even Vishnu needs wealth to get himself a wife and home on earth. One who rejects Lakshmi cannot expect to have a home or a spouse.

Popular images of the rage and reconciliation of Lakshmi

News of Vishnu's marriage to Padmavati upset Lakshmi who came to the wedding and demanded her place in Vishnu's chest. So Vishnu expanded his chest to accommodate his two wives. He placed the celestial Lakshmi (Sri-devi) on the left side of his chest, near his heart, and the terrestrial Padmavati (Bhu-devi) on the right.

This Vishnu at Tirumala is trapped and needs the help of his devotees to repay his debt, so that he can return to Vaikuntha. He is called Venkat, he who can destroy (kata) bondage (vem), for in exchange of the wealth received, he grants his devotees the wisdom of yoga that explains the relationship one should have with wealth in order to be truly happy. This is further demonstrated in the ritual of giving wealth to transform Daridra-Narayana (the poor Vishnu) into Lakshmi-Narayana (the rich Vishnu): when Lakshmi is used to enable others to repay their debts, Vaikuntha is established and Lakshmi becomes a tool for liberation.

# 6. Saraswati's Secret

*Imagination can expand or contract the mind*

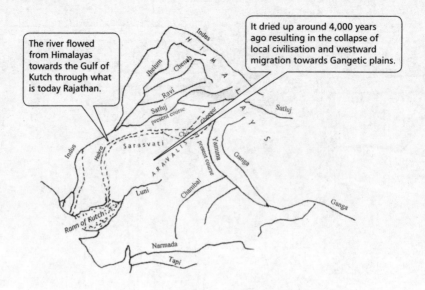

The now-dry river Saraswati referred to in the *Rig Veda*

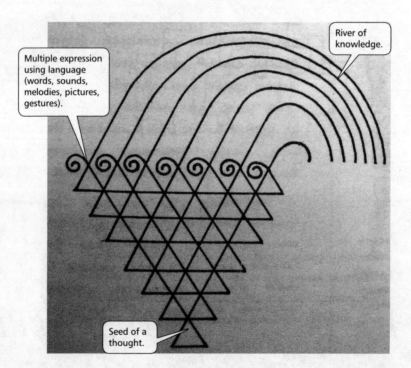

Symbol of Saraswati used in schools

*E*xperts on the Vedas often say how the Saraswati has dried up. No one is sure what this means exactly. Does this refer to a river that flowed four thousand years ago in Punjab, Sindh and Rajasthan, on whose banks many of the hymns of the *Rig Veda* came to be composed? Or does it refer to the metaphorical river of language and imagination that is used more to control the world, rather than break free from fear? No one is sure. Different scholars approach Vedic verses differently, either literally or symbolically.

In the Puranas, Saraswati is a well-defined goddess. Her stories are rare, though always related to language. The devas, for example, invoke her just when the demon Kumbhakarna is about to ask Brahma for a boon and request her to twist the rakshasa's tongue so that instead of Indra-asan (seat of Indra), he asks for Nidra-asan (sleep).

In these Puranas, Saraswati is identified as the first creation of Brahma, even the first woman created by Brahma. Brahma gets infatuated with her. Such 'incestuous' affection is frowned upon and Rudra-Shiva, who embodies renunciation, either beheads Brahma or simply pins him to the sky to stop him from pursuing her. Like Vedic hymns, this Puranic story can be seen literally or symbolically. Symbolically, it refers to the tension between a creator claiming ownership over his creation and the renouncer destroying this relationship and advocating detachment. The daughter is sometimes called Shatarupa, she of many forms. When Brahma steps back and observes his creation, not with the desire to control it but from the desire to understand it, he realises it reflects his own mind. His creation is a mirror that reflects his

Poster art showing Brahma and Saraswati

own personality. Shatarupa then becomes his teacher Saraswati, she who flows in the mind.

Some sociologists are of the opinion that the absence of Brahma temples in later Hinduism was a symbolic rejection of the old Vedic way that was highly materialistic. The rise of Vishnu and Shiva temples marks a shift in thought in Hinduism. In the Puranas, Saraswati who shuns the vile Brahma becomes consort of Vishnu according to Vaishnavas, the companion of Ganesha according to Shaivas and the daughter of Shakti according to Shaktas. In the new form of Hinduism, where answers were sought in temples, beyond materialism, but always through materialism, the all-male triad of Brahma, Vishnu and Shiva was replaced by the triad of Devi, Vishnu and Shiva.

While Shiva is commonly paired with Shakti who is Durga/Kali/Gauri, and Vishnu is paired with Lakshmi, it is not clear who Saraswati should be paired with. To maintain symmetry between the male triad (Shiva, Vishnu, Brahma) and the female triad (Durga, Lakshmi, Saraswati), it is common to link Brahma with Saraswati. The explanation given for this is that the creator needs knowledge, the sustainer needs wealth and the destroyer needs power. This is a more convenient explanation than an accurate one, for everyone knows that all three resources are needed for all three jobs. To assume that you can create with knowledge alone, without wealth and power, or you can sustain only with wealth, without knowledge or power, is fantastic to say the least.

In medieval times, it was common to show Lakshmi and Saraswati as the two consorts of Vishnu, and Shakti as his sister.

Folk Bengal art showing Saraswati with Kartikeya

Pahari miniature painting showing Ganesha with Saraswati

The rival sect of Shiva-worshippers also appropriated Lakshmi and Saraswati by placing them on either side of Ganesha, Shiva's more worldly son. As Ganesha's consorts, they are more popularly known as Riddhi (goddess of material treasures) and Siddhi (goddess of mental powers). In Bengal, Lakshmi is associated with the food-loving Ganesha, who is associated with learned Brahmins; and Saraswati with the art-loving Kartikeya, associated with affluent landowners or zamindars.

Despite being linked to Brahma, Vishnu, Ganesha and Kartikeya, images of Saraswati with a male consort are rare. She is shown as aloof and distant, always alone, content in her own company, an indicator of true wisdom. Unlike other goddesses who turn 'hot' and fiery and dangerous when kept away from matrimony and maternity, Saraswati remains calm and composed despite her isolation. A cynic may equate Saraswati's white sari not with asceticism but with widowhood, revealing the loneliness of women especially, but also men, who are extremely intelligent or intellectual or smart.

Saraswati, like Lakshmi, is essentially an independent goddess. Her origins can be traced to the four thousand-year-old *Rig Samhita*. There she shares her name with the river Saraswati and her qualities with Vak, goddess of speech, language and meaning. She is sometimes also linked to Gayatri, the goddess of Vedic hymns and melodies.

The Vedas paid great attention to language. Language was at one time called 'brahman', which etymologically means that which expands (brah, in Sanskrit) the mind (manas). Later, the word

Poster of Sharada, patron goddess of Shankar-acharya

Devdutt Pattanaik

brahman came to mean divinity. Language is the one thing that distinguishes humans from other animals. Animals communicate with each other but they are just signals; human language is more complex, allowing people to explore and express abstract concepts, intangible ideas, such as 'past', 'present', 'beyond', 'love' and 'friendship'.

Language can be expressed using gestures (mudras), using speech (vak) and of course, script. The vowels or matras were associated with goddesses, the Matrikas. And early Indian scripts, Brahmi and Sharada, were both personified as women and goddesses. Brahmi was the daughter of the Jain Tirthankara Rishabha, to whom he bequeathed the first script. Sharada became another form of Saraswati and Vak, who was especially worshipped by Adi Shankara, the great 8th century Vedanta scholar, who probably read works of earlier philosophers in the Sharada script.

Language emerges from imagination and it also expands imagination. Imagination is one thing that animals do not have, at least not on the scale of humans. Imagination is fluid (saras), and can either be contained as a lake (sarovar) or made to flow like a river (sarita). From saras, comes Saraswati.

Imagination allows humans to travel through space without moving and through time in a single moment. Imagination allows humans to conjure up worlds that do not exist. Humans communicate these thoughts through language. Saraswati is the goddess of fluid thoughts and words, an exclusively human goddess, who grants humanity to humans. Perhaps that is why Hindus paint their forehead with sacred marks, for the head contains the brain, the home of Saraswati. A dot, or the bindu, in

Varied attributes of Saraswati

the centre of the forehead is an indicator of human potential, our ability to make sense of the world, and solve any of its problems.

Because Saraswati enables us to understand and appreciate nature, she eventually became the goddess of arts, associated with literature and music, and holds in her hands a book and a lute (vina, in Sanskrit). She is even called Veda-mata, the mother of the Vedas. She is also the mother of svaras (musical notes) and ragas (melodies).

In imagery, Saraswati is often associated with a goose (hamsa) because legend has it that a goose can separate milk from a mixture of milk and water. In other words, it can separate truth (milk) from falsehood (water), making it the symbol of analysis. Saraswati is also associated with the heron, which is the symbol of concentration. And in modern calendar art, with a peacock which does not spread its feathers in her presence as it knows that humility is the true measure of wisdom.

She is associated with white and transparent things to indicate her purity. She is associated with white champa flowers and the white autumn moon and white transparent crystal beads.

She is often invoked during Vasant, or springtime, because the season of spring inspires poets to compose songs. In this month, she is dressed in bright yellow clothes, the colour of mustard flowers.

Many scholars trace the modern Saraswati to Tara, a Buddhist goddess who had a major role to play in the transformation of Buddhism. Buddha was initially uncomfortable with the female

Tibetan painting of the Buddhist Tara

form and women in general. Women were seen as daughters of Mara, the demon of desire. Gradually Buddha softened, especially after he saw the sorrow of his step-mother when his father died, and so he allowed women to be part of the monastic order. Still women played a secondary role. With the rise of the Mahayana, the later school of Buddhism, the idea of a feminine force that empathises with humanity and is less intellectual in its approach emerged. This was Tara. Like Parvati, Tara is known for her ability to turn the indifferent monk into an engaged saviour. Like Lakshmi, Tara holds a lotus in her hand. But she is, like Saraswati, renowned as the embodiment of pragnya, or wisdom.

Saraswati was closely associated with dancers, musicians and courtesans as she was seen as the mother of the arts and theatre. Through songs and plays and literature, she could evoke a variety of aesthetic experiences (rasa) in the audience that could grant both entertainment and enlightenment at the same time. This is one reason why, in Bengal, she was associated with Kartikeya, who was visualised as an affluent rasik, a connoisseur of the arts who frequented the houses of talented singers and dancers.

But as monastic orders rose in India, knowledge was divided into pure knowledge that grants spiritual bliss (yoga), and impure knowledge that arouses the senses and generates wealth (bhoga). The former was associated with priests, philosophers, ascetics and devotional poet-saints, while the latter was associated with entertainers, dancers, singers, musicians and performers. The former came to be more associated with Saraswati, and the latter more with Vidya-Lakshmi, vocational and transactional knowledge. This is one reason why 'commercial' artists have historically been frowned upon. Art for them is about making

Odisha patta painting showing Maha-vidya Baglamukhi

money and not about expanding the mind.

This disdain for the commercial artist is the reason why the 'nat' (entertainer) or the 'ganika' (courtesan) was always looked upon with suspicion. This suspicion combined with the puritanical nature of the Victorian era lead to the banning of devadasi practices and of classification of the caste of entertainers as 'criminal tribes' in British India.

In Vaishnava literature, Lakshmi became bhoga-patni, who entraps with pleasure, and Saraswati became moksha-patni, who liberates with wisdom. Stories emerged in Bhagavat parampara of how Krishna has to balance the demands of his rich wife, Satyabhama, and his gentle, wise wife, Rukmini. For the audience, the rich Satyabhama who dominates and shows off her wealth is Lakshmi, while the poor Rukmini who has nothing except devotion and wisdom is Saraswati.

One belief related to Saraswati that is common in almost every Hindu household is this: she never stays in the same house as Lakshmi, as they quarrel all the time.

The difference between the two goddesses is stark. Lakshmi is dressed as a bride, in red, embellished with ornaments; Saraswati is dressed as a widow, in white, with no regard for ornamentation even though artists deck her with crystal beads and white flowers. Lakshmi is attractive while Saraswati is aloof. Lakshmi comes and goes on a whim, but can be held in place using force and cunning. Saraswati comes only with great effort, but once she comes she does not leave.

In one folk tale, tired of the quarrels between his two wives,

Pala sculpture from Bengal showing Vishnu with Lakshmi and Saraswati

Vishnu separates them by placing Saraswati on his tongue and Lakshmi in his heart (or some say, his feet). Thus he gets the best of both — the invisible Saraswati and the visible Lakshmi.

The quarrel revolves around this one single idea: what matters more in worldly life, wealth or knowledge. This quarrel can be traced to the conflict between three major Vedic communities: the brahmins who were keepers and transmitters of Vedic knowledge, the kshatriyas who were warriors and so held bows and rode chariots, and the vaniks or vaishyas who were traders and so had access to wealth. In other words this conflict was not just about Saraswati of the brahmins and Lakshmi of the vaishyas but also Durga of the kshatriyas. It asks a deeper, philosophical question: what really matters in society — knowledge, wealth or power.

At the root of this conflict is the human desire to dominate. Why do humans seek to dominate? Animals dominate so as to get more access to food and mates. They cannot help themselves; it is in-built as part of nature's survival strategy. Humans however have the choice whether to dominate or not. And this choice comes from imagination, from Saraswati.

With imagination, humans come up with ideas and inventions that enable them to create surplus food. So there is really no need for a pecking order — there is enough for everyone to go around. And yet humans want to dominate. This comes from a deeper anxiety, a unique human anxiety — the quest for identity. Who am I? This quest also comes from Saraswati.

Animals have no doubt about where they are in nature's food chain and pecking order. But the imagination of humans creates doubts. Every human being can imagine themselves in a particular way. But those around may not imagine them in the same way. This

Poster of Gayatri, a personified Vedic hymn

creates conflict. We seek to impose and assert our imagining of ourselves on others. We want others to see us as we see ourselves.

In early societies, strength and cunning was used to dominate. But later, with surplus wealth, the idea of property emerged. He who had more property could dominate even the strong and the smart. Property could be inherited, and so one did not really need strength, skill or even cunning to acquire it. Social laws and concepts of ethics and morality ensured no one could usurp someone else's property. This secured the wealth of the wealthy. So, naturally, those who inherited wealth did not care much for knowledge. They did not even care for strength, skill or social status. With wealth everything could be bought — even people who were strong, skilled, talented and beautiful.

One group of people suffered greatly because of the rise in the importance of property. They were the keepers of Vedic lore. Vedic hymns had to be transmitted orally; they could not be written down as scripts could not adequately capture the intonations of Vedic mantras. This meant the entire day was spent chanting hymns using various techniques known as pada-patha. The focus remained so much on chanting that even understanding the hymns was ignored. Such a community dedicated to securing Vedic lore had no time to generate wealth for themselves. Wealth came only in the form of gifts and donations. Thus the idea emerged that where there is Lakshmi, there is no Saraswati, and where there is Saraswati, there is no Lakshmi.

Over time, Vedic priests created vocations for themselves, became astrologers, grammarians, temple priests, scribes and bureaucrats to generate Lakshmi for their households, but the relationship with wealth remained a tricky one. It was seen as

Mysore painting of Saraswati, the goddess of the arts

corrupting and distracting. Strangely, no one noticed that even knowledge could be corrupting and distracting. Because those who were too busy memorising and transmitting the Vedic hymns and rituals remained clueless about their meaning or significance.

Vedic knowledge is all about expanding the mind, outgrowing fear, in the quest for self-realisation. As long as the mind is contracted, there is fear, and hence the desire to dominate. While the kshastriyas dominated society using power (Durga), and the vaishyas dominated society using their wealth (Lakshmi), the brahmins dominated society by claiming to be 'purer' than others as they were keepers of esoteric knowledge (Saraswati). This hierarchy of purity is unique to Indian society and it wreaked havoc in Indian society.

Everything that the brahmin could not partake of as the keeper of Vedic lore became a source of impurity: meat, alcohol, sexual pleasure, wealth, property, trade, even vocations that involved physical labour and contact with nature. So the purest man was one who shunned all things worldly and material. Impurity became contagious and so to establish purity, the brahmin avoided contact with all things 'impure'. He isolated himself from other communities and even from his own wife when she was menstruating with a feeling of superiority. This idea caught on and spread across all communities.

Everyone who wanted to climb up the social ladder realised it was possible to do so even without wealth and power or even knowledge, by simply embracing the concept of 'purity'. The pure could look down upon the impure. Eventually, communities or jatis started locating themselves on the purity hierarchy. On top were the brahmins. At the bottom were a whole bunch of professions

Cosmic form of Saraswati

such as tanners, cobblers, sweepers, toilet-cleaners, butchers, who were considered so impure that they were even denied access to the village well.

Thus, Saraswati who was supposed to expand the human mind and help humans discover atma, ended up becoming the cause of contracting the human mind and amplifying aham. Self-awareness was overshadowed with self-delusion. The draconian caste system became the hallmark of Hinduism. It continues to haunt Hinduism today as people continue to strive to be 'purer'.

To be pure is to assume there is dirt in the world. Dirt is a cultural concept, not a natural one. In Tantra, where Devi worship takes centre-stage, great value is therefore given to what is shunned by purity-conscious mainstream society. Thus, the Goddess is offered meat and alcohol and blood. Even menstrual blood, seen as dirty and polluting by most communities, is seen as sacred and auspicious. It is described, as everything else in nature, as valid (satyam), energising (shivam) and beautiful (sundaram).

To outgrow the human need to dominate using wealth, status, knowledge, beauty, success and notions of purity, is to truly let Saraswati flow in our minds.

# 7. Vitthai's Secret

*Affection dissolves boundaries*

Photograph of a statue of Vitthal, a form of Krishna worshipped in Maharashtra

*I*n the 13th century, a young sage from Maharashtra called Dyaneshwar did something revolutionary for the times: he translated the Sanskrit *Bhagavad Gita* into the local tongue of Maharashtri Prakrit (old Marathi). But with one difference: while in the Sanskrit *Bhagavad Gita*, Krishna is the valorous masculine warrior-charioteer, in Dyaneshwar's *Dyaneshwari*, Krishna is Vitthai, or 'mother Vitthal'.

Vitthal, who is enshrined in Pandharpur, is the popular name of Krishna in Maharashtra. Dyaneshwar saw him in feminine terms. For him, Krishna was the affectionate cow who comforts the lost and frightened calf, Arjuna, with his milk of wisdom. He used other metaphors for Krishna, all feminine, like the mother turtle who watches over her baby turtles with loving sidelong glances. This idea of 'mother Krishna' was carried forward by other poet-saints of Maharashtra, like Janabai and Tukaram. For these poets, gender was but a tool to communicate a very particular emotion. Love and wisdom mattered more than Krishna's gender. And no one took offence.

This feminisation of the masculine is fairly common in Hindu mythology. Hypermasculine characteristics of a village god, like a moustache, diminish with the rise in his status. Features become gentle and soft. Muscles disappear.

This contrasts with the trend to masculinise the feminine in modern society. While feminism, in principle, has been about reclaiming humanity by restoring the balance of power between men and women, in popular culture, a feminist is often projected as one who does everything that a man can. Thus, for society to

Surya is a Vedic god whose key role in astrology ensured he survived as a Puranic god too, though not as popular as Vishnu and Shiva.

Surya has children by Saranya (Yama, the god of death, and his sister, Yami), Chhaya (Manu, Tapti and Manu, leader of humans) as well as Aruna/Usha (Sugriva of the Ramayana).

Surya rides a chariot pulled by seven horses across the sky.

Popular representation of the sun-god Surya and his wife Saranya

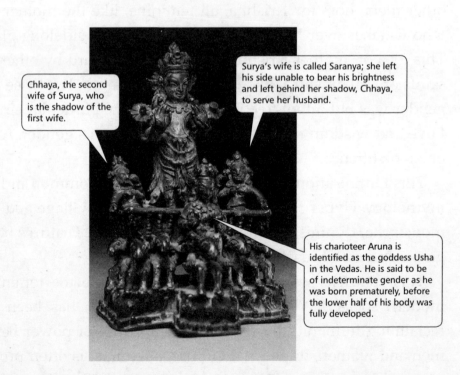

Chhaya, the second wife of Surya, who is the shadow of the first wife.

Surya's wife is called Saranya; she left his side unable to bear his brightness and left behind her shadow, Chhaya, to serve her husband.

His charioteer Aruna is identified as the goddess Usha in the Vedas. He is said to be of indeterminate gender as he was born prematurely, before the lower half of his body was fully developed.

17th century image from Nepal, of Surya with his wives and charioteer

progress, women have to compete with men. It is a race where she, not he, has to catch up.

This anxiety can be traced to monotheistic religions such as Islam and Christianity, where God is avowedly masculine with no room for the feminine. The relationship between God and Goddess in the stories and rituals of Hindu mythology has always been tumultuous. But there was never a time when the Goddess was dismissed.

In the Vedas, the gods have gender and there is a clear preference for the male. There are many more hymns dedicated to male devatas such as Surya (sun), Indra (sky), Agni (fire), Marutta (storm), Soma (herb/moon), Varuna (order) and Mitra (pact) than female devatas such as Prithvi (earth), Saraswati (river), Ushas (dawn), Nritti (death), and Aranyani (forest). The male deities reside above the earth, in the sky, and are associated with cultural order, while the female deities are associated with the earth and natural order. There are invocations to male ancestors (pitrs) and prayers for male offspring (putra). The gender divide is clear.

In the Upanishads, however, the idea of a cosmic consciousness or brahman starts to become more important than gods and goddesses. Cosmic consciousness is identified with atma, consciousness of the individual. Both the cosmic brahman and individual atma are described as nirguna, without form, unfettered by the body, hence genderless. The Upanishads are also called Vedanta, the philosophy milked out of the Vedas.

But all talk of consciousness remained with the elite. The ordinary village folk preferred their grama-devas who satisfied their basic

Stone sculpture of Lakshmi-Vishnu on the 12th-century Khajuraho temple wall

needs: the virile guardian gods who granted protection and the fearsome fertility goddesses who granted prosperity. These viras (heroes) and matas (mothers) were both powerful. Sometimes, the heroes served the loving mother. At other times, the hero controlled the wild mothers. Most times, the hero and the mother formed the perfect pair, their powers complementing each other's.

From the 5th century BCE, Buddhism along with other shramana (ascetic) movements started decrying the value placed on desire and rejected the householder's worldview. In their very monastic perspective, pleasure was frowned upon. Naturally, women, associated with pleasure and the household, became 'daughters of Mara', Mara being the demon of desire. Women were, however, admitted into monastic orders so that, through meditation and ascetic practices, they could, in their next life, acquire a male body, and achieve nirvana.

The popularity of Buddhism and other shramana orders forced Hinduism to redefine itself. The new Hinduism, based on the Puranas, put great value on desire, on household, hence relationships between men and women. In this new Hinduism, God was no longer formless; it acquired form. But neither the male nor the female form was given preference. God was seen as male: Shiva was ishwar (the lord) and Vishnu was bhagavan (all encompassing), but these male forms of the divine owed their divinity to their female counterparts. This is why both are addressed as 'husbands of the Goddess'. Shiva is Uma-pati (husband of Uma) and Vishnu is Lakshmi-vallabha (beloved of Lakshmi). Male gods can be addressed only after the name of the consort is mentioned. Thus, Shiva is Uma-Mahesh and Vishnu is Lakshmi-Narayana. Devi here is not a supplement; she is a complement.

Photograph of a typical Shiva shrine with the invisible Goddess

This was the time when monotheistic religions were on the rise around the world and Goddess cults were being wiped out, following the conversion of the Roman Emperor and his Empire to Christianity. In Christianity, God was a man and his son, the saviour, was also a man. Mary, the mother of God, was but a holy vessel, untouched by mortal man, hence virgin and mother, but not Goddess. Women were no longer priestesses; those who continued to be faithful to ancient Goddess lore and rites were deemed witches and burned at the stake.

Meanwhile, in India, the feminine provided the canvas that projected the divinity of God. This is evident in a Shiva temple. What dominates the shrine is the linga-stone representing Shiva. Some scholars see it as the phallus, but devotees see it as the form of a formless divinity (linga of that which is a-linga). What keeps this linga in place is the yoni-trough below representing Gauri (another name of Uma) and what keeps it wet and dynamic is the perforated pot above representing Ganga (another wife of Shiva, junior to Gauri, in some traditions). The shrine itself is called the garbha-griha, the womb room. Whose womb? The Devi's of course. Thus Shiva is housed inside a goddess and is between two goddesses, but only he is seen, for the temple is attributed to him. Some choose to interpret this as patriarchy: the two goddesses have been shoved into the background, granted inferior positions (consort?) in the power hierarchy. Others choose to interpret this as feminism: only through Devi can God be established. Still others see this as wisdom: the Goddess withdraws so that the devotees engage with the ascetic Shiva and force him to participate in their worldly affairs, much as a mother withdraws to encourage her child to interact with strangers.

Tanjore painting of the marriage of Meenakshi

Popular representation of Meenakshi, the goddess-queen of Madurai, Tamil Nadu

The value placed on desire and sexuality and engagement with the world in this new form of Hinduism can easily be read as a direct attack on monastic Buddhism and explains the sexual imagery on Hindu temple walls. Vishnu became an enchanting man (Mohan) for women and an enchanting woman (Mohini) for men. And just as Devi domesticates the hermit Shiva, she herself is domesticated by the handsome hermit, Shankara Sundareshwara.

From Tamil temple lore comes the story of one Meenakshi of Madurai, warrior princess with three breasts, who conquers the world but loses her masculinity and her extra breast when she sees Somasundaram, as beautiful as the moon, who is none other than Shiva. In her temple today, she may be his coy bride with a parrot in one hand, but the dagger hanging on her hip indicates her once free spirit. Amongst Tamilians, a household dominated by a woman is called Madurai (temple-town of the Goddess), while a household dominated by a man is called Chidambaram (temple-town of God).

So important is the Goddess that any attempt to worship God without Goddess is discouraged violently as explained by the story of Bhringi found in Tamil temple lore. Bhringi, an ardent devotee of Shiva, paid a visit to Mount Kailas, abode of Shiva, intent on going around his lord. But Parvati stopped him. 'Shiva and I make a pair. You cannot worship him in his totality without acknowledging me. Hence you must go around both of us.' But Bhringi was determined to only go around Shiva, not Parvati. To make this impossible, Parvati sat on Shiva's left lap. Bhringi tried squeezing between them to have his way. So Parvati fused her body with Shiva's and became his left half. Determined not to include Parvati in his worship, Bhringi turned into a bee and tried to bore

Poster art of Shiva as half woman

a path between the left and right halves of Shiva's body. Peeved at his insolence, Parvati cursed Bhringi that he would lose that part of his body that emerged from the female seed. Immediately, Bhringi lost all flesh and blood and collapsed to the ground. Reduced to nothing but bones, Bhringi apologised and sang songs to the glory of the Goddess. Finally Parvati showed mercy and gave him a third leg to enable him to stand upright. He still had a skeletal frame to remind him of the importance of the Goddess.

The half-woman form of Shiva, Ardhanareshwara, does suggest equality of God and Goddess but it is not so. This half-woman form is clearly identified with Shiva. There is no corresponding half-male form of Devi. This makes sense only when we appreciate the symbolic meaning of God and Goddess as mind and nature. The mind cannot exist without nature, but nature can exist without the mind. The Puranas thus present an idea shared by evolutionary biologists. While the visible form is gendered, the idea being communicated is genderless. This was clearly an attempt to present sophisticated ideas of Upanishad-Vedanta to the laity in narrative form. Miscommunication was a very real risk.

The Puranas also reiterate that the essence of all male gods is female. But the opposite is not true. Thus when an asura attacks and the devas run to Brahma, then Vishnu, then Shiva, they are advised to release their inner strength. This emerges in female form. From Indra comes Indrani. From Vishnu comes Vaishnavi. From Varaha comes Vairahi. From Narasimha comes Narasimhi. From Kumara comes Kumari. From Vinayaka comes Vinayaki. These become the Matrikas who collectively defeat asuras. They also merge to become Durga, the supreme defender of all devas. Durga may fight battles, emulating male heroes, but at no point does she become a man.

Miniature painting of Matrikas, the female form of devas,
accompanying the Goddess into battle

While apsaras (damsels) were known to seduce tapasvins (ascetics), we find stories of Vishnu himself turning into an enchantress called Mohini to seduce not just asuras but also Shiva. Thus is born their son variously named Sastha or Aiyanar.

By the 5th century CE, temples offered legitimacy to kings who, in turn, patronised the temple. Grand temple complexes became centres of commerce, craftsmanship and culture. They housed singers, musicians, performers and, most importantly, devadasis, women who were well-versed in the arts. These were very different from the secular courtesans or ganikas of yore. They got validation by being the spouse and servant of God. They offered pleasure just as the king, the other servant of God, offered protection to pilgrims who thronged these temple towns. We find this concept in temple-cities like Puri in Odisha, Tanjavur in Tamil Nadu, and Thiruvananthapuram in Kerala. During the height of summer, the devadasis of Puri Jagannath temple, known as Maharis, were encouraged to dance for the ascetic Balarama in the hope that his seduction would herald rain. Thus monasticism was associated with drought, and sensuality with fertility. Marriage of God and Goddess was critical for the prosperity of the realm. Hence the many temple marriage festivals such as the Brahmotsavam of Venkateshwara Tirupati Balaji. The popularity of Hinduism over Buddhism as the centuries passed owes much to the sensual vibrancy of the temples that overshadowed the austerity of the monasteries.

From the 7th century onwards, a new religion gained a foothold in India — Islam. It came via trade in the south and via warlords in the north. Like Christianity, it was a monotheistic religion where

Mural from Kotakkal palace, Kerala, showing Parvati, Shiva and Mohini

God was masculine, his prophet was masculine and women had a clearly defined inferior position. Islam frowned upon idol worship and its followers could not understand the use of song, dance and theatre in worship. As Muslim warlords gradually became the rulers of north and east India, Hinduism had to redefine itself once more.

Both for internal reasons (rejection of the excessive sensuality of temple devadasis) as well as external reasons (arrival of Islam), from the 10th century onwards, we see a gradual rejection of all things sensual and feminine. This is evident in the popular ballads of the Nath-jogis (vernacular of the Sanskrit yogis), followers of Matsyendra-nath and Gorakh-nath, who are always in confrontation with sensuous Tantrik sorceresses called yoginis who get their power through sex.

Far removed from the sensuous temple culture, the Nath-jogis were wandering ascetics who attributed their power to celibacy. Some jogis even destroy their genitals, which ensures the semen does not slip out of their body but instead rises up towards their head. In Tantra, this is called urdhva-retas, the upward flow of semen that grants them powers known as siddhi, by which men have the power to fly through the sky, walk on water, give fertility to the land and children to the childless. The acquisition of siddhi turned the Nath-jogis into Siddhas, powerful men who had no time to waste on sensory worldly pleasures.

The attitude of the Nath-jogi tradition towards celibacy is very different from that in Buddhist times. In Buddhist tradition, it was more about the conquest of desire. In Nath tradition, it is about the rejection of all things feminine. The Nath-jogi's hyper-masculinity did not come from dominating women; it came from turning away

Circular temple of 64 yoginis in Odisha

Painting of Vajra-yogini from the Tantrik tradition

from women altogether. Femininity was seen as stripping men of their masculinity.

Matsyendra-nath was born a fish but he overheard the secret conversation between Shiva and Shakti, during which Shiva revealed the mysteries of Vedas and the Tantras to Parvati. That knowledge transformed him into a human male with enough siddhi power to enter the banana grove unharmed. He entered this land of women and stayed there, enchanted by the women, unable to return. He had to be rescued by his student, Gorakh-nath.

Even the story of the great Vedanta teacher Shankara has these elements when challenged about his knowledge of the erotic arts by Ubhaya Bharati, wife of Mandana Mishra. Since he is a celibate ascetic, Shankara knows nothing, so he resurrects a dead king, Amaru, by entering his body at the moment of his death and then going on to experience sensory pleasures in the inner quarters of the palace with queens and courtesans for several months. Unlike Mastyendra-nath, however, Shankara does not succumb to the pleasures of the flesh and eventually leaves the king's body and returns to being an ascetic, thus establishing the superiority of his mind over his flesh.

Alongside violent Muslim warlords came the poet-saints known as Sufis from Persia. With them came music and the idea of love for God expressed in passionate, even romantic terms. Hindus connected with this idea and it amplified the bhakti or devotional movement.

The idea of devotion is found in the *Bhagavad Gita* written centuries before the rise of Islam. Tamil songs of Alvars and

Miniature painting of Radha and Krishna

Nayanars that speak of devotion to Vishnu and Shiva predate the arrival of Islam into India. But the tone of devotion here is one of surrender. The arrival of Sufism made devotion more romantic. It also encouraged the expression of devotion through regional literature.

Indian poets took the idea of romantic attachment for the divine to another level through the idea of Radha. Krishna had always been associated with milkmaids who yearn for him, but in the songs of the poet-saints, Krishna also pines for Radha and Radha demands and gets Krishna's attention. It is no longer about submission; it is now about mutual longing. The devotee becomes a woman, a maid, a servant, even a wife and a queen who God indulges with affection.

Those who could not handle the romantic and the sensual turned to the parental. But it was not always God who was the parent. The devotee could be parent too: Yashoda to Krishna and Kaushalya to Ram.

Most early bhakti songs were directed at Vishnu and Shiva. Later bhakti songs are directed at the Goddess too. Shyama Sangeet in Bengal and the Jagrata songs sung all night for the pleasure of Sheravali in Punjab and Jammu, for example. The relationship here is never romantic. It is always parental. Here the Goddess is mostly mother. At times she appears like a daughter, virginal and powerful, rarely mischievous and playful. In Sri Vaishnavism, strongly influenced by the teachings of Ramanuja, the 12th century Vedantic scholar who turned away from married life and became a monk, Shri or Lakshmi is the mother who the devotee approaches so that she will negotiate with the stern father, Vishnu.

In Sufi songs, God is decidedly male, and the male singer-

Gopeshwara Mahadeva of Mathura represents Shiva who became a gopi in order to dance with Krishna.

Popular image of Vinayaki, the shakti of Ganesha, who is visualised in female form.

Painting of Srinathji who is Krishna, showing him in sakhi-vesha, or the costume of a lady friend.

Gods embracing the feminine

devotee does not shy away from making himself feminine. In Bhakti literature, this gender shifting extends to God. Love for the devotee turns the masculine into feminine and the feminine into masculine.

In Trichy, Tamil Nadu, Shiva turns into a midwife in order to help deliver the child of a devotee whose mother is unable to reach her house in time. In Mathura, Shiva turns into a gopeshwara, a milkmaid, who wants to join Krishna in his raas-leela.

Krishna exchanges clothes with Radha to experience what it means to be Radha. And in imagery found on temple walls of Odisha, he does not mind sporting a woman's plait and anklets. In his Nathdvara temple in Rajasthan, he indulges in stri-vesha, or cross-dressing, in memory of his mother and his beloved, unafraid that such activities will undermine his masculinity.

There is an oral tradition in Bengal about a time that came when Kali's violence became so excessive that the world lost its balance. She had to be stopped. So Shiva lay on his back, on the ground, in her path. As soon as she stepped on him, she was so enchanted by his beauty that her strident march came to a halt and she decided to make love to him, with her on top. With this, the balance of the world was restored and the earth regenerated itself. But then the asuras returned. The devas begged Kali to come to their rescue and rid the earth of asuras. But Kali was so full of love that she could not resume her violence. So she decided to take another form, that of Krishna. From female, she became male. Shiva could not bear the thought of being without Kali so he decided to follow Krishna as Radha. Krishna was as dark as Kali and Radha was as fair as Shiva. Kali had sat on top of Shiva and so Krishna allowed Radha to sit on top of him. Thus their respective gender and positions

Odisha patta painting of a composite image of Krishna and Kali

were reversed. Krishna was Kali. Shiva was Radha. They were not two but one.

By worshipping Krishna then, one did not exclude Kali. And by worshipping Radha, one did not exclude Shiva. The gender fluidity of the narrative seeks to unite Vaishnava, Shaiva and Shakta orders. It allows for negotiations and interactions between the vegetarian Krishna cults and the non-vegetarian Kali cults. It also unites the ascetic Shaiva traditions with the sensuous Radha traditions.

When there is wisdom, there is affection. When there is affection, there is no fear of predators, hence no need for boundaries. Rigidity then gives way to fluidity: God becomes Goddess and Goddess, God.

In the 16th century, Europeans came to India as traders. By the 18th century, they had complete control over the subcontinent, turning this land into a source of taxes as well as raw materials for their industries back home. The Europeans had Christian roots and saw themselves as children of the enlightenment who came with a scientific temperament. They mocked Hindus for being so 'effeminate' and described Hinduism as paganism as they worshipped the Goddess.

Hindus reacted by masculinising themselves, distancing themselves from all things sensual, and redefining the Goddess in virginal and maternal terms, just like the biblical Mary. All things Hindu were seen as foul. So rather than reform devdasi traditions of their exploitative side, they were simply wiped out, and all dance and song sanitised. Freedom fighters projected themselves

Randhal-ma who embodies Saranya and Chhaya, the two wives of Surya.

Chamunda and her sister Chotila.

Ashapura and her companion, Piplaowali.

Jyestha and Kanishtha, the elder and younger sister, who are forms of Gauri, mother of Ganesha.

Twin goddesses who are autonomous, without male companionship

as celibate monks more determined to serve Mother India as yogis. They refused to be seen as rasiks and bhogis who enjoyed art and pleasure.

The impact of the European Orientalist gaze was so powerful that it continues to haunt modern political Hinduism where leaders are especially respected if they are celibate. Posters have been created of Ram without Sita and Shiva without Gauri, both sporting firm muscular bodies with determined expressions, and no trace of feminine softness. Durga, the protective mother who rides lions and does battle, has become the preferred form of the Goddess, not Kamakshi, who sits on Shiva holding the symbols of Kama, god of desire, or the restless whimsical Lakshmi.

The 20th century saw the rise of American academia. It had two powerful influences. One was the Protestant rejection of Catholic feudalism, even though it still remained masculine and monotheistic at its core. The other was scientific thinking that rejected all matters of faith. It established a neo-Orientalist lens that started explaining Hinduism through the lens of fairness and justice, where it positioned the researcher as the saviour and the research subject either as villain or victim. Suddenly, the Ramayana and Mahabharata became patriarchal epics. The differences between many Ramayanas were more valued than the commonalities. The Ram of devotees was no longer the gentle God but the stern imperialist, a wife-abusing villain, and Sita became his whimpering silent victim, stripped of her Goddess status. This reading was reinforced when Ram became the mascot of Hindu fundamentalism. Shiva was admired as the rule-breaker who allows the wild Kali to stand on his chest, while Vishnu was frowned upon because he makes Lakshmi a subservient consort

The Western gaze sees Lakshmi massaging Vishnu's feet as indicative of subservience.

The Indian gaze sees Lakshmi's subservience as indicator of nature's unconditional affection for a mind that truly appreciates her.

The Western gaze considers the Indian gaze as being apologetic and in denial.

The Indian gaze sees Kali's dance as nature's determination to awaken the withdrawn, passive, corpse-like mind embodied by Shiva.

The Western gaze sees Kali standing on Shiva as indicative of female rage and rebellion.

The Indian gaze is outraged by the literal reading of images that the West sees as objective truth, disregarding the opinions of the devotees.

**The difference between Western and Indian gaze**

who has to massage his feet. This literal and rather rudimentary reading shaped by Western ideologies and templates continues to have a huge impact on young students who go to American universities to pursue studies in humanities and liberal arts. It endorses the Western imagination that there is nothing redeeming about India: it is essentially chaos where order has to be brought in from outside; its many hierarchies have to be replaced by equality; and it is desperately in need of a Western-style revolution.

The Goddess smiles. It is in the nature of the beast to compete and dominate. Like young lions who challenge old ones, like dogs who bark at strangers, every society mocks older alien cultures. The West is no different, despite the veneer of rationality and science. And like animals who do not recognise themselves in the mirror, societies often fail to see themselves as others see them. India is no different when they turn chauvinistic.

Vitthai asks: what is wrong with gods being feminine and men being effeminate? Why should women be like men? Why should there be a race that someone has to win? Why can't people be themselves? The nature of man cannot be domesticated by rules that enforce fairness and justice. Such rules will only suppress and eventually provoke the beast within humanity to strike back, defy and subvert the very same laws. For what starts as a tool to create equality invariably ends up as a tool that establishes new hierarchies.

The Goddess has seen it before and she will see it again. As long as Brahma seeks to control nature, he will find himself being beheaded by Shiva. As long as Indra believes he is entitled to Lakshmi, he will always wonder why she is drawn to Vishnu.

The point is not about domesticating the Goddess outside

Clay image from Bengal of Jaga-dhatri, the mother of the world

us; the point is to evoke the God within us. It is not about being righteous, about proving the validity of one God or one truth; it is about expanding the mind so that we can affectionately include multiple truths. And that can only happen when we appreciate that idea that is Goddess, hence God, without the bias of gender.

# 7 Secrets of
# Vishnu

*Anointed with perfumes*
*Draped in silk*
*He reclines on the ocean of milk*
*Eyes open*
*Ever smiling*
*Securing the world with his attention*
*He is God who is chased by fortune*
*Perumal, Balaji, Narayana, Vishnu*
*Who walks the earth as Krishna, and as Ram*

Locked in his stories, symbols and rituals are the secrets of our ancestors. *7 Secrets of Vishnu* attempts to unlock seven.

# Author's Note
## On communicating ideas

$\mathcal{I}$t is significant that the stories of Vishnu rose to prominence after the rise of Buddhism. Prior to that, Hinduism was a religion of elite-based complex rituals known as yagna, and esoteric speculations captured in texts known as the Aranyakas and the Upanishads. These seemed very distant to the common man who focused on fertility rituals, worship of plants and animals and nature.

Buddhism spoke directly to the common man in the language of the people and addressed everyday concerns. It naturally became very popular. But the Buddhist worldview leaned towards monasticism. By contrast, the Hindu worldview made room for both the hermit and the householder. To fire the imagination of people moving towards monasticism, this had to be communicated using a tool that the masses relished — stories.

Stories of Vishnu communicate the Hindu worldview from the point of view of the householder. This is complemented by stories of Shiva that communicate an equally valid but alternate viewpoint, that of the hermit. Since both Vishnu and Shiva were forms of God, both worldviews, that of the householder and that of the hermit, were held in equal regard.

To ensure that these stories were not reduced to entertainment, they were deemed sacred and anchored with symbols and rituals. The symbols and rituals of Vishnu are different from the symbols and rituals of Shiva. For example, Vishnu is visualised bedecked in gold while Shiva is worshipped smeared in ash; Vishnu is offered sprigs of the tulsi that is grown inside the house while Shiva is offered leaves of the bilva that is grown outside the house; Vishnu dances with his eyes open while Shiva dances with his eyes shut. Through these differences, different ideas were communicated.

Wisdom that was once restricted to a few now reached everyone who chose to hear the stories, look at the symbols, and perform the rituals. Vishnu represents a key figure in the new story-based Hinduism. He is a critical piece of what can be called the grand Hindu jigsaw puzzle.

- To help readers unravel the secrets of Vishnu, the chapters have been arranged as below:

- The first chapter focuses on how gender is used to explain fundamental metaphysical concepts integral to Hinduism.

- The second chapter discusses the difference between man and animal.

- The third and fourth chapters focus on the Devas and the Asuras, both of whom are unhappy, as one struggles with insecurity and the other with ambition.

- The fifth and sixth chapters revolve around the Ramayana and Mahabharata, as man struggles with his humanity.

- The seventh chapter is about the wisdom of letting go with faith in renewal.

This book seeks to make explicit patterns that are implicit in stories, symbols and rituals of Vishnu firm in the belief that:

> *Within infinite myths lies an eternal truth*
> *Who knows it all?*
> *Varuna has but a thousand eyes*
> *Indra, a hundred*
> *You and I, only two.*

# 1. Mohini's Secret

*Spiritual growth need not exclude material growth*

A festival image or utsav-moorti of Vishnu
as Mohini from a south Indian temple

$\mathcal{M}$ohini is the female form of Vishnu. She is an enchantress, an alluring damsel, a temptress. But she is not a nymph, or Apsara, such as Menaka, Rambha and Urvashi, renowned in Hindu mythology for their ability to seduce sages and demons. Mohini stands apart because she is identified as Vishnu and Vishnu is conventionally visualised as male. Mohini is his female form.

Hindu mythology uses gender as a vehicle to communicate metaphysical ideas. A fundamental theme in Indian metaphysics is the existence of two realities: material reality and spiritual reality. Material reality is tangible reality that can be perceived through the senses. Spiritual reality is intangible reality that cannot be perceived through the senses. Material reality is represented using female form while spiritual reality is represented using male form.

Mohini is female in form but male in essence, unlike Apsaras who are totally female. Both enchant, but their intentions are different. An Apsara enchants to distract humanity from spiritual reality and entrap all in material reality. Mohini enchants to draw humanity's attention to spiritual reality within material reality. Mohini is thus spiritual reality wrapped in material reality. This is the central theme of Vishnu lore.

In metaphysics, material reality is known as prakriti, and spiritual reality is referred to as purusha. Prakriti means nature. Purusha means human.

Humans are accorded a special place in nature over minerals, plants and animals, because only humans have the ability to reflect, introspect, imagine and choose. All these qualities make it

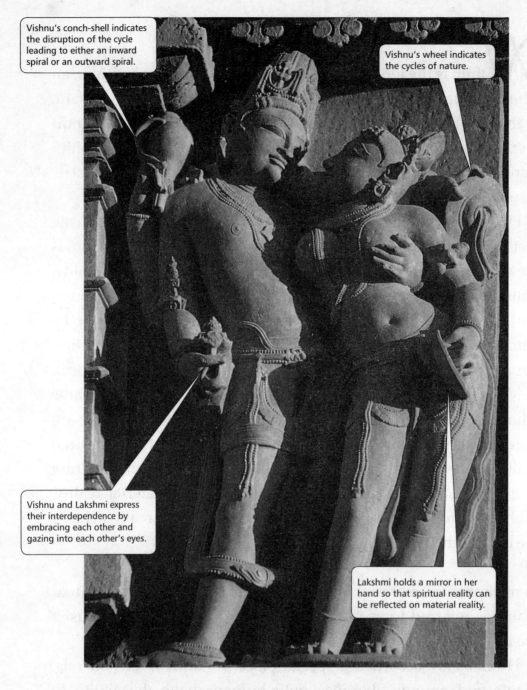

Vishnu's conch-shell indicates the disruption of the cycle leading to either an inward spiral or an outward spiral.

Vishnu's wheel indicates the cycles of nature.

Vishnu and Lakshmi express their interdependence by embracing each other and gazing into each other's eyes.

Lakshmi holds a mirror in her hand so that spiritual reality can be reflected on material reality.

Vishnu and Lakshmi on the walls of a Khajuraho temple, built in the 12th century, by Chandela kings

possible for humans to rise above physical limitations, transcend the boundaries of nature, and discover infinity. Human life is thus special. Therefore, the ancients represented both metaphysical principles using human symbols.

Material and spiritual reality are interdependent. Without material reality, spiritual reality cannot be discovered, and without spiritual reality, material reality has no purpose. This idea of complementary realities is expressed in Hindu mythology as a human couple. The interdependence of material and spiritual reality is best expressed through the interdependence of woman and man. This is the reason why temple walls are adorned with intimate conjugal images or dampatya.

In the Puranas, common nouns become proper nouns; an idea becomes a god or a goddess. Thus purusha becomes Purusha, or God, and prakriti becomes Prakriti, or Mother Nature. In Vishnu lore, Purusha is called Vishnu while Prakriti is called Lakshmi. He sustains the world; she is wealth personified. He cannot perform his role without her and she has no role without him. He gives her purpose and she gives him wherewithal. Thus Vishnu and Lakshmi validate each other. One cannot exist without the other.

But the mythological association of women with material reality irks many people. Why not the other way round? Why not represent spiritual reality through Lakshmi and material reality through Vishnu?

The reason for the irritation lies in the tendency to place spiritual reality on a higher plane than material reality. When this is coupled with the subordinate position of women in a male-dominated society, it seems that the use of women to represent material reality

The white lines, made from sandal paste, indicate spiritual reality. They meet at the bottom to form a cup that anchors material growth.

The central red line indicates material reality. The upward orientation indicates growth. Thus the central line represents material growth.

Making sandal paste demands tremendous faith and patience. It takes years before the wood of the tree can produce fragrant paste. The wood of a mature tree has to be rubbed on a wet surface in rhythmic circular motion. The more one rubs, the more paste one gets. At first the paste is transparent and the sandal invisible, but one must have faith. In time, the water evaporates and the sandal colour will be seen.

**The sacred mark of Vishnu or the urdhva-namam or the vertical mark**

is yet another attempt to impose patriarchal values. However, this is not true. Yes, mythological scriptures do use the female form to depict material reality, but the reason has less to do with gender politics and more to do with human physiology.

The fundamental difference between a man's body and a woman's body is that a man creates life outside his body while a woman creates life inside her body. He provides the trigger to life; she gives form to life. Both are essential to life in different ways. In metaphysics, spiritual reality triggers the observation while material reality embodies observation. The male body is doing in the reproductive context what spiritual reality is doing at a metaphysical context. So is the case with the female body. The male body is therefore best suited to represent spiritual reality while the female bod / is best suited to r present material reality. This does not mean men are spiritual and women are materialistic. In mythology, all forms are symbolic.

Vishnu's sacred mark, the vertical namam, includes both material as well as spiritual reality. Material reality is represented by red, the colour of blood that sustains life as it flows through the veins. Spiritual reality is represented by white, the colour of bones that upholds life by being still.

The central red line and the adjacent white lines are oriented upwards indicating growth. From the verb 'to grow', which is 'Brh' in Sanskrit, comes the Vedic word for God, which is brahman. Brahman is that which grows, that which is vast, that which is infinite. Vishnu means 'that which expands to occupy everything'. In other words, Vishnu is God who celebrates infinite growth, both material and spiritual.

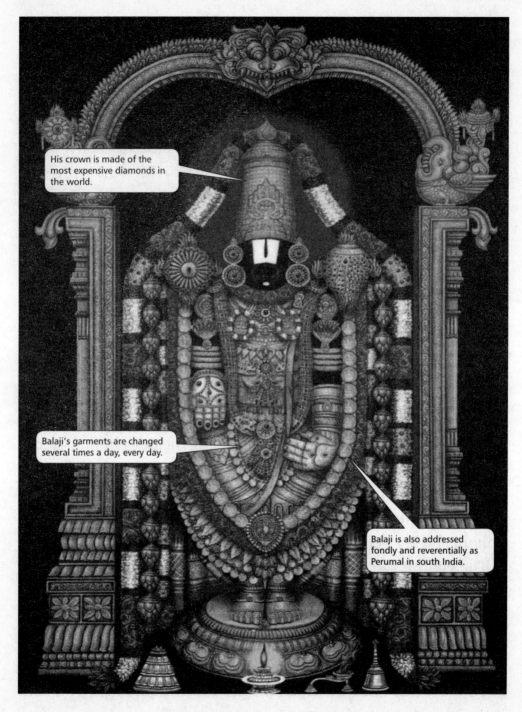

Venkateshwara Balaji of Tirupati, Andhra Pradesh

What does material growth mean? It means access to all the wonderful things the material world has to offer to please the five senses: food, clothing, shelter, music, dance, art, entertainment, relationships, peace, pleasure and prosperity. A visit to any Vishnu temple — whether it is Venkateshwara Balaji in Tirupati, or Srinathji in Rajasthan or Jagannath in Puri or the grand complexes of Ranganatha on the river-islands of the Kaveri — shows how material splendour is an intrinsic part of Vishnu worship. The rituals include colour and fragrance and music and flavours.

But material things are impermanent. Sooner or later, they wither away or cease to pleasure the mind. This causes pain, frustration, anxiety, stress, insecurity and fear, emotions that are most undesirable. Left unchecked, they can evoke in the mind greed and jealousy, rage and attachment.

Spiritual growth is the ability to overpower these emotions so that one has the wisdom to appreciate and enjoy all things material without getting needy or clingy. One is happy when the material world favours us and not unhappy when it does not. This can only happen when material growth is accompanied by intellectual growth. Only intellectual growth can control emotional turmoil caused by dependence on material things.

This is why the sacred mark of Vishnu is placed on the head, container of the human intellect. That is why the two white lines of spirituality form a cup at the base to anchor and support the single red line of materialism that stretches upwards in aspiration. Fetterless material growth is not a desired state.

The first step in the pursuit of spiritual reality is to take birth as a human being, for only the flesh can sense material reality and only

An image from Nepal known as Budhanilakantha that is Vishnu as Narayana sleeping on the serpent Sesha

Temple wall sculpture from Belur, Karnataka, showing Vishnu seated on the serpent Ananta

human flesh can fathom spiritual reality.

Perhaps it is the idea of an unborn human child floating in the water of its mother's womb that inspires the visualisation of Narayana, a form of Vishnu that sleeps on the waters. When Vishnu slumbers, the world does not exist, in form, or in thought. So it is with the unborn child.

In the unborn state, the child is innocent and ignorant of the world outside. It is not exposed to the form of the world, nor does it have any thoughts on the world. No thoughts on spirit or matter, no thoughts of male or female, white or red. Nothing. The unborn child is like Narayana in dreamless slumber.

Narayana sleeps on the coils of a serpent with many hoods. This serpent is called Adi-Ananta-Sesha, and it represents time. Adi means primal, Ananta means infinite and Sesha means the residue. These three names refer to three states of time corresponding to when one is awakening, when one is awake and when one is slumbering. When we awake, we first sense the flow of time. This is Adi, the primal sensation, represented mathematically as one, the first number. When we are fully awake, we can potentially perceive the world in infinite ways. This is Ananta, the ultimate sensation, represented mathematically as infinity. While we are in deep slumber and do not dream, we have no sense of time, hence no perception of the world. Nothing exists. What remains then is nothingness or Sesha, the residue, equal to what is mathematically represented by the number zero. Thus the name of Vishnu's serpent, Adi-Ananta-Sesha, draws attention to the three states of being all human beings go through cyclically: awakening, waking and slumber states.

Calendar art showing Brahma rising from Vishnu's navel

When Narayana awakens, a lotus blooms from his navel. In it sits Brahma.

Brahma is the child slipping out of the mother's womb. He senses the sudden rush of stimuli from the outside world. It is different from the experience in his mother's womb. This is his first brush with nature.

Brahma recognises himself as distinct from Prakriti. This ability comes from Purusha within him, but he does not know it yet. He knows he is not Prakriti. He objectifies nature as he becomes increasingly self-aware. The birth of Brahma thus marks the birth of human consciousness.

Brahma represents consciousness that is finite; it has the capability to realise infinite consciousness which is brahman. Hence the Vedic maxim, 'Aham Brahmasmi', which means both 'I am Brahma' as well as 'I am brahman'. The first meaning is acknowledgment of the finite truth that has been unravelled. The second meaning is the aspiration for the infinite truth that awaits unravelling.

The human mind, or Brahma, observes that nature is never still. As one moves from place to place, nature changes: wet rainy forests turn into deserts, cold icy mountains turn into vast oceans. Even when one sits in a place, one observes nature restless, changing with time: plants wither and die, animals mate and migrate, seasons change, sun rises and sets, moon waxes and wanes, the celestial sphere rotates around the Pole Star. Everything that is born eventually dies.

In the mother's womb everything is static and comfortable. Nothing is expected. But outside, in nature, everything is moving, and one is expected to act if one has to survive. As far as Brahma is

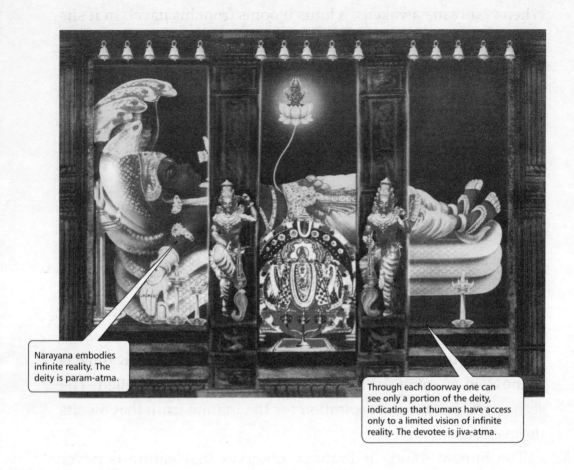

Narayana embodies infinite reality. The deity is param-atma.

Through each doorway one can see only a portion of the deity, indicating that humans have access only to a limited vision of infinite reality. The devotee is jiva-atma.

Calendar art depicting the inner shrine of the temple at Thiruvananthapuram, where lies a giant image of Padmanabhaswami

concerned, Prakriti is Shatarupa, the restless goddess with myriad forms. She frightens him.

Brahma's mind is blessed with manas or imagination. He is able to imagine a time Shatarupa dances to his whims. This gives him joy. He is also able to imagine a time when Shatarupa overwhelms him. This frightens him. Most critically, he is able to imagine a time when he will not be able to experience Shatarupa. In other words, he imagines death. This frightens him the most.

Brahma passes on this fear of mortality to all living creatures, the jiva-atma, who are his children and his grandchildren. That is why all babies cry when they are born. That is why Brahma is not worshipped.

Vishnu has no such fear. He knows that what Brahma considers death is merely the death of the body that encases the Purusha. He does not depend on material reality for his identity. He knows that he is Purusha, infinite and immortal. He is param-atma. That is why Vishnu is worshipped. He is what all jiva-atma aspire to be.

Brahma shuns those aspects of nature that frighten him and he yearns for those aspects of nature that comfort him. This shunning of fear and yearning for comfort gives birth to a goddess called Maya.

The word Maya has its root in 'Ma' which means 'to measure'. Maya is a measuring scale. Like Prakriti, Maya is an aspect of material reality. But while Prakriti is physical, Maya is mental. Prakriti existed before Brahma, Maya comes after. Prakriti is Brahma's mother while Maya is his daughter; or one can say wife, because Brahma does not know he created Maya.

Brahma needs Maya to survive Prakriti. Brahma observes

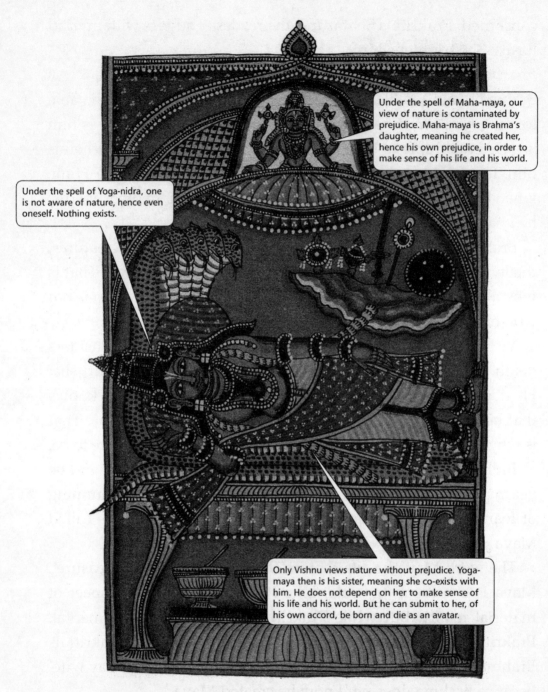

Mysore painting showing the goddess Maya watching
over the reclining Vishnu

Prakriti, and tries to make sense of her, through the lens of Maya. Maya is the measuring scale. Brahma is doing the measuring. Prakriti is that which he measures. With the help of Maya, Brahma is able to judge Prakriti as good or bad, right or wrong, beautiful or ugly. No more is Brahma intimidated by Shatarupa and her transformations. This ability to judge the world around him makes Brahma feel very powerful.

Unfortunately Maya is not static. She is continuously informed and coloured by Brahma's experiences and expectations. When experience changes, when expectation changes, Maya recalibrates herself. As a result, what was right in the past may be wrong in the future; what was good in one part of the world may be bad in the other; what one person may find beautiful may be ugly for another. This confuses and confounds Brahma. It leads to conflicts between his children. One wonders what the perfect truth is. One questions reality. One wonders what the point of life is. This amplifies fear.

Maya often is taken to mean delusion. A world seen through a measuring scale is a delusion, because it is a perception, dependent on a measuring scale. It is a delusion that comforts Brahma as well as perplexes him. Without it, Brahma is lost. With it, he has meaning, purpose and direction.

The world of delusion constructed by Brahma with the help of Maya is called Brahmanda or Brahma's sphere. Brahmanda is not objective reality; it is Brahma's version of reality, his very own personal construction, his opinion of nature.

Prakriti is objective material reality. Brahmanda is subjective material reality. The former exists without the aid of Maya; the

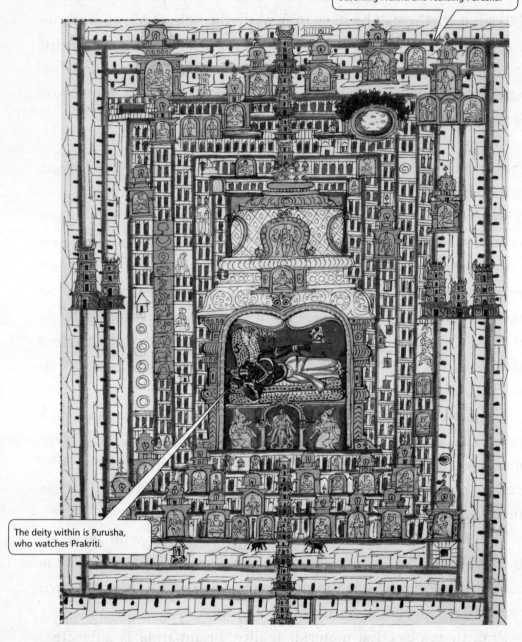

Mysore painting of the deity Ranganatha within the temple

latter is a product of Maya. Prakriti is the forest — in the forest, man is no different from other animals. Maya, however, makes man feel that he is superior to animal and that he is the master of the forest.

Objectively speaking, nature treats man no differently from any other living creature; we have been given a different set of strengths, and cunning, to survive. Subjectively speaking, however, man is different from all other living creatures — he can imagine, and this gives him the right to domesticate nature and create culture. Culture, the world imagined and constructed by man, with the aid of Maya, is Brahmanda.

Without Maya, man would be at the mercy of nature; with Maya, man is able to dominate nature and establish culture. Maya thus elevates man from being an animal. Life is no longer about survival alone; it is about meaning. The quest for meaning provokes man into action or karma, from the root 'Kri'(to do). In the quest for meaning, man creates society. Brahma thus becomes creator.

When Vishnu is in deep slumber, he is not aware of Prakriti. That does not mean nature does not exist. It is simply not sensed. This state is described as Yoga-nidra. It is a state similar to when we are in deep slumber; we do not remember our name or anything about our life or our world. From a practical standpoint, our subjective reality does not exist. Subjective reality or Brahmanda is reborn only when we awaken, when the serpent Sesha transforms into Adi.

When awake, Vishnu observes nature just like Brahma. But unlike Brahma, he is not intimidated by Prakriti. Vishnu experiences no fear. He does not need a measuring scale to appreciate Prakriti. He sees Prakriti for what she is, without the aid of Maya, because

South Indian painting of Vishnu and his consort, Yoga-maya

he knows he is brahman. Brahma depends on Maya to survive Prakriti; Vishnu does not. Brahma is thus a slave of Maya while Vishnu is her master. Brahma needs to construct a subjective reality to make sense of existence, while Vishnu has no such need.

For Brahma, Maya is Maha-maya; he is under her spell. For Vishnu, Maya is Yoga-maya; she is under his command. That is why Vishnu is called Mayin, the great deluder.

Vishnu can, if he wishes, choose to engage with Maya. When he does, he takes the form of an avatar. For example, he can become Ram or Krishna. Both Ram and Krishna experience birth and death, like all human beings, but being realised souls, they are not afraid of Maya. Both know they are Vishnu; their identity is not dependent on any measuring scale or subjective reality.

Vishnu thus has a threefold relationship with Maya. As Narayana, he is ignorant of Maya. As Vishnu he is aware of Maya but chooses not to be under her spell, and as Vishnu's avatars, like Ram and Krishna, he willingly submits to Maya, engages with subjective realities, but is never dependent on her.

By engaging with Maya, Vishnu makes himself accessible to Brahma. As Ram and Krishna, he brings joy and breaks hearts, he participates in worldly affairs, seduces, fights, draws the jiva-atma towards him. The tangible world is the ranga-bhoomi or playground where one encounters spiritual reality. In the tangible world, Vishnu is both Mohan, the deluder, as well as Mohini, the enchantress.

There is a story of Vyasa's son, Suka. Suka refused to leave his mother's womb even after the stipulated ten lunar months had passed. His father begged him to come out and after twelve

Brahma blesses Suka-muni as he shared his wisdom with the world and encouraged everyone to realise infinity through Krishna.

The parrot-head indicates he shared with humanity exactly what his father said without any editing.

Calendar art showing Suka-muni, the parrot-headed son of Vyasa

The stories and images of Krishna aim to enchant the senses and overwhelm the emotions, thus giving value to subjective reality and worldly issues.

Temple image of Krishna as Man-mohan, the enchanter of the mind

years of coaxing, Suka finally relented, not because he wanted to experience worldly life, but because he did not want to trouble his pregnant mother anymore.

Soon after birth, rather than step on earth, he rose skywards. He did not see the point of dealing with Maha-maya, and the subjective reality she would help him construct. While in his mother's womb, he had heard his father chant hymns of the Veda. He knew the difference between Maha-maya and Yoga-maya. He was not interested in creating his Brahmanda; he preferred the truth of Prakriti. He was not interested in finite truths; he wanted to experience infinity. This meant rising to the abode of Vishnu, and becoming one with him.

As Suka rose, his father cried out, 'Come back, come back.' But Suka refused to look back. It was then that Vyasa began describing Krishna's beauty. Vyasa said, 'His lotus feet, his curly hair, his winsome eyes, his mysterious smile, the peacock feather on his crown, the sandal paste marks on his long dark limbs, his broad chest with the curl of hair in the centre, his long legs draped in fine yellow silk, the garland of forest flowers round his neck, his dolphin-shaped earrings.'

So beautiful was the description that Suka stopped midway between the earth and the sky to hear his father. As the description progressed, he longed to see Krishna; somehow bondage did not seem so terrible anymore. It was enchanting. He realised that the only way to experience what he was hearing was to surrender to Maha-Maya. Only in a limited, finite world of measurement could beauty be truly relished. Brahmanda had its value. Only in subjective reality does Krishna manifest himself.

Brahma's many heads indicate the gradual modification of the mind as it is conditioned by prejudices that comfort the mind and allay fear.

Brahma holds in his hand instruments of ritual, for Vedic rituals are said to contain the secret that will take man from a prejudiced vision towards unprejudiced vision, from fear to fearlessness.

Brahma is the creator of all measuring scales and subjective realities. He is not worshipped.

Temple wall sculpture from Belur, Karnataka, showing the many-headed Brahma

Brahma created many sons to engage with Prakriti in order to realise brahman. He encouraged his sons to marry.

Marriage is a metaphysical metaphor for engagement with material reality. Marriage results in the construction of Brahmanda. Only through marriage can Brahma and his sons access Ram and Krishna, and through them discover Vishnu, and ultimately Narayana. Marriage is thus necessary for realising spiritual reality.

Amongst Brahma's many sons was one Narada. Narada refused to marry. He did not want anything to do with the mat-erial world. Like Suka, he preferred the realm of Narayana, when time and space do not exist, where Maya casts no spell. He went a step further; he encouraged Brahma's other sons to stay celibate like him. He did not see the point of engaging with Prakriti. He did not understand the point of constructing Brahmanda.

Many of Brahma's sons agreed with Narada. They also refused to marry. This happened several times, until an enraged Brahma cursed Narada, 'You will stay trapped in the material world until you appreciate the value of Maya.'

Narada went to Vishnu and asked him the meaning of Maya. In response, Vishnu said, 'I will explain after you quench my thirst. Go fetch me some water.'

Narada went to a river to fetch water. But as he was collecting the water, he saw a beautiful girl. He was so drawn to her that he followed her to her village and asked her father for her hand in marriage. The father agreed and the two got married. Before long, Narada was a father and then grandfather and then great grandfather. Narada felt content. Suddenly one day, it rained. And the rains refused to stop. The river swelled and broke its banks. Water rushed into Narada's house, and to his horror, swept away his

Popular modern images of Narada with his lute

wife, his children, his grandchildren and his great grandchildren. He screamed and shouted for help as the water dragged him under. Suddenly he was pulled up. He found himself in Vaikuntha beside Vishnu.

'Narada,' said Vishnu, 'where is my water? I am still thirsty.' Narada did not understand. Where was his family, his wife's village, the river?

'Where does this pain and suffering come from, Narada?' asked Vishnu with a smile. 'I thought you had full knowledge of Maya before you set out to fetch water for me.'

Narada bowed his head in realisation. He knew Maya but had never experienced Maya. Brahma was encouraging his sons to marry so that they could experience Maya. Knowledge of Maya is not experience of Maya. Unless one experiences Maya, one will not be able to empathise with those who are trapped in Maya.

Said Vishnu, 'You knew all about measuring scales and subjective realities. Yet you forgot all about them as soon as you experienced material pleasure — home, family, children, and village. Your understanding of Maya and Brahmanda could have helped you in the tumult of pleasure and pain, but it did not. Such is the spell of Maya. Now that you have experienced Maya, I want you to go and meet people, shake up their measuring scales, challenge their subjective realities, until they realise that the only way out of Maya is seeking answers outside material reality. I want you to provoke them into following the spiritual path.'

That is why Narada is renowned in Hindu mythology as a trouble-maker. He disturbs the equilibrium of a happy material life, spreads turmoil through comparison and gossip. Once, Narada came to Krishna's house. Krishna's wives offered him a gift. 'I want

A woodblock print from Bengal showing Krishna being weighed

you to give me Krishna,' said Narada. The wives were shocked by the request and naturally reluctant, but they could not go back on their promise. 'Then, in that case, offer me something that is equal to Krishna in weight.' A measuring balance was brought and Krishna was made to sit on one pan. On the other pan, one of the wives, Satyabhama, placed all the gold she possessed. Despite the vast quantity of gold, Krishna's pan remained lower, revealing that there is more to life than wealth. Then another of Krishna's wives, Rukmini, placed a sprig of the tulsi plant from her courtyard on top of the gold. It was the symbol of a devotee's love for Krishna. Instantly, Krishna's pan rose up, thus revealing that what matters more in life is not possession but affection. A person who is loved is always happier than a person with wealth. Thus, Narada's mischief led to wisdom even in Krishna's household.

Whenever Narada arrives on the scene, he does two things: he ignites a conflict and then chants 'Narayana, Narayana.' Conflict stems from things material and measurable, hence in the realm of Maya. Most people get embroiled in the conflict and pay no regard to the chant. The few who do listen to the chant surrender to a power that is indifferent to Maya: Narayana. This results in peace, realisation of brahman and entry into Vishnu's paradise, Vaikuntha.

In the many tales of mythology, Brahma never makes the journey out of Brahmanda into Vaikuntha. He convinces himself that his subjective reality is objective reality. He ends up trying to control the world. Rather than looking beyond pleasure and pain, he works towards enhancing pleasure and reducing pain. He gets trapped in his own delusion. The material world stops being a medium, it

Tulsi plants growing in a courtyard

becomes the destination. Brahma spends all his life securing his own version of reality. He does everything in his power to defend his measuring scale.

Brahma forgets Brahmanda is his creation. He forgets Maya is also his creation. He forgets Prakriti is his mother. Instead he seeks to control reality, dominate her, and make her dance to his whims. But Prakriti cannot be controlled by Brahma. The story goes that Brahma tries to get Shatarupa to dance to his whims. In other words, he tries to establish his control over Brahmanda. But the goddess runs away.

Brahma pursues her, desperate to possess and control her. It is a futile effort that he refuses to abandon. This Brahma, who chases Brahmanda, under the spell of Maya, is the unenlightened man, who seeks control over material reality, who seeks to dominate the world around him, seeks to make it function according to his whims. This is Brahma, the creator of all measuring scales and subjective realities, who is never worshipped.

In his obsession, Brahma sprouts many heads. The many heads of Brahma represent the gradual crumpling of human consciousness as it becomes increasingly contaminated by prejudices and conditioning. Finally, Brahma sprouts the fifth head, his own imaginary understanding of who he is. This is Brahma's self-image. It makes him demand significance in the world that he has created. Sometimes called the ego, this fifth head of Brahma is destroyed by Shiva.

Shiva rejects Brahma's infatuation with material reality and beheads him. Shiva is therefore called Kapalika, the beheader. Shiva is Bhairava, the conqueror of fear. He liberates Brahma from

Stone image showing Shiva and Vishnu merged into one,
a form known as Hara-Hari

fear. But he does not stop there. He reverses the process started by the blooming of the lotus from Vishnu's navel.

Without his head, Brahma stops seeing nature. There is no imagination, no measuring scale, no subjective reality. There is no karma. There is no growth. There is nothing. There is a return to the dreamless slumber of Narayana. There is Sesha, zero. A return to entropy! No movement, only stillness. No sound, only silence.

Brahma, Vishnu and Shiva are the three aspects of spiritual reality. These three aspects of the spiritual engage with material reality in three different ways. Brahma is spiritual reality trying to find himself through material reality. Brahma creates measuring scales and subjective realities in his quest of self-realisation but ends up getting attached to it. Vishnu facilitates Brahma's liberation by celebrating the material world while Shiva facilitates Brahma's liberation by rejecting the material world.

Vishnu's way is called pravritti-marga or outward-looking path while Shiva's way is called nivritti-marga or the inward-looking path. Vishnu plays with Maya, without getting overwhelmed by her, while Shiva rejects her totally. Vishnu is therefore a more worldly form of the divine, a king and a warrior and a lover, while Shiva is a more monastic form of the divine, a hermit, who shuts his eyes to all things worldly.

Shiva shuts his eyes to the material world. He refuses to engage with Prakriti. In mythological narratives, he withholds all heat inside his being so that he becomes a pillar of fire. Around him nothing moves or flows. Water becomes snow. All things become still. The world ceases to be. When Kama, the god of love, tries to strike an arrow of desire in his direction, he opens his third eye, releases a missile of fire and reduces Kama to ashes.

A Kerala mural of Vishnu as the voluptuous Mohini

Shiva needs to open his eyes to material reality. He needs to be seduced. And so, Vishnu takes the form of an enchantress. He becomes Mohini and dances before Shiva. Shiva is compelled to open his eyes and look at Mohini. He recognises Mohini is Vishnu. She is spiritual reality cloaked in material reality. She is Vishnu playing with Prakriti and Maya. She is Vishnu in full control of time and space and subjective realities. Immersed in brahman, she is inviting spiritual reality to enter her playground, rangabhoomi, and join the game of material reality, the leela.

# 2. Matsya's Secret

*Only humans can empathise, and exploit*

A saint with the mark of Vishnu

Image of a temple gate

*T*he sacred mark of Vishnu is always worn on the forehead, perhaps to draw attention to the one thing that distinguishes humans from animals: the larger brain.

The larger brain, especially the frontal brain, enables humans to imagine. Imagination allows us to conjure up a better world where we are not at the mercy of the elements. Imagination inspires us. We are driven to realise what we imagine. We inquire about the elements, and means to control it or improve upon it. We work towards creating technologies that will empower us to look beyond survival. In other words, it is this larger brain that compels us to create culture.

This larger brain transforms Pashu or animal into Purusha or human. It creates Brahma who seeks brahman. The larger brain is the physical manifestation of spiritual reality. It is born of Vishnu so that we can realise Vishnu.

Because humans have manas, the ability to imagine, humans are called Manavas. The first human is called Manu. The first story in the lore of Vishnu tells us how Vishnu engages with Manu in the form of a fish.

While Manu is performing his ablutions in a river, a fish approaches him and says, 'Save me from the big fish, and one day I will save you.' This request of the fish seems insignificant until one is informed that, in Hindu mythology, the phrase 'big fish eating small fish' refers to matsya nyaya, or the law of the fishes, which is jungle law.

That Vishnu first takes the form of a fish to engage with humankind is no coincidence. It is a deliberate attempt to draw

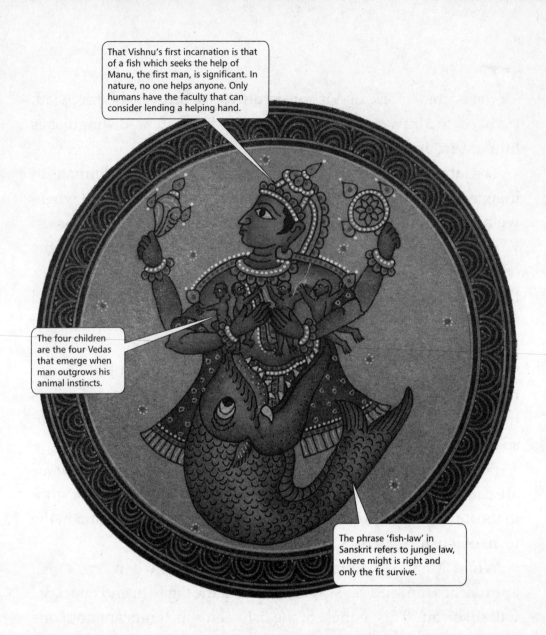

Mysore painting of Vishnu's fish incarnation

attention to the jungle law — a law that only humans can overturn.

In the jungle, there are no rules. Only the fit survive and might is right. Might here does not mean physical strength, it also means intellectual strength. One can use one's strength and cunning in any way to survive. There is no right or wrong, no appropriate or inappropriate conduct. Anything goes as one fends for oneself. A goat is allowed to chomp on tender fresh grass. A lion is allowed to eat the goat. A wounded lion is abandoned and left to fend for itself. A hawk is allowed to swoop down and eat a snake that is just about to lay its eggs. A hyena is allowed to attack a doe in the middle of childbirth. Humans may judge animals as being cruel and insensitive, but animals do not see themselves this way. All their actions are driven by the need to survive. They do not judge the appropriateness of their actions. In fact they do not judge at all, because they cannot.

Of all living creatures, only humans can imagine a world where might is not right. Where the tiger and the goat live in harmony, where the hawk and serpent are friends. From this imagination comes the notion of heaven — the paradise of perfection. Desire to create this paradise of perfection provokes man into creating culture.

Manu does what no other creature can do. He responds to the cry of the little fish, collects it in the palm of his hand and puts it in a small pot. In other words, Manu interferes with nature. This interference has its roots in empathy. Manu feels the fear of the little fish and does something to allay it. The presence of Manu transforms nature. The little pot in which the fish is kept represents culture, a man-made creation, where the little fish is safe from the big fish.

Mysore painting of Matsya, Vishnu's first incarnation

It is this emotion and action that enables man to create society, a world where jungle law is challenged, where the mighty take care of the meek, where the weak are given opportunities by the strong. The thought that creates this secure world is called dharma, from the root 'Dhr' which means 'to make secure' or 'to bind'.

Dharma thus is an artificial construct. One can argue that Dharma is what is natural to man. In overturning matsya nyaya lies purusha-artha, the validation of human existence. That is why humans were created. So long as we follow jungle law, we are pashu or animals. Only when we rise above it and start establishing dharma do we become purusha or human.

Manu's water pot that contains the fish is Manu's property, his to give to the fish. The notion of property reminds us that, fundamentally, Manu is still animal and relies on the notion of territory.

In nature, animals have territory. They mark it by spraying their urine. This territory ensures the animal has enough to eat. The territory also ensures that the animal has exclusive rights on a mate, so that it can reproduce and create the next generation. Territory is critical to the survival of the beast. If another animal seeks access to this territory, it has to contend with the previous master. And in keeping with the laws of the jungle, the contention is usually violent.

But Manu's notion of property is quite different from an animal's notion of territory. Territory cannot be inherited. Territory cannot be bequeathed. One has to fight for territory. No rules and laws protect it. Without territory, animals will not survive.

Human property is not just about need. At one extreme, human

Kerala mural of a king

property is based on compassion — to provide for more and more people, even unrelated people, like the fish, for example, that Manu provides for. This compassion stems from empathy, imagination of other people's fear. At the other extreme, human property is based on greed — to hoard more and more for oneself, even when there is no immediate need. This greed stems from fear, an imagination of scarcity that is unique to humans. In greed, we exploit the earth's resources. We also exploit fellow human beings. Thus property has its roots in imagination. When the imagination leads to empathy, property becomes inclusive; this is dharma. When the imagination amplifies fear and supports exploitation, property becomes exclusive; this is adharma.

Animals give up territory only when forced to but humans have the ability to give up property voluntarily. This is made explicit in the Ramayana, an epic which tells the story of Ram, a form of Vishnu that walked the earth.

In the Ramayana, the Rakshasa-king Ravana drives his half-brother Kubera, the Yaksha-king, out of Lanka and claims the island-city as his own. Ram, however, is more than willing to let his brother, Bharata, become king of his kingdom, Ayodhya. When asked by his father to give up his claim to the throne in favour of his younger brother, Ram does so willingly, without hesitation or regret. Ram is therefore identified with dharma while Ravana is identified with adharma. Ram realises his human potential, which makes him God, Bhagavan, worthy of worship. Ravana fails to realise his human potential, which makes him Rakshasa, a demon, unworthy of respect.

Mysore painting showing Vali and Sugriva fighting

The fish grows in size and so Manu transfers it from a small pot to a bigger pot. The fish keeps getting bigger and to accommodate it, out of compassion for the poor creature, Manu keeps providing it with bigger and bigger pots.

In the Ramayana, two monkeys fight over territory, the kingdom of Kishkinda. They are two brothers, Vali and Sugriva, the sons of Riksha. The two brothers are supposed to share the kingdom, but following a misunderstanding, Vali drives his brother Sugriva out of the kingdom. Vali even forcibly claims Sugriva's wife, Ruma, for himself. When Vishnu descends on earth as Ram, he interferes in this fight between the alpha male, Vali, and the contender, Sugriva. While the two brothers fight, Ram shoots an arrow from behind a bush and strikes Vali dead. Vali protests. 'This is against dharma,' he says. Ram argues that a monkey who lives by the law of the jungle must die by the law of the jungle.

Vali has no right to quote the rules of dharma because dharma is based on sharing property, on inclusion not exclusion. Vali behaved like an animal when he refused to share his kingdom and when he forcibly deprived his brother of the kingdom and his wife; Sugriva was therefore entitled to use cunning to deprive his brother of his life. The law of the jungle is a valid option in the realm of adharma.

With Vali dead, Sugriva becomes lord of Kishkinda. Ram now demands that Sugriva follow dharma and appoint Vali's son, Angad, as his heir. In the animal world, when the alpha male takes over, it kills the children of the overthrown leader. Dharma must, however, be rooted in compassion. Ram demands Sugriva change: if Vali followed matsya nyaya, Sugriva must follow dharma. Vali saw Kishkinda as territory and refused to share; Sugriva must see Kishkinda as property and pass it on to his erstwhile rival's son.

Mughal painting showing Shibi saving a dove from a hawk

Thus the pot of Ram, containing dharma, once limited to Ayodhya, now expands to include Kishkinda.

The desire for the larger pot can also indicate a lack of sensitivity and a lack of contentment. As more of the forest is domesticated and turned into fields to provide for human society, more and more of nature is destroyed for culture. Human laws tend to include some and exclude some and in doing so push nature to its limits. This is evident in the following story from the Mahabharata.

A king called Shibi, in compassion, rescues a dove being chased by a hawk. The hawk asks the king, 'What will I eat now?' The king suggests he eat another dove. The hawk retorts, 'So that you can indulge your compassion for this dove, you are willing to sacrifice another dove. Is that fair?' The king then asks the hawk to eat a rat or a serpent. 'Why should they die so that the dove can live?' This question has no answer.

In being kind to the dove, the king is being cruel to the hawk. The king has included the dove but excluded the hawk. Why should the dove be saved? Why should the hawk be made to starve? These questions, which have no answers, challenge the human construct of society.

Man creates society as he pursues his imagination of paradise, a place where all creatures are safe. However, in the process, he creates a world where some are more safe than others. Human society invariably favours a few over others. Culture is thus always imperfect. Vishnu lore always draws attention to this truism, for Vishnu is a worldly god and knows that seeking answers by controlling material reality will never be satisfactory.

In the Mahabharata, the Pandavas seek to build a city in the

Balarama, like his brother Krishna, wears fabric made of cotton and silk. To get cotton one needs to farm. To establish a farm one has to destroy a forest. To get silk one needs to kill silkworms to claim their cocoon. Thus culture favours humans at the cost of nature.

Mysore painting of Balarama

Balarama's plough indicates his association with farming activities.

The dragging of Yamuna is suggestive of canal-building, a violent activity that results in the destruction of riverbanks but irrigates fields and orchards.

Pahari miniature showing Balarama and Yamuna

forest given to them by their uncle. The only way to do this is by burning down the forest. Vishnu in the form of Krishna encourages them to do so. As the forest burns, the birds and the beasts of the forest try to run away to save themselves only to be shot down by arrows released by the Pandavas at the behest of Krishna. This reeks of cruelty until one realises that until the forest is burnt, a field cannot be established. Culture is built on the destruction of a natural ecosystem.

In the *Bhagavata Purana*, Krishna's elder brother, Balarama, also a form of Vishnu, wants the river Yamuna to come to him so that he can bathe without making the effort to go to the river. The river-goddess refuses to come to him. Enraged, Balarama grabs the river-goddess by her hair and forces her to come to him. In some versions, he uses his plough to hook her side and bring her to where he is. The act is described in extremely violent terms, for material reality has been subjugated with force against her will. The story alludes to the practice of canal irrigation, which is not natural. It entails the destruction of riverbanks and with it the destruction of many animals that may have depended on an intact riverbank for their survival.

Manu's motivation may be noble, but it includes only the fish in the pot, not the other fishes outside. Thus, what begins as empathy for one ends up becoming rather exclusive — lack of empathy for the rest.

Humans can never include everybody. Plants and animals are excluded if they do not serve the needs of society. Crops are included, weeds are not. Domesticated animals are welcomed but wild animals are shunned. People whose points of view align

Stone carving of fish

with ours are included; the rest are excluded. Society will always exclude somebody. And this exclusion eventually claims a huge price.

So the fish gets bigger and bigger, utilising all the resources provided by Manu, and Manu keeps transferring it to bigger pots to satisfy its ever-growing needs. At no point does Manu think the fish can fend for itself and so he does not bother to throw the fish back into the sea. At no point does the fish think it can fend for itself and ask Manu to throw it back into the sea. The fish in the pot gradually becomes dependent on Manu and displays no desire to be independent. Eventually the fish has to be put in a pond, then a larger pond, then a lake and finally a river. A point comes in the story when dark clouds gather overhead and it rains relentlessly. The sea begins to swell and swallow the earth. It is Pralaya, death of the world.

This is what happens when human society becomes so focussed on itself that it loses touch with the rest of nature, when culture expands at the cost of everything else, when the needs of culture override the needs of nature. Eventually something will snap. Nature will strike back.

At first Manu wonders why he is suffering even though he spent his life doing a noble deed: caring for the small fish. He blames the rain and curses the sea. But then realisation dawns.

This is not explicitly stated in the scriptures as Manu is the reader of the tale. Manu is all of humanity. This wisdom has to be figured out by the story-listener, not communicated by the story-teller.

Manu realises that his obsession with the small fish is the cause of the great calamity. This obsession made him insensitive to the fact that the fish had grown and could take care of itself.

Miniature painting showing Vishnu killing Panchajana, the conch-shell demon

Miniature painting of Manu's ship being towed by the horned fish

He became insensitive to the consequences of his action on the rest of the world. Every action has a reaction that one is bound to experience. This is the law of karma. Just as society is created by an act of compassion, when Manu saves the fish, society is destroyed when the compassion becomes exclusive, and fails to include all of nature. When Manu realises this, he takes responsibility for his role in Pralaya. It is then that the fish reappears before Manu. This time, the fish has a horn on his forehead.

Why a horn on his forehead? Is it to direct Manu towards his larger brain, that source of imagination, that root of empathy and exploitation? The horn is very much like the vertical mark of Vishnu, reminding Manu that life is about growth. Manu grew from animal to human when he saved the fish; but he was unable to make the move from human to divine when he focused exclusively on the fish, and became too insensitive to include the rest. While there was material growth, indicated by the larger pots, there was no emotional and intellectual growth to realise that he has to expand his vision to include all.

The horned fish guides Manu to build a boat, much like the Biblical Noah's ark. The fish asks Manu to tie the boat to his horn using the serpent Adi-Ananta-Sesha. The fish then tows the ship to safety to Mount Meru, the centre of the world. When the waters recede, an enlightened Manu saved by the fish and its horn starts the world anew.

In some versions of the story, a demon called Panchajana steals the Veda and hides at the bottom of the sea as Pralaya claims the earth. Vishnu in the form of a fish defeats the demons, rescues the

Photograph of Shalagrama stones, considered a form of Vishnu

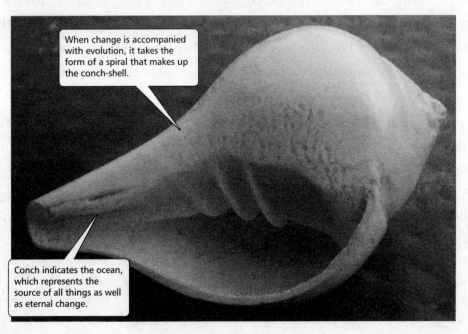

Photograph of a conch-shell

Vedas and hands them over to Manu. Having killed the demon, Vishnu turns the conch-shell in which the demon had hidden into a trumpet called Panchajanya. This Vishnu blows so that everyone hears the secret of the Veda.

And what is this secret? In nature, all plants and animals move cyclically and predictably. They have no choice but to stay within this wheel. But humans have the power to break this cycle, turn the wheel into a spiral that winds outwards and inwards. The break in trajectory happens when humans break free from fear, empathise, follow dharma and transcend animal instincts to realise divinity.

The spirals of the conch-shell, sacred to Vishnu, are reminders of this unique human possibility.

# 3. Kurma's Secret

*Wealth eludes the insecure*

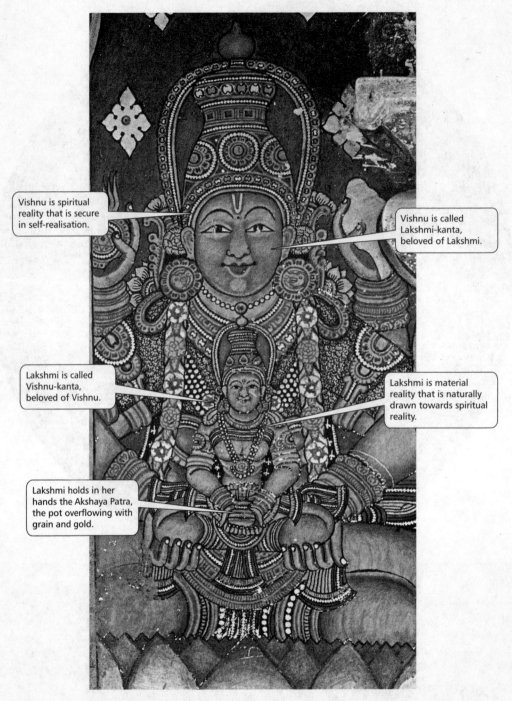

Vishnu is spiritual reality that is secure in self-realisation.

Vishnu is called Lakshmi-kanta, beloved of Lakshmi.

Lakshmi is called Vishnu-kanta, beloved of Vishnu.

Lakshmi is material reality that is naturally drawn towards spiritual reality.

Lakshmi holds in her hands the Akshaya Patra, the pot overflowing with grain and gold.

Kerala mural showing Lakshmi in the arms of Vishnu

*L*akshmi is the goddess of wealth. She is described as dressed in red, bedecked with gold, seated on a lotus, holding a pot overflowing with grain and gold. Everyone worships her as she provides sustenance to all beings. She is the food that we eat, the clothes that we wear, the house that we live in. Without her, we cannot survive.

Lakshmi does not discriminate. A bowl of rice will satisfy a saint and a sinner. A blanket will provide the same warmth to a king or a beggar. A house will equally shelter a man or a woman.

But Lakshmi is restless. She never stays in one place for long. And no one knows what makes her move. Some describe her as cockeyed; one may think she is going in one direction but then she ends up going somewhere else.

Since wealth in its most primal form, metal and plants, comes from under the ground, Lakshmi is described in scriptures as Patala-Nivasini, she who lives in Patala. 'Pa' means foot and 'tala' means below. Lakshmi is thus the resident of subterranean realms. This is the realm of the Asuras.

Asuras are the grandchildren of Brahma. Their father is Kashyapa and their mother is Diti. For humans, who seek access to wealth, Asuras are demons who withhold Lakshmi under the earth. Humans worship Devas who they declare as gods because they help release Lakshmi and draw her to the surface out of her subterranean prison. Devas are the half-brothers of the Asuras. They have the same grandfather, Brahma, and the same father, Kashyapa, but a different mother, Aditi.

The leader of the Devas is Indra, who strikes clouds and brings

In Kubera's hand is a mongoose that spits jewels.

Stone image of Kubera, king of Yakshas

Yakshini holds a child in her arms, indicating the earth's fertility.

Yaksha holds a bag of gems and coins in his hand, indicating subterranean mineral wealth.

Stone image of a Yaksha with a Yakshini

rain. He is both sky-god and rain-god. His brothers are Agni, the fire-god, who sits on the ground; Vayu, the wind-god, who moves between the earth and the sky; Surya and Chandra, the sun-god and the moon-god, who reside in the sky. His guru is Brihaspati, lord of the planet Jupiter, associated with rationality and mathematics.

Brihaspati performs a yagna for Indra, giving him the power to draw Lakshmi from under the earth. Agni and Vayu melt rocks and release metal. The wind and the sun and the rain draw plants from under the earth.

Stories of Devas killing Asuras are thus stories of Lakshmi's release from subterranean confinement. That is why the acts of mining, hunting, fishing, farming and harvesting, which generate wealth, are so violent. Unless the rock is broken, metal cannot be released. Unless the grain is threshed, grain will not be released. In other words, for Lakshmi to be obtained, Asuras need to be killed.

For Indra, Lakshmi is Sachi, his wife. But for Asuras, she is Pulomi, daughter of Puloman, their king. She is also Bhargavi, daughter of their guru, Bhrigu, also known as Shukra, lord of the planet Venus, associated with intuition and creativity. Considering the close association of Lakshmi and the Asuras, it is not surprising that the abode of Asuras is Hiranyapura, or the city of gold.

Lakshmi is also associated with other 'demonic' subterranean and wild creatures like Yakshas and Rakshasas. Yakshas live near water bodies and are visualised as misshapen beasts. The king of Yakshas is Kubera, who is sometimes described as a treasurer of the gods, hoarding wealth and keeping a count of every penny. Kubera built the golden city of Lanka, which was usurped by his brother, Ravana, king of the Rakshasas.

Wood carving of Indra, king of the Devas

When Lakshmi sits beside Indra as Sachi, Indra's city of Amravati, located above the sky, transforms into Swarga, or paradise. It houses Kalpataru, the wish-fulfilling tree, Kamadhenu, the wish-fulfilling cow, and Chintamani, the wish-fulfilling gem. All this wealth should make Indra, secure and happy. But it makes him insecure. He fears Sachi will leave his side and choose someone more worthy to be her husband.

King Sagara once performed the Ashwamedha yagna. This involved letting loose the royal horse and following it with one's army. All the land that the horse traversed unchallenged came under the king's rule. King Sagara was so powerful that no king dared stop his horse. As a result he was on his way to becoming Chakravarti, ruler of the circular horizon, meaning the ruler of the whole world. He would then be powerful enough to overthrow Indra. An insecure Indra stole the horse and hid it in the hermitage of a Rishi called Kapila. Sagara's sons found the horse and accused Kapila of theft. Kapila glanced at them so angrily that they all burst into flames. Having thus lost his sons, Sagara lost all interest in his yagna. And Indra felt safe.

Another time, a Rishi called Kandu was busy performing tapasya. This was a practice involving the control of the five senses so as to generate inner heat or tapa. With this tapa, Kandu would have the power to control nature, manipulate it to his whims. Indra feared that if Kandu was successful in his practice, he would overthrow him. To prevent such an eventuality, he sent an Apsara called Pramlocha to seduce Kandu. Pramlocha was successful in her quest. Such was the passion of her lovemaking that Kandu lost sense of time; a hundred years seemed like one night. When Kandu finally recovered his senses, he realised he had been

Cambodian temple carving showing Indra on elephants

beguiled by the nymph on Indra's instruction and he could do nothing about it.

Indra does not trust Sachi, because he does not trust himself, and he does not trust himself because he does not know himself. Like Brahma, he is not aware of spiritual reality. Thus he is plagued by ideas of impermanence and mortality.

To distract himself from his fears, Indra immerses himself in pleasure and becomes a hedonist. Sachi eventually runs away, not because she is attracted to another king or sage, but because she is repelled by Indra's behaviour.

Once, the Rishi Durvasa, known for his temper, offers Indra a garland of beautiful lotus flowers. But Indra, surrounded by damsels, and in a state of intoxication, takes the garland and simply tosses it on the floor, allowing it to be trampled by his elephant, Airavata. Enraged, Durvasa curses Indra, 'You will lose it all — the wish-fulfilling tree, the wish-fulfilling cow, and the wish-fulfilling gem. Lakshmi will slip out of this realm.' And that is precisely what happens.

In other stories, misfortune follows after Indra angers his guru, Brihaspati, with his insolence. One way or the other, Indra always loses his fortune, and he is always to blame for it, no one else.

With Lakshmi gone, a mortified Indra rushes to his father, Brahma. 'Help me bring her back,' he cries. But Brahma does not know how to help the Devas. He advises them to seek the help of Vishnu. And Vishnu says, 'The goddess has dissolved herself in the ocean of milk. Churn her out. Use the king of the mountains, Mandara, as the churning staff. And use the king of serpents, Vasuki, as the churning rope.' In other variants of this tale, the

The turtle is patient enough to witness alternative victories of Devas and Asuras, and of Nagas and Garudas.

That the second incarnation of Vishnu is amphibious while the first incarnation of Vishnu, the fish, is aquatic, suggests an ancient understanding of evolution.

Mysore painting of Kurma, the turtle form of Vishnu

Temples dedicated to Kurma avatar are rare; one is located in Karnataka (Gavirangapura) and another in Andhra Pradesh (Srikurmam).

A rare image of Kurma worshipped in a temple at the village of Gavirangapura, Karnataka

churning staff is Meru, the axis of space, and the churning rope is Adi-Ananta-Sesha, the serpent of time.

The Devas try to carry the king of the mountains, but Mandara is too heavy even for all of them put together. They try to drag out the king of serpents from the subterranean realms, but Vasuki refuses to budge. So they beg Vishnu to help. Vishnu tells his hawk, the mighty Garuda, to pick up the mountain and pull out the snake and bring them to the ocean of milk. 'But how will the spindle stay afloat. Mandara will surely sink to the bottom of the ocean,' cry the Devas. To their astonishment, they find a giant turtle called Kurma, rising up to the surface of the sea. It is none other than Vishnu. Garuda places Mandara on Kurma's back and then winds Vasuki around the mountain. The churn is ready.

The Devas start churning the ocean of milk. But they lack the strength to serve as the force and counterforce. Vishnu advises them, 'You need to take the help of your half-brothers, the Asuras. You hold the tail of Vasuki and serve as the force of the churn. Make the Asuras hold the neck of Vasuki and serve as the counterforce.'

Though born of the same father, the Devas and the Asuras hate each other. The Asuras feel Lakshmi belongs under the earth and the Devas feel she belongs above. But with her disappearance, both have no choice but to cooperate and bring her out. And so the Asuras join the Devas and agree to serve as the counterforce of the churn.

The churning starts in earnest. When the Devas pull, the Asuras relax and when the Asuras pull, the Devas relax. By placing them as the force and counterforce, Vishnu successfully makes two opposing sides work towards a common goal.

Calendar image of Kurma, the turtle form of Vishnu

But the exercise is not an easy one. It involves a great deal of time and a great deal of effort. The Devas and the Asuras have to work as never before.

Milk is a common metaphor in Hindu narratives. It represents the material world full of possibilities. But to get the best out of milk, it has to be churned. It has to be turned into butter and finally clarified to make ghee. The whole process involves a lot of effort. In Vishnu temples, Vishnu always demands butter and ghee, unlike Shiva who is content with raw unboiled milk, for Vishnu is the God who celebrates the best the material world has to offer, while Shiva is God who is indifferent to material reality. Lakshmi is the best that the material world has to offer. Vishnu celebrates her.

Eventually, as butter rises when milk is churned, the ocean of milk begins to spew out its many treasures. There is the flying horse, Ucchaishrava, and the white-skinned elephant with seven trunks, Airavata. There is the Parijata tree, another name for Kalpataru, and there is Kamadhenu and there is Chintamani, also known as Kaustubha. There is the nymph called Rambha and wine called Varuni.

All these are the treasures that once adorned Indra's Swarga. Significant amongst these are Rambha and Varuni, women and wine. It is these indulgences that cost Indra his fortune and yet the scriptures acknowledge that these are pleasures that are very much a part of worldly life. Ancient texts are not embarrassed by sensual pleasures. They appreciate their value but also warn of the dangers of overindulgence. Thus Indra's Swarga is a place where women dance and wine flows, and it is precisely these luxuries that make Indra lose his sensibility.

The horse and the elephant represent dharma, or righteous

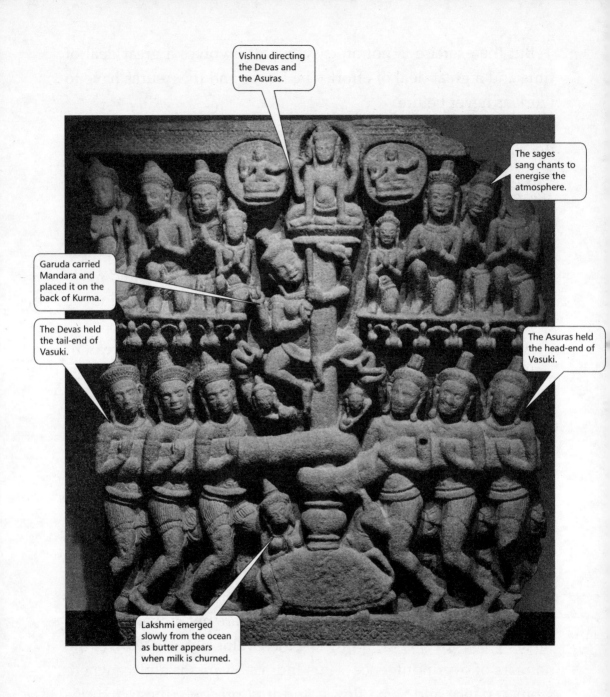

Cambodian temple wall sculpture showing the churning of the ocean of milk

conduct. The tree, the cow and the gem represent artha, or wealth. The nymph and the wine represent kama or pleasure. Thus from the ocean came righteous conduct and wealth and pleasure. These are the gifts of the ocean. These are the gifts that announced the arrival of Lakshmi, the goddess of wealth.

As soon as Lakshmi rises, everyone gets excited. She is draped in a red sari, covered with jewels and seated on a lotus. In her hand is the Akshaya Patra, the vessel that is eternally overflowing with grain and gold. The Devas and the Asuras sing praises to this beautiful and enchanting goddess. White elephants that reside in the cardinal and ordinal directions rush to welcome her; they raise their trunks and sprinkle her with fragrant water.

Everyone waits with bated breath to see where Lakshmi will go. Will she be the wife of the Devas or the daughter of the Asuras? But to everyone's surprise, she moves towards Vishnu and garlands him, thereby declaring him her husband.

The Asuras want Lakshmi, so do the Devas, but Lakshmi wants Vishnu who does not yearn for her. This is significant. Why does Lakshmi choose Vishnu? Because Vishnu is enterprising — he designs the churn and gets enemies to work together. She also selects him because he is detached from the entire enterprise. He helps the Devas but does not seek the treasures the ocean has to offer.

Vishnu knows he is spiritual reality, brahman, infinite and immortal, and hence knows the truth about Lakshmi who is material reality. He does not derive any significance from her but knows she enables him to understand himself. Therefore he does not attempt to control her. Instead, he enjoys her whimsical nature. His knowledge of Lakshmi makes him smile.

North Indian miniature painting showing Lakshmi flanked by
two elephants pouring water on her

A temple sculpture from Belur, Karnataka,
showing Lakshmi seated on Vishnu's thigh

In the Ramayana, Ram does not lose his composure when he is asked to leave the palace and live in the forest. He is as much at peace in the palace as he is in the forest. He does not derive his identity from material reality. This quality of Vishnu makes him attractive to Lakshmi. Vishnu is therefore called Shri-nivasa or Shri-vatsa, which means abode of Lakshmi. He is Lakshmi-vallabha or Lakshmi-kanta, which means the beloved of Lakshmi. He is Shri-natha or Thiru-pati, which means he who is the lord of Lakshmi. He does not chase her, but she always follows him.

In art, Vishnu is shown sleeping on the coils of the serpent Adi-Ananta-Sesha, who floats on the ocean of milk. Lakshmi sits at his feet, massaging his legs, demure and domesticated. This is totally unlike her character. Lakshmi is a flamboyant goddess who goes where she wills. Neither the Devas nor the Asuras, who fight to possess her, can control her. There is something about Vishnu that makes her willingly surrender her autonomy. He does not seek her and this is precisely why she wants to follow him and serve him. Vishnu is therefore Shrivatsa, the one whose abode is Lakshmi. Where he is, so is she.

Lakshmi has a sister, Alakshmi. She is the goddess of strife. Whenever wealth enters a house, so does Lakshmi's sister, causing quarrels. Alakshmi is the chaff of the grain that is Lakshmi. Alakshmi is the pollutant that accompanies the metal that is Lakshmi. Alakshmi is the skin and seed that cannot be eaten of the juicy fruit pulp that is Lakshmi. The two always come together. So when Lakshmi rises from the ocean of milk, so does Alakshmi, in the form of Halahal, a terrible poison.

Black viscid scum fills the air with a putrid stench. Light

Poster art from Bengal showing an owl seated beside Lakshmi

disappears and the Devas and the Asuras choke as vile fumes envelope everything in sight. 'Save us,' they cry to Vishnu.

Vishnu immediately invokes Shiva, the God whose indifference enables him to accept all that which everyone rejects. Everyone accepts Lakshmi and yearns for the wonderful gifts that accompany her, but no one accepts Halahal. Someone has to accept Halahal, otherwise it will destroy the world. So Shiva is summoned and Shiva consumes Halahal in one gulp.

In some folk narratives, Alakshmi emerges from Halahal and demands she be given a husband. If Vishnu has accepted Lakshmi, someone must accept her. Since neither the Devas nor the Asuras want her, she is given to the only one who has no preferences or prejudices. Shiva!

Some scholars are of the opinion that Alakshmi represents wild and undomesticated Kali. Others believe that Alakshmi and Lakshmi together embody Prakriti. Lakshmi is the desirable aspect of nature, while Alakshmi is the undesirable aspect of nature. If Lakshmi is love, then Alakshmi is conflict. If Lakshmi is alluring nourishment, then Alakshmi is venomous pollution. One cannot exist without the other. The difference between the two is created by Maya. Vishnu does not see the difference. He embraces Lakshmi in her totality, with Alakshmi. He knows what is the place of Lakshmi and what is the place of Alakshmi. He knows that Alakshmi must never be ignored or disregarded.

What distinguishes Vishnu from Shiva is that Vishnu is a very discerning form of God, unlike Shiva. Shiva takes no sides; he neither loves nor hates the Devas or the Asuras. By consuming Halahal, he saves both Devas and Asuras. Vishnu, by contrast,

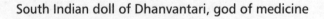

The wheel and conch-shell in Dhanvantari's hands are reminders that he is a form of Vishnu.

The pot contains Amrita, the nectar of immortality.

Dhanvantari holds a leech in his hand; leeches are used by Ayurvedic doctors to clean wounds and suck out impurities from blood.

South Indian doll of Dhanvantari, god of medicine

takes the side of the Devas and nowhere is this more evident than in the story of Amrita.

Amrita is the nectar of immortality. And it is the final treasure to emerge from the ocean of milk after Lakshmi and Halahal. It emerges from the sea in the arms of a deity called Dhanvantari, the god of health and healing. He is the god of Ayurveda, which is the traditional Indian medicine.

Dhanvantari is a form of Vishnu. Like Vishnu he holds a conchshell trumpet and a wheel, but what distinguishes him from Vishnu is the pot of nectar in one hand and the leech that he holds in another. This leech is used by those who practise Ayurveda to drain pus from infected ulcers. Sometimes, instead of the bowl of Amrita, he is shown holding herbs in his hand or a pestle and mortar to make pastes and ointments.

Everybody wants Amrita, the nectar of immortality. All the children of Brahma, whether they are 'gods' or 'demons', fear death. Everyone wants to live forever. So both the Devas and the Asuras rush to grab the pot of nectar. The partnership that helped the churning collapses. A fight ensues, each one claiming full right over the nectar. Everyone agrees that all those who churned the ocean have a right to the nectar, but who shall drink first? The Devas and the Asuras do not trust each other.

Vishnu then takes the form of Mohini and appears before the Devas and the Asuras. She is so beautiful that everyone is overwhelmed with desire. It is said that Shiva, having consumed Halahal, was about to retreat to his mountainous abode when he sees Mohini. He is so enchanted by her beauty that he embraces her. From that union of Shiva and Mohini is born Hari-Hara-Suta, the son of Vishnu and Shiva, a child who possesses the ascetic

Poster art of Aiyappa, or Hari-Hara-Suta, the son of
Vishnu and Shiva, worshipped in Kerala

qualities of Shiva, hence refuses to marry, as well as the warrior qualities of Vishnu, hence is ever-willing to defend society. In Tamil Nadu, this warrior-ascetic is called Aiyanar. In Kerala, he is Manikantha or Sastha or Aiyappa, whose shrine is built atop the Sabari hill. No women are allowed to this shrine. And men have to practise weeks of celibacy and simplicity to gain access there.

Mohini is so enchanting that, for a moment, everyone forgets the nectar. She speaks in a melodious voice. 'May I distribute the nectar.' No one can say no to so delightful a creature.

The pot of nectar is given to the enchantress and all the Devas and the Asuras sit down awaiting their turn. Mohini sails amongst them, smiling invitingly, her eyes twinkling, pouring Amrita down their throats.

Suddenly, the Asuras notice that Mohini is pouring the Amrita down the throats of only the Devas. Nothing is being given to the Asuras. They realise there is mischief afoot. They are being tricked by the damsel. They raise their weapons and rush towards Mohini, determined to snatch the pot of nectar once again. But now all the Devas have been nourished with Amrita; they are immortal. They run to Mohini's rescue. A great battle follows. The weapons of the Asuras have no effect on the Devas and with great ease the Devas are able to defeat the Asuras.

With the Asuras dead, the Devas, now unafraid of death, rise to their celestial abode, Amravati, with all the wonderful treasures that had emerged from the ocean of milk.

At first glance, this story of how Mohini tricks the Asuras and gives the Amrita to the Devas seems like a trickster story. The demons are duped by a damsel. Since the Asuras are villains, one is told,

South Indian stone carving showing Mohini, the female form of Vishnu

they deserve being cheated so. But this is a simplistic and incorrect understanding of the tale.

One must remember that the Devas and the Asuras are half-brothers, children of Brahma who, like Vishnu, is a form of God. English translations that equate Asuras with demons are more judgmental than descriptive. No one is sure what is the 'villainous' deeds for which the Asuras are condemned so. Yet, one is quick to visualise them as horrible monstrous ogres. And this impatient conclusion prevents one from seeing the big picture.

The big picture is that while the Devas do not die, the Asuras are also blessed with a power that enables them to survive death. When killed in battle, they can be resurrected, because their guru, Shukra, son of Bhrigu, has access to the secret occult lore known as Sanjivani Vidya. And Shukra obtained this lore from Shiva, the indifferent ascetic.

If Brahma, the creator, is equally passionate about the Devas and the Asuras, Shiva in his role of destroyer is equally indifferent to both the Devas and the Asuras. So both Brahma and Shiva neutralise each other, giving equal boons to both the Devas and the Asuras. As a result there is no motion in the world, no movement, no change, no happening. The only way to create motion is to create a gradient of power, generate opposition between two equal forces so that they serve as the force and counterforce of a churn. Vishnu, in his role as preserver, spurs this motion in the cosmos by creating an imbalance of power, by giving Amrita to the Devas and denying it to the Asuras.

The Devas always kill the Asuras and take Lakshmi to Swarga. Sometimes they do this on their own and sometimes with a little help from Vishnu. However, thanks to Indra's insecurity, and

Poster art showing Mohini favouring Devas

consequential hedonism, they cannot hold on to Lakshmi for long. She goes away and, to get her back, the Asuras are needed once more. The resurrection of Asuras by Sanjivani Vidya ensures the fertility of the land is restored every year and the crops rise every year, despite the 'killing' during the last harvest. Every time the Asuras rise, the battle of the Devas and Asuras starts anew. The Asuras die, Lakshmi is gathered by the Devas and the cycle begins anew.

Both Devas and Asuras are critical to ensure the movement of Lakshmi. Devas distribute her and Asuras create her. That is why, in yagnas, offerings are made to Suras, which means Devas who consumed Amrita, and to the Asuras, who were denied Amrita. Vishnu does not seek the absolute and eternal defeat of the Asuras. For if that happens, the churning will stop and the world will come to an end.

Conflict between two forces is a recurring theme in Hindu mythology. One conflict is that between material and spiritual reality, between the hermit and the nymph, between Shiva and Mohini. The other is within material reality, between the Devas and the Asuras.

The conflict within material reality, presided over by Vishnu, also manifests as the conflict between the Nagas and Garuda, the serpents and the king of the hawks, both being sacred to Vishnu.

Like the Asuras, serpents live under the ground, and like the city of the Asuras, the city of the Nagas, Bhogavati, is made of gold and gems. Like the Devas, the hawk flies in the sky above. Like Asuras and Devas, the serpents and the king of the hawks are half-brothers, children of Brahma, of two wives.

South Indian painting of Garuda

Brahma takes the form of Kashyapa, a Rishi, and accepts two wives, Kadru and Vinata. Kadru says she wants to be the mother of many children, so she becomes the mother of serpents. Vinata says she wants fewer but stronger children. As a result she becomes the mother of Garuda, a mighty hawk.

Garuda is born into slavery. He learns that, having lost a bet, his mother is forced to serve Kadru. Garuda cannot bear the humiliation of serving the Nagas; he is desperate for a way out. The Nagas say, 'The price of your freedom and your mother's freedom is the pot of Amrita that the Devas jealously guard.'

Garuda rises to the sky, with great ease defeats the Devas, and descends from Swarga, pot of Amrita in his hands. Despite having it in his hands, Garuda does not take a sip of the nectar. This detachment pleases Vishnu. He feels Garuda would make a worthy companion. Vishnu blocks Garuda's descent and says, 'If you serve me as my mount, then I will show you the way to liberate yourself and your mother without making the Nagas immortal.' Garuda is all ears.

Instructed by Vishnu, Garuda demands his liberation and his mother's liberation before he hands over the pot of Amrita to the Nagas. 'So be it,' said the Nagas. 'You are free.'

Garuda then places the pot on grass, as promised. He then advises the Nagas to purify themselves with a bath before drinking the nectar. The Nagas, who had waited patiently for Garuda to return with the nectar, rush to the river. While they are away Garuda invites Indra to swoop down and reclaim the pot. Much pleased, the king of the Devas gives a boon to the hawk, 'Henceforth Nagas will be your food. You will incur no sin when you kill them.'

When the Nagas return, they are furious to see that the pot had

Poster art showing Vishnu and Lakshmi riding Garuda, the eagle

Vishnu and Lakshmi resting on Ananta Sesha, the serpent

disappeared. They shout at Garuda for not securing it. 'I am under no obligation to do so; I am no longer your slave,' snarls Garuda.

The unhappy snakes slither on the grass where the pot of Amrita had been placed. This has a magical effect. Since Amrita had been placed on the grass, the grass acquires the power of regeneration — every time a blade of grass is plucked, it grows back. Likewise, the serpents by rolling on the grass also acquire the power of regeneration. From time to time, they can replace their old skin with new skin and stay youthful forever.

Just as the Devas and the Asuras are eternal enemies, so are the Nagas and Garuda. Garuda and the Devas refer to the forces of the sky: the sun, the moon, the wind, the rain and the fire. Nagas and Asuras refer to the regenerating forces of the earth. The former release Lakshmi from the confines of the earth, but only the latter can give birth to her. Vishnu may side with the Devas but he knows the value of Asuras. That is why both the Garuda and the Naga are sacred to Vishnu.

# 4. Trivikrama's Secret

*Ignorance breeds insecurity and arrogance*

Image from 13th century Bengal showing Vishnu
flanked by Lakshmi and Saraswati

*L*akshmi is the goddess of wealth while Saraswati is the goddess of learning. Lakshmi is dressed in red and bedecked in gold while Saraswati is dressed in white and bereft of gold. Lakshmi brings prosperity wherever she goes, while Saraswati brings peace. The two are rarely seen together.

Lakshmi is typically drawn towards places where Saraswati resides. That is why prosperity always follows peace. However, when Lakshmi comes, attention shifts from Saraswati to Lakshmi. Enraged, Saraswati leaves. In her absence, Alakshmi comes to give her sister, Lakshmi, company. With Alakshmi comes strife. Strife ends peace. And in the absence of peace, prosperity eventually wanes. Lakshmi leaves and there is nothing left.

This is what repeatedly happens to the Devas. When Lakshmi sits beside Indra, he ignores Saraswati and remains an insecure hedonist, which results in the loss of Lakshmi. Lakshmi returns only when good sense prevails and Indra, adequately chastised, surrenders to Vishnu.

This is also what happens to the Asuras. Deprived of all the treasures that come from the ocean of milk, they pursue ascetic practices and attain Saraswati. They obtain a variety of boons from either Shiva or Brahma that makes them near invincible. They defeat Devas, overrun Amravati and acquire Lakshmi. But with the acquisition of wealth and power, they ignore Saraswati, become arrogant, and the resulting hubris heralds their downfall at the hands of Vishnu.

Devas and Asuras focus on either Saraswati or Lakshmi at any one time. Vishnu, however, focuses on both goddesses at all times.

Poster art of Saraswati, goddess of knowledge

Lakshmi is Vishnu's bhoga-patni, connecting him with the earthly needs of man. Saraswati is Vishnu's moksha-patni, connecting him with the spiritual needs of man. He knows the two of them do not see eye to eye and so he keeps Saraswati hidden in his mouth while he keeps Lakshmi at his feet. Thus he manages to create harmony between them.

In the Mahabharata, shortly after establishing the kingdom of Indra-prastha, the Pandavas gamble it away, just like Indra, and lose rights over it for thirteen years. Following this loss of Lakshmi, the Pandavas are subjected to a humiliating exile in the forest during which they regain Saraswati and understand the role of Lakshmi in their life. When the exile is complete, they ask the Kauravas to return their kingdom but the Kauravas cling to Indra-prastha, go back on their word and refuse to part with it. A war is declared between the Pandavas and the Kauravas, each one claiming rights over Indra-prastha. Both go to Krishna for help. Krishna offers them either himself or his army. Arjuna, representing the Pandavas, chooses Krishna. Duryodhana, representing the Kauravas, chooses Krishna's army. The Pandavas thus choose what Krishna 'is' while the Kauravas choose what Krishna 'has'. In the war, the Kauravas lose everything while Pandavas gain both wisdom and kingdom.

The quest for Saraswati is the journey from Brahma to brahman, from jiva-atma to param-atma, from finite to infinite. This is a journey of 'what I have' to 'what I am'. But in Maya, we equate 'what I have' with 'what I am'. Mine becomes me. The more I have, the greater I feel I am. We construct a self-image of ourselves. This is a delusion. This is the path the Asuras take after they are denied wealth and immortality after the churning of the ocean of

Miniature painting of Varaha

Cave temple carving from Tamil Nadu showing Varaha with Bhu-devi in his arms

milk. Rather than pursuing Saraswati, they pursue Lakshmi. They delude themselves that the acquisition of Lakshmi will make them immortal and all-powerful. They do not realise that despite having Lakshmi, Devas are insecure and eternally anxious.

And so, an Asura called Hiranayaksha drags Bhu-devi, the earth-goddess, to the bottom of the sea and claims her for himself. He declares himself to be her master. This is a delusion. The earth belongs to no one. To claim ownership of her, or parts of her, stems from ignorance.

The abduction of Bhu-devi by Hiranayaksha alarms the Devas who complain to their father, Brahma. Brahma hears Bhu-devi's wailing. In rage, Brahma's nostrils flare. From one of the flaring nostrils emerges a wild boar with long resplendent tusks. It is Vishnu in the form of Varaha!

Varaha plunges into the sea and challenges the Asura, Hiranayaksha, to a duel. The fight is fierce as Hiranayaksha clings to Bhu-devi, refusing to let her go. But in the end, Varaha gores him to death. Varaha then rises up towards the surface, holding Bhu-devi on his snout. The goddess sings songs praising Vishnu. She declares him Bhu-pati, the lord of earth, her husband. He promises to take care of her. 'If anyone treats you with disrespect, they will answer to me,' says Vishnu.

From that day, Vishnu becomes the guardian of earth, watching over Bhu-devi, stretching himself as the sky above. That is why Vishnu is blue as the day-sky and black as the night-sky.

Some say that, as they rose, Bhu-devi accepted Varaha as her consort and named him Bhu-pati, lord of the earth. They made love and so passionate was Vishnu's embrace that the

Burning of the effigy of Naraka in Goa during Diwali

North Indian palm leaf painting showing the attack on Naraka's citadel

earth crumpled, causing mountains and valleys to form. As Vishnu plunged his tusks into the earth, the earth became impregnated with the seeds of all kinds of plants.

From the union of Varaha and Bhu-devi, a child was born. His name was Naraka. Though the son of Vishnu, he was an Asura, and like all Asuras he craved power. He invoked Brahma and asked for immortality. When denied that, he said, 'May I be killed if I attack my mother,' sure that he would never harm the earth. Brahma gave Naraka the boon he sought and sure enough, empowered by the boon, he overran the abode of the Devas and laid claim to Indra's umbrella and Aditi's earrings. Naraka was challenged to a duel by Krishna. Naraka saw that beside Krishna sat his queen, Satyabhama. He did not realise that Krishna and Satyabhama were the mortal incarnations of Vishnu and Bhu-devi, in other words they were his parents. He hurled his weapon at Krishna; it hit Satyabhama. In doing so, Naraka had struck his mother. Instantly, he became vulnerable to the weapons of Krishna and was killed as a result.

Images of Naraka, the Asura, are burned along the Konkan coast during Diwali celebrations. Diwali, the festival of lights, coincides with the autumn harvest. It is the festival that celebrates the arrival of Lakshmi. Here the creator of the Asura and the destroyer are both Vishnu, perhaps alluding to the fact that the farmer who sows the seed is also the one who cuts the crop. The festival once again reminds us that to obtain Lakshmi, the Asura needs to be killed year after year.

Bhu-devi is the tangible form of Lakshmi. Lakshmi has another form called Sri-devi, which indicates intangible wealth. It refers to the glory and fame that everyone craves for. Sri-devi is Sachi who

Calendar art showing Vishnu with two forms of Lakshmi: Sri-devi and Bhu-devi

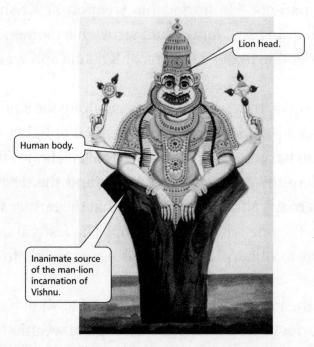

Mysore painting showing Narasimha emerging from a pillar

sits besides Indra. Bhu-devi is Pulomi who the Asuras abduct. Neither is able to hold on to either. Both Bhu-devi and Sri-devi end up with Vishnu.

Nature has given all living creatures two things to survive, either strength or cunning. In the quest for immortality, Hiranayaksha uses strength. He fails. So his brother, Hiranakashipu takes recourse to cunning. He invokes Brahma and says, 'If you cannot grant me immortality then let me be killed only by a creature that is neither man nor animal, by neither a weapon nor a tool, neither inside a dwelling nor outside, neither on earth nor in the sky, neither at day nor at night.' The boon is given and naturally Hiranakashipu assumes he can never be killed, hence he will never die. 'If I cannot die,' he says, 'I must be spiritual reality. I must be God.'

Here Hiranakashipu uses Saraswati to acquire immortality, hence Lakshmi. Saraswati is thus, for Asuras, only a means, and not the end. When Saraswati is used for acquisition of Lakshmi, she is called Vidya-Lakshmi. Vidya-Lakshmi increases 'what I have' but does not take 'what I am' towards brahman. Jiva-atma remains jiva-atma, trapped in Maya.

Immortality alone is not the attribute of God. Devas have immortality but they are merely gods, not God, because they are eternally unhappy and insecure, unable to attract or withhold Lakshmi. Besides, Devas are located only above the ground. They do not exist below the ground. God or param-atma exists everywhere.

Hiranakashipu's son, Prahalad, refuses to acknowledge his father as God. He prays to Vishnu alone. An angry Hiranakashipu therefore tortures his son. He has him thrown in water, but

Kalighat painting showing killing of Hiranakashipu

Vishnu saves his devotee from drowning. He has him thrown off a cliff, but Vishnu makes his devotee glide down to the ground. Hiranakashipu then orders his sister, Holika, to walk into fire with Prahalad in her arms. Holika has a boon that fire will never harm her, but to the Asura-king's astonishment, when Holika and Prahalad walk into a huge bonfire, Holika is reduced to ashes while Prahalad escapes unscathed, for Vishnu could reverse a boon given by Brahma. This story is told during the festival of Holi when a huge bonfire is lit as winter gives way to spring.

Finally Hiranakashipu asks his son for an explanation. Prahalad says, 'Vishnu is the master of space and time. By tricking death away, you may have conquered time. But you have not conquered space. You are here but only Vishnu is everywhere. That is why Vishnu is God but you are not.'

Hiranakashipu is not convinced. He challenges Prahalad, 'Are you saying this Vishnu is even in the pillars of my palace?' Prahalad nods his head. To prove him wrong, Hiranakashipu kicks and breaks one of the stone pillars of his palace. As the pillar falls apart, to his astonishment a living creature emerges from the stone. It is a strange creature, neither human nor animal. It is Narasimha, half-lion and half-human. Narasimha catches the Asura with his claws, which is neither a weapon nor a tool. He drags the Asura to the threshold of the palace, which is located neither inside a dwelling nor outside. He places the Asura on his thigh, which is neither on earth nor in the sky. At twilight, which is neither day nor night, Narasimha rips open Hiranakashipu's entrails and drinks his blood. Thus the cunning Asura who tried to outsmart death is outsmarted by God.

Having consumed an Asura's blood, Vishnu is said to have

Clay doll from Andhra Pradesh showing Lakshmi seated on Narasimha's thigh

become bloodthirsty. The goddess Lakshmi had to appear and sit on his lap to calm him down. Having calmed down, Narasimha blessed Prahalad.

Hiranakashipu cannot imagine the existence of a creature that can be part human and part animal. He cannot imagine an organism that can be born out of a stone pillar. In other words, Vishnu defies his imagination. This episode in Vishnu lore is a reminder that divinity cannot be limited by human imagination or human memory. There is always something in the universe that surprises us.

This is a recurring theme in Vishnu lore. In the Ramayana, when Sita sees a golden deer and begs Ram to fetch it for her, Lakshman says that such a creature cannot exist; it is unnatural. To this Ram says, 'Never presume to know the limits of nature. Prakriti is infinite. The human mind is finite.'

In the Mahabharata, the warlord Bhishma, commander of the Kaurava army, reveals that he cannot be killed unless he is made to lower a bow and he will lower a bow before no man. In other words, to kill Bhishma one must bring a woman before him. But women are not allowed on the battlefield. This makes it impossible to kill Bhishma and so for nine days the battle on Kurukshetra between the Pandavas and the Kauravas is a stalemate. Finally, Krishna advises the Pandavas to let Shikhandi ride into battle on his chariot with Arjuna and challenge Bhishma to a duel. Shikhandi is born a woman but later in life, with the help of a Yaksha, has acquired male genitals. Thus Shikhandi believes he is a man. But Bhishma does not accept this gender transformation and insists on treating Shikhandi as a woman. Bhishma lowers his bow as

Patta painting of Nava-gunjara, the composite beast, described in
the Odia Mahabharata

Shikhandi rides before him on Krishna's chariot and provides Arjuna with the opportunity to strike him down. Thus the story shows Vishnu accepting gender ambiguity. Bhishma dies because he refuses to make room for ambiguity.

In the Tamil retelling of the Mahabharata, one finds the story of a warrior Aravan, son of Arjuna. In order to win the war, the Pandavas are advised to sacrifice a man with sacred marks on his body. There are only three such men in the Pandava camp: Krishna, Arjuna and Aravan. Since Krishna and Arjuna are indispensable, Aravan volunteers to be the sacrifice. But he has one condition, 'I want to marry, experience conjugal bliss before I die. I want to leave behind a widow who will weep for me with true feelings when I die.' So the Pandavas go in search of a bride for Aravan. But no woman is willing to marry a man doomed to die after the wedding night. Finally Krishna decides to take matters into his hands. He takes the form of Mohini and marries Aravan. They spend a night together and at dawn, when Aravan is beheaded, Krishna weeps for him as a widow would.

In the Odia retelling of the Mahabharata, the great archer Arjuna is once confronted by a beast that is a composite of nine animals: it has the head of a rooster; the neck of a peacock; the back of a bull; the waist of a lion; the feet of an elephant, a human, a deer, and a tiger; and a serpent for a tail. At first Arjuna is terrified by this strange beast and raises his bow to shoot it. But then he notices the creature holds in his human hand Krishna's sacred wheel. Arjuna stops. He ponders on his inability to identify the monster or explain its existence. It is clearly beyond all known definitions; it challenges conventional classifications. It seems to emerge from beyond the limits of human comprehension. Arjuna concludes this

Image of Vaman from a step-well in Patan, Gujarat

is no monster but a manifestation of the divine. This is Krishna. This is God. For what is impossible in human reason is possible in divine thought. Arjuna drops his bow and salutes this magical manifestation of God.

Hiranayaksha uses strength to overcome his discontent and become all-powerful. Hiranakashipu uses cunning. The Asuras who follow, Virochan and Bali, use generosity to win the affection of subjects to achieve the same end. While Hiranayaksha and Hiranakashipu are self-absorbed, Virochan and Bali are concerned about others. This indicates growth. Unlike Hiranayaksha and Hiranakashipu who exclude others, Virochan and Bali include others. Though Asuras, they are revered in the scriptures.

But still, the focus of Virochan and Bali remains 'what I have' rather than 'what I am'. They feel that happiness comes when material needs are met. They fail to realise that as long as man is in Maya, material needs can never be fully satisfied. Contentment comes only when material growth is accompanied by spiritual growth.

Virochan is Prahalad's son. And like all stories of Asuras, he becomes very powerful until Vishnu comes to him in the form of Mohini and secures a gift from him. 'Whatever you wish,' says Virochan. Mohini immediately asks him for his head. Virochan, true to his word, severs his neck, to the delight of the Devas.

Virochan's son, Bali, becomes more powerful than any other Asura before him. And like his father, he is very generous. This makes Bali a very popular Asura. In his realm there is prosperity everywhere. His fame spreads far and wide and in time eclipses even the glory of the Devas. Humans turn to Bali with reverence

Modern sculpture in Kerala, of the giant Trivikrama

and eventually even Sachi leaves Indra's side to sit beside the wise and noble Bali. So great is Bali that in his kingdom everything is perfect; all needs are satisfied and all wants are met; there is no disease or death. People conclude that Bali must be God. Even Bali comes to believe that he is God, after all he can give everyone whatever they desire.

That is when Vishnu approaches Bali as a dwarf or Vaman. 'Whatever you wish shall be yours,' says Bali. Vaman asks for three paces of land. Without a thought, Bali agrees to give what Vaman wants. But Shukra, advisor to Bali, recognises Vishnu. He tells Bali to hold back, but Bali refuses to go back on his word.

To complete the act of charity, Bali has to ritually pour water from the snout of his water pot. To block the ritual, Shukra reduces his size, enters the pot and blocks the snout. Vishnu divines what Shukra is up to and so when no water comes out of the pot, he offers to unclog the snout. Vishnu takes a blade of grass, sharpens its end and shoves it up the snout, blinding Shukra in one eye. Shukra leaps out of the pot howling in pain and water gushes out from the snout. The ritual is thus completed and Vaman is officially entitled to three paces of land.

Vaman then, right before Bali's eyes, transforms into a giant and with one stride claims the sky and with another stride claims the earth. 'I have no other place to place my foot now,' says Vishnu in a voice that booms across the three worlds. Bali, overwhelmed by the sight of the giant Vishnu, bows his head humbly and replies, 'Please place it on my head then.' Vishnu places his head on Bali's head and shoves him under the ground, into Patala, the subterranean world that is the rightful place of Asuras.

All those who see this gigantic form of Vishnu conclude that only

Calendar art showing Vishnu as Trivikrama

Vishnu is Trivikrama, conqueror of the three worlds of the Devas, the Manavas and the Asuras. He spans all worlds. He is God.

Bali is a good king who, like his father, assumes that if he satisfies the desires of all living creatures, all will be well. By transforming into a giant, Vishnu draws Bali's attention to a reality that Bali ignores: human desires are infinite while material resources are finite. Bali can never satisfy *all* the desires of living creatures. Material resources are limited but human want is unlimited. To make Bali realise this, Vaman turns into a giant. Before Vaman's gigantic form, Bali realises his insignificance.

In Vishnu lore, there is a general discomfort with the idea of offering people whatever they desire. A man who offers another 'whatever he or she desires' is in effect being arrogant and over-estimating his capability and capacity. This offer always lands them into trouble.

In the Ramayana, Dashratha offers his wife, Kaikeyi, whatever she desires, not once but twice. So she asks that Ram, the heir to the throne, be sent into forest-exile for fourteen years while Bharata, her son, be made king instead. Thus the boon of the king causes trouble and disturbs the serenity of the land.

In the Mahabharata, Shantanu offers the same boon to his wife Ganga and she demands that he never question her actions. He agrees only to find to his horror that she drowns their children as soon as they are born. Thus no good comes from these apparently magnanimous boons which in effect are products of delusion for no one, but God, can offer another 'whatever he or she desires'.

Every jiva-atma in the cosmos has boundaries and limits. Devas therefore are restricted to the celestial realms, Manavas are restricted to the earthly realms while Asuras are restricted

Moksha-patni is the wife who enables spiritual growth, which means emotional and intellectual growth which grants man detachment, generosity, faith and patience.

Bhoga-patni is the wife who enables material growth, which grants man the pleasures of worldly life.

Lakshmi, dressed in red, is Bhoga-patni.

Ignored by Asuras and Devas.

Fought over by both Asuras and Devas.

Saraswati, dressed in white, is Moksha-patni.

Vishnu balances both wives, hence is greater than Asuras and Devas.

Clay doll from Andhra Pradesh — Vishnu with two consorts

to the subterranean realms. Asuras, in their quest for fulfilment, constantly seek conquest of realms beyond their own. They rise and occupy other worlds, until Vishnu shows them their place, as in the story of Vaman and Vali.

But each year, Bali is allowed to rise up above the ground. His arrival is marked by many festivals such as Diwali in north India and Onam in Kerala. It is a time of bounty and prosperity. To get the harvest to the granary, Bali has to be killed, like all Asuras. Only when shoved underground, will he return the following year, nourished by Sanjivani Vidya, with yet another bountiful harvest.

Asuras and Devas are quite similar to each other. Both are children of Kashyapa, grandchildren of Brahma and hence very aware of their mortality. They both crave Lakshmi, believing that her presence will give them happiness. Both ignore Saraswati and end up losing Lakshmi and with it, happiness.

Asuras and Devas are also very dissimilar. While Devas seek stability, Asuras seek growth. Devas are content with what they have but are insecure about losing it. They do not aspire for more. They do not seek to go beyond the limits of Swarga. Indra never tries to be ruler of the three worlds. But Asuras yearn to be masters of the three worlds. They are never content with what they have. They do not want to be restricted to the subterranean realms. They also want to be masters of the earth and the sky.

Devas and Asuras reflect two aspects of human personality: our need for stability and our need for growth. The former makes us either insecure or complacent. The latter makes us frustrated and restless. We crave for Lakshmi mostly. Sometimes we crave for Saraswati, with the sole pursuit of obtaining Lakshmi; for

Mysore paintings of (clockwise) Varaha, Narasimha and Vamana

when Lakshmi arrives we ignore Saraswati to our peril. That we experience these emotions is an indicator that we have not yet realised or experienced spiritual reality, which is Vishnu.

Vishnu overpowers Hiranayaksha with force and outsmarts Hiranakashipu with cunning. In the case of Vaman, it is Vishnu who transforms and humbles Bali, reminding him that the point of existence is not conquest of the three worlds, but the realisation of infinite potential or brahman. This demands not just material growth but also emotional and intellectual growth, which manifests into generosity of spirit and humility.

⊙≋

Vishnu's actions against Hiranayaksha, Hiranakashipu and Bali in favour of Indra may seem like God is taking sides. So one can quickly conclude that Asuras are bad and Devas are good. But this is a simplistic explanation. Devas are insecure and complacent, and highly susceptible to overindulgence. This hardly makes them models of appropriate conduct. By contrast, the Asuras, at least Virochan and Bali, are generous and they seem more like wronged heroes rather than villains. And Prahalad, though Asura, is one of the greatest devotees of Vishnu.

The idea of bad gods and good demons is confounding. But it emerges from the presumption that the division of gods and demons is made on ethical and moral terms. This is, more often than not, the result of poor English translations of Hindu mythology in the 18th century, which declared Devas as 'good' and Asuras as 'bad'.

Devas and Asuras, in mythology, are just two sets of beings, one residing in the sky and the other residing under the earth. Vishnu's actions are driven by the need for social order. He keeps pushing Asuras back where they belong each time they cross their frontiers.

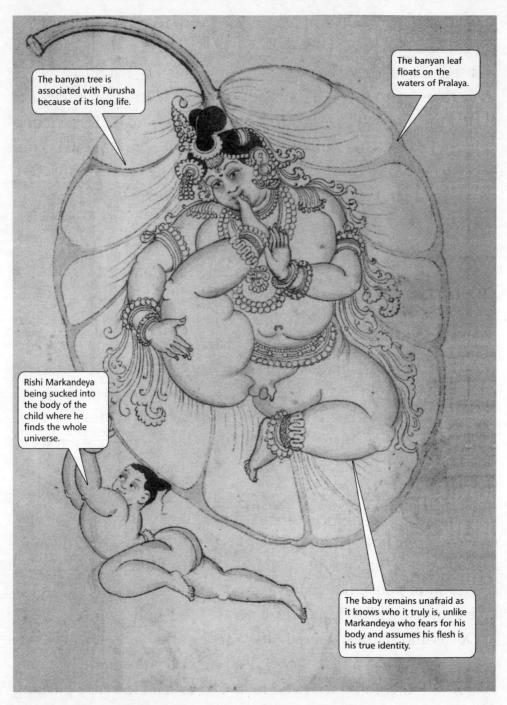

Mysore painting of the child on the banyan leaf

The act of killing Asuras generates Lakshmi for the Devas. But while the Devas can enjoy Lakshmi, they are unable to create her. For that they always need the Asuras. Thus Asuras are an essential part of the Hindu universe.

The word evil is often used to describe Asuras. But this word 'evil' makes no sense in Hinduism. Evil means 'the absence of God'. This idea does not exist in Hinduism because, for Hindus, the whole world is a manifestation of the divine. So, nothing can be evil. This notion that everything is divine is made explicit in many stories of Vishnu.

Once when Yashoda sees her little son eating dirt she forces him to open his mouth and is stunned to find in his mouth the earth and all the planets and the stars and everything that makes up the universe. The son is Krishna, Vishnu incarnate.

Once the sage Markandeya has a vision of the world coming to an end. He sees the ocean rise up and consume the earth. Everything is dissolved — the plants, the animals, the rocks and every creature imaginable until there is not a single trace of life. Markandeya weeps for the world there was until he observes a banyan leaf floating on the waves of the ocean. On the leaf is a child; it is Vishnu. The baby inhales and the sage finds himself being sucked into Vishnu's body. Within he sees a magnificent sight: all the oceans and the continents and the stars and the planets. He sees all creatures, those that walk the earth, those who live in the sky and those who live under the earth. He sees every plant and animal and creature, human and celestial, inside Vishnu. He then is exhaled out of God's body. He realises that all things exists within God.

On the battle field of Kurukshetra, when Krishna gives his

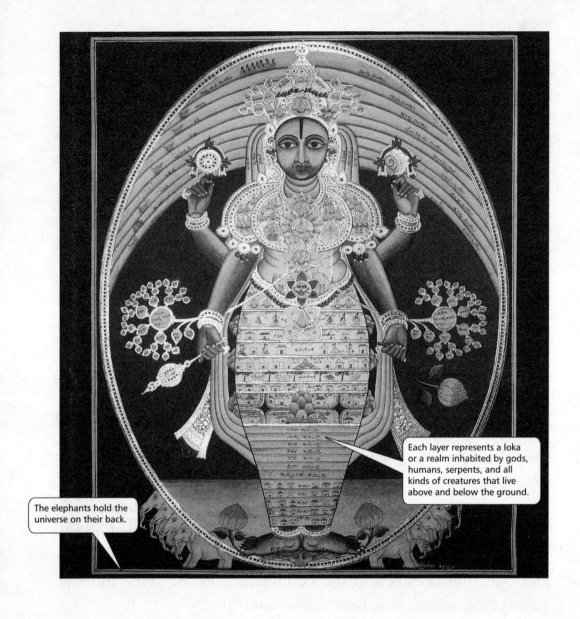

Tanjore painting of Virat-Swarup

discourse known as the Bhagavad Gita to Arjuna, Arjuna is convinced that his friend, Krishna, is no ordinary man. 'Show me your true form,' he begs Krishna. And so Krishna shows his Virat-Swarup or cosmic form. He expands till his head reaches beyond the stars and his feet below the deepest recesses of earth. He sprouts innumerable heads and arms and legs. The sun and moon are his eyes. He breathes in worlds and breathes out fire. He grounds planets between his teeth. Within him is time, past and present and future. Within him is space, all dimensions, known and unknown. He is the container of all things.

All things contain the Asuras too. Everything contains the spark of divinity, even those deemed demons and villains by storytellers.

Evil refers to an act that has no cause or explanation, an act that cannot be justified. But in Hinduism, all actions have a cause. The Hindu world is governed by the notion of karma: no event is spontaneous, everything is a result of past action, either performed in this lifetime or in the ones before.

The idea of evil is typically found in cultures and religions that believe in one life; Hinduism believes in rebirth where deeds of past lives explain everything. Thus in the Hindu world there is no need for the word evil. This idea is made explicit in the story of Jaya and Vijaya.

The behaviour of Hiranayaksha and Hiranakashipu is traced back to their past life, when they were Jaya and Vijaya, doorkeepers of Vaikuntha, the abode of Vishnu.

When the Sanat-kumars seek entry into Vaikuntha, they are stopped at the gates by Jaya and Vijaya as Vishnu is asleep at that

Poster art of Sanat-kumars, the four boy sages

time. Annoyed, the four sages cursed the doorkeepers, 'May you be born as Asuras away from Vishnu.' The curse immediately takes effect and the two doorkeepers emerge as Asuras from the womb of Diti.

Jaya and Vijaya, now Hiranayaksha and Hiranakashipu, are eager to return to Vaikuntha and so perform vile deeds that will force Vishnu to descend and liberate them. Hiranayaksha uses his strength to drag the earth below the sea. Hiranakashipu uses cunning instead; he tortures his son, Prahalad, who is a devotee of Vishnu.

The villainy of the two brothers is cited as examples of viparit-bhakti or 'reverse-devotion'; in hating God, one remembers God constantly and thereby earns God's affection.

The cries of Bhu-devi and Prahalad reach Vaikuntha and trouble Vishnu. He descends to rescue both them and his former doorkeepers. Vishnu feels sad that the doorkeepers have been punished for doing their duty; he feels it is his duty to liberate them from the Asura flesh. And so as Varaha and Narasimha he kills the two brothers. Death liberates the brothers. Shedding their Asura forms they return as guardians of Vaikuntha.

When this story is told, the act of violence committed by Varaha and Narasimha transforms from an act of divine retribution to an act of divine love. No more are Asuras seen as villains. There is an explanation for their villainy. While it does not condone their act, it makes one judge them less harshly and with more understanding.

༺≋༻

The names of both Jaya and Vijaya mean victory. But Jaya means spiritual victory, while Vijaya means material victory. Vijaya is conventional victory, victory over the other, over other's minds,

Jaya and Vijaya, the doorkeepers of Vishnu's paradise
known as Vaikuntha

a victory where there are winners and losers. Jaya, on the other hand, is victory over oneself, over one's mind, a victory where there are no losers.

At any moment of life, things either go our way or the other way. In the former situation, when things go our way, we are happy. It is the state of Vijaya, material victory, for we have got what we wanted, often at the expense of others. In the latter situation, when things do not go our way, we are unhappy. But unhappiness propels us to introspect on the nature of material things, and question the reason for our emotions. This introspection and questioning reveals to us the mysteries of the world; we realise the true nature of the world. It is the state of Jaya, spiritual victory, for we have learnt something vital.

In Jaya, Saraswati can walk in our direction. In Vijaya, Lakshmi walks in our direction. But the point of life is to experience the two states together. Lakshmi and Saraswati need to arrive simultaneously, not sequentially. Only when Jaya and Vijaya come together does the gateway to Vaikuntha open up on our lives.

# 5. Ram's Secret

*Outgrow the beast to discover the divine*

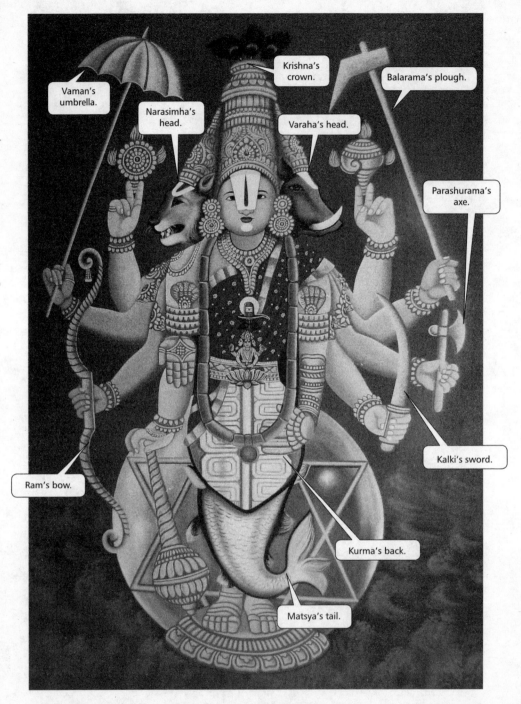

A composite modern painting showing the animal and human forms of Vishnu

$V$ishnu's stories can be divided into two sets: those who function in a timeless realm and those who function within time. The first set deals mostly with Devas and Asuras. The second set deals with Manavas and Rakshasas.

The battle of Devas and Asuras has more to do with timeless issues revolving around wealth creation, emotional security and intellectual growth. The battle between Manavas and Rakshasas has more to do with appropriate social conduct, ethics and morality that is a function of history and geography.

Devas live in the sky and Asuras live under the earth. Their battle is aligned vertically, between the celestial realms and the nether regions. Manavas and Rakshasas live on earth. Their battle is aligned horizontally between culture and nature, between dharma and adharma.

Words like justice, righteousness and goodness do not adequately explain the term dharma because notions of justice, of what is right and good, change over time and are different in different parts of the world. Dharma is the underlying principle that enables man to realise his divine potential through social behaviour.

To understand the words dharma, and adharma, we have to realise the stark divide between humans and the rest of nature. Only humans have the ability to reject the law of the jungle, both positively and negatively. Positive rejection of the law of the jungle means that we empathise and include others in our quest for security and growth. This is dharma. Negative rejection of the law of the jungle means that we exploit others and include all in our

Miniature painting of Ram

quest for security and growth. This is adharma.

Dharma manifests as rules that seek to provide for, and protect, all creatures. This means actions that help the helpless, where the mighty care for the meek. Adharma is the very opposite; taking advantage of the law of the jungle for the benefit of a few at the cost of the rest. Adharma is about domination, territoriality, hoarding, attachment and power. Dharma is about outgrowing these cravings.

Humans who uphold dharma are called Manavas, after Manu, the first human who rejected the law of the fishes. Humans who uphold adharma are called Rakshasas and are often described as demons. Both Manavas and Rakshasas are grandchildren of Brahma, indicating that they are two different frames of mind. The conflict forms the keystone of the epic, Ramayana.

Ramayana tells the story of Ram, the only avatar of Vishnu to be worshipped as king. It is the story of a man who upheld the code of civilisation and refused to succumb to animal instincts despite every provocation. To appreciate the Ramayana one must first hear the story of Prithu and his father, Vena.

The *Bhagavata Purana* refers to a king called Vena who plundered the earth so much that the earth in disgust ran away in the form of a cow. This naturally resulted in chaos. The plants refused to bear fruit and the seeds did not sprout. There was hunger everywhere. Animals cried, humans wailed. The sages then decided to do something about it. They picked up a blade of grass, chanted magical hymns, turned the grass into a potent missile and used it to kill the greedy king. The Rishis then churned Vena's corpse, removed all that was savage and untamed in it, and created a new

Miniature paintings showing Prithu chasing and milking the earth-cow

king from the distilled, purified positive elements. This king was called Prithu, a form of Vishnu.

Prithu went to the earth-cow and requested her to provide milk for his subjects but the cow refused. She was still angry. So Prithu raised his bow and threatened to shoot her down with his arrow. 'If you kill me,' said the earth-cow, 'then all of nature will be destroyed and so will all life.' Prithu then argued that without domesticating the earth, he could not feed humanity. He had no choice but to tame the earth, turn the forests into fields, route the water of rivers with canals. 'Do so then in moderation,' said the earth-cow. So Prithu promised to institute dharma through rules that allow culture to thrive without destroying nature.

This is not easy, it must be remembered. Because human life is validated when there is growth. Animals have no such desire to grow. Growth of human civilisation involves the domestication of nature, the uprooting of forests and destruction of ecosystems. This material growth can destroy the world if unchecked. The only way to check it is by tempering it with intellectual growth and emotional growth, which are the two limbs of spiritual growth.

Dharma balances nature and culture, between the needs of animals and the needs of humans. The symbol of dharma is the bow, which the gods gave to Prithu. The bow indicates balance — the string cannot be left loose or too taut. Prithu is described as the first responsible king of earth. This is why the earth is called Prithvi.

As human society creates settlements, forests are turned into fields and animals are domesticated. This gives man extra resources — more food and time. This enables man to move from material

Kerala mural showing Ram in court

pursuits to other pursuits, such as art and philosophy. But to ensure that there is no excessive material exploitation of earth, rules are put in place. These rules are known as varna-ashrama-dharma.

Varna-dharma means every human being has to function as per his station in life, while ashrama-dharma means every human being has to function as per his stage in life. Thus, in dharma, humanity is governed by duty, not desire. Rules are not ends in themselves; they are warning signs so that greed does not rear its ugly head.

There are four stations in society: Brahmana, the station involved with spiritual activities; Kshatriya, the station involved in administrative activities; Vaishya, the station involved in wealth-generating activities; and Shudra, the station involved in service-providing activities.

Varna means disposition. Jati means profession. In an ideal world, varna corresponds to jati. But this is rarely the case. If it were so, then varna would supersede jati, as varna is natural while jati is man-made. When jati supersedes varna, when professional station is given more importance than natural disposition, problems emerge.

There are four stages, or Ashramas, of life: Brahmacharya, the student stage; Grahastha, the householder stage; the Vanaprastha, the retirement stage; and Sanyasa, the hermit stage. Ashrama ensures that not more than two generations utilised the earth's resources at any one time. When the grandson is born, it is time to retire, eat less food than the householder. And when the great grandson is born, it is time to become a hermit, eat what the forest, not the field, provides.

The role of instituting and maintaining dharma in society

Vishnu serves as the model for kingship.

The wheel represents rhythm and regularity.

The mace represents discipline.

The conch represents communication.

The downward pointing palm means the willingness to give.

The bird on which Vishnu travels represents the ability to be long-sighted and have a broader vision of things.

Stone sculpture of Vishnu seated on Garuda

is given to the king, who is treated as the diminutive double of Vishnu.

Like Vishnu seated on a hooded-serpent, he has to stay alert and ensure everybody behaves as expected of their station and stage. If things go wrong, he has to rush as Vishnu would rush on his eagle to set things right. Like Vishnu, he has to blow the conch-shell trumpet to remind people of their obligations to outgrow animal instincts. Like Vishnu, around whose index finger rotates the wheel, he has to review things periodically to ensure things keep moving. Like Vishnu, he has to wield his mace and lotus, punish law-breakers and reward law-abiders.

Only this will ensure peace and prosperity in the kingdom. And if all kings function as Vishnu does, there will be peace and prosperity across the world. The needs of humans will be satisfied without affecting the needs of animals and plants and the regenerative capacity of earth. Only if the king does his duty will the earth cow be happy.

But in the material world nothing is permanent. As faith in spiritual reality collapses, fear resurfaces, duty gives way to desire, ambition rears its ugly head, and eventually rules are compromised. Humans refuse to function as per their station in society and stage of life. The excesses of man breaks the back of the earth-cow and makes her udders sore. In despair, she turns to her guardian, Vishnu. And he responds by descending in various forms, sometimes animal, sometimes human. These descents are known as avataranas and the form Vishnu takes each time is known as avatar.

The number of avatars varies. The most popular list based on Jayadeva's 12th-century song, *Gita Govinda*, has ten: Matsya,

Matsya, aquatic.

Kurma, amphibian.

Varaha, terrestrial.

Narasimha, half human.

Vaman, dwarf.

Parashurama, priest who does not marry.

Ram, prince who is married.

Balarama, farmer who shunned war.

Krishna, cowherd with many wives.

Kalki, outsider who destroys everything.

**Avatars of Vishnu**

Kurma, Varaha, Narasimha, Vaman, Parashuram, Ram, Krishna, Buddha and Kalki. In the *Bhagavata Purana*, there are twenty-two avatars. The other twelve are: Chatursana, Narada, Nara-Narayana, Kapila, Dattatreya, Yagna, Rishabha, Prithu, Dhanvantari, Mohini, Vyasa and Balarama. Others included in the list of avatars are: Hamsa and Hayagriva.

Vishnu's rescue is material — destruction of forces that threaten the natural and social order. The rescue is also spiritual — enlightening creatures so that they do not threaten natural and social order.

It has often been commented that the order of Vishnu's descents follows the evolution of man: the aquatic Matsya, then the amphibian Kurma, then the terrestrial Varaha, followed by the half-human Narasimha and finally the human Vaman.

The human avatars, in turn, follow the varna system: Parashurama is a Brahmana who behaves as a Kshatriya, Ram is a Kshatriya by birth and action, Krishna is a Kshatriya by birth but functions as a Vaishya (cowherd) and Shudra (charioteer). They also follow the ashrama-system: Parashurama is a Brahmachari, Ram and Krishna are Grihastis, Buddha becomes a Vanaprasthi and finally, Sanyasi.

While material reality is bound to transform, Vishnu makes the transformations predictable by anticipating the changes and acting accordingly.

Thus, over time, all organisations and systems and pro-cesses and codes lose their relevance. This inevitable and gradual collapse of all systems is expressed in the concept of yuga.

Just as a human life has four phases: childhood, youth, maturity

Clay doll of Vishnu reclining on the serpent with Lakshmi at his feet

and old age, every organisation or system goes through four phases: Krita, Treta, Dvapara and Kali. It is said that the bull of dharma stands on four legs in the Krita yuga, on three legs in Treta yuga, two in Dvapara yuga and one in Kali yuga. After this, the bull of dharma and the society it upholds is washed away by the waters of Pralaya. This is death of the world, followed by rebirth. In the new life, the four yugas will follow each other once again. This is the kala-chakra, or the circle of time.

In the Bhagavad Gita, Krishna says, 'Whenever dharma is threatened, I descend to set things right.' This line has to be read with an understanding of yuga. Vishnu does not stop the march of time, nor does he reverse it. An avatar does not restore the ideal dharma, because there is no ideal dharma. An avatar re-defines dharma for a particular age. Dharma of Krita yuga is not the dharma of Treta yuga; times are different, needs are different, hence the code of civilisation is different. One can look at Vishnu as a doctor who appears whenever there is a disease. He restores health but does not stop aging. Eventually, a patient will die. The doctor's duty is to help the patient live a full and healthy life. This is what avatars do: balance human demands with nature's needs for as long as possible. Pralaya is an eventuality, but an avatar prevents it from happening prematurely.

One can say that when one age has reached its ebb, an avatar appears to facilitate the transition to the next age. Parashurama thus appears when the golden age of Krita yuga gives way to the silver age of Treta yuga. Ram appears when the Treta yuga gives way to the bronze age of Dvapara yuga. Krishna appears when the Dvapara yuga gives way to the iron age of Kali yuga. Buddha shows the way in Kali yuga and when Kali yuga comes to a close,

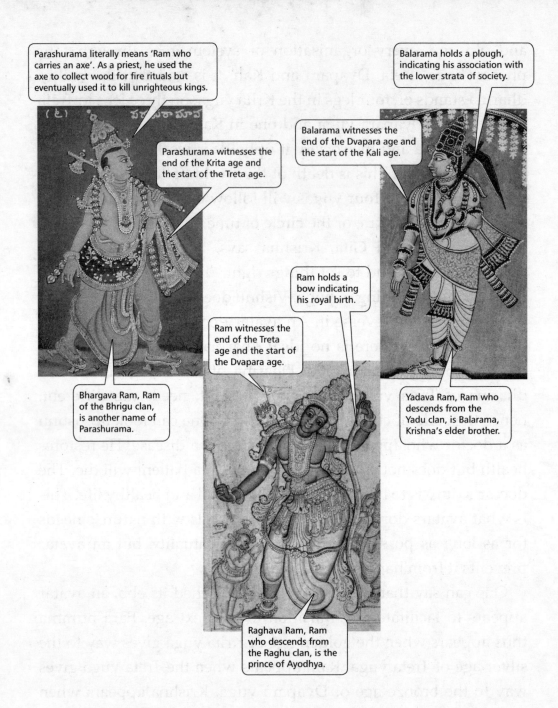

Mysore painting of three incarnations of Vishnu, all known as Ram

Kalki heralds Pralaya — death that leads to rebirth.

The shift from Krita yuga into Treta yuga happens when the notion of property emerges. Property relates to several things: domesticated animals, land, and even women.

The wife is visualised as property. She is expected to be obedient and faithful to her husband. In the Krita yuga, this is voluntary. But as the golden age draws to a close, desire and passion changes all this. Fidelity is enforced.

Renuka, a princess, marries Jamadagni, a priest. And she bears him five sons, the youngest of whom is Parashurama. Renuka is a faithful wife, so faithful that she can collect water in unbaked pots made of clay from the riverbank. But one day, Renuka sees a handsome Gandharva bathing in the river and sporting with his wives. Some say, it is not a Gandharva but a king called Kartavirya. She is smitten with passion for the handsome man. This momentary adulterous thought causes her to lose her magical powers; she can no longer collect water in unbaked clay pots. When her husband realises this, he is furious. He orders his sons to behead their mother. The elder four refuse and so die instantly. Parashurama, however, picks up the axe and severs his mother's neck. Pleased with this unconditional obedience, Jamadagni offers Parashurama a boon. 'Resurrect my mother back to life,' says Parashurama. Jamadagni does so, for he is a priest of the Bhrigu clan, and like Bhrigu and Bhrigu's son, Shukra, who serve the Asuras, he possesses Sanjivani Vidya, the secret lore of bringing the dead back to life.

In Krita yuga, cows are distributed freely by kings. The act of Kshatriya generosity ensures Brahmanas can carry out their

Mysore painting of Parashurama

Mysore painting showing Parashurama
beheading his mother, Renuka

Miniature painting from north India showing Parashurama killing Kartavirya,
the Haihaiya king

rituals and other spiritual and philosophical obligations without worrying about income. But then Krita yuga draws to a close and Kartavirya, king of the Haihaiya clan, seeks the return of a cow gifted to Jamadagni. Jamadagni finds the very idea preposterous. No one takes back gifts once given. But the king insists and begins to take the cow by force. Kartavirya is a powerful king, blessed with a thousand arms, a metaphor for his military might, and no one can stop him. Jamadagni begs the king to stop but the king refuses. Parashurama cannot bear to see his father demean himself so. He cannot bear to hear the piteous cries of the cow being dragged away by the king. So he picks up his axe and hacks the king to death. This is a shocking event — the killing of a king by a priest. When the sons of Kartavirya hear of this, they avenge their father's death by raiding Jamadagni's hermitage and cutting his head off. An infuriated Parashurama, takes an oath. To rid the earth of all warriors and kings. So a massacre begins. He kills twenty-one generations, some say twenty-one clans, of Kshatriyas. So much blood flows that it forms five lakes. Parashurama uses the blood of fallen kings to make funeral offerings to his father. He then swears to keep a watchful eye over the kings of the earth who abuse their military might to gain power.

But then one day Parashurama encounters Ram; he realises his work is done, for Ram is the model king, one who never uses his royal power for personal gain. Ram, like Parashurama, is an avatar of Vishnu, but the only one to be visualised and worshipped as a king.

Parashurama, though born in a family of priests, behaves as a warrior, thus transgressing the rules of varna. Ram, however, is

Miniature painting showing brothers

Chitrakathi painting from Maharashtra showing brothers

born in a family of kings and all his life behaves in keeping with what is expected of royalty.

He is the eldest son of Dashratha, king of Ayodhya, born of the first wife, and rightful heir to the throne. But on the eve of his coronation, his step-mother, Kaikeyi, reminds Dashratha of a promise made long ago, that he would give satisfy any two of her wishes. She demands that Ram go into exile and live as a hermit in the forest for fourteen years, and her son, Bharata, be made king instead. When informed of the situation, Ram, without regret or resentment, abandons his royal robes and goes to the forest followed by his dutiful wife, Sita, and his loving brother, Lakshman. To Kaikeyi's despair, Bharata refuses to take the throne acquired through deceit. He decides to live like a hermit himself and wait for his brother to return and reclaim his right to the throne.

The behaviour of Ram's brothers are very unlike the behaviour of other brothers Ram encounters as he moves from north to south during his exile. Far to the south is the kingdom of Lanka, ruled by Ravana, the Rakshasa who has usurped the throne from his brother, Kubera, the Yaksha. In between Ayodhya and Lanka is Kishkinda, land of monkeys, ruled by Vali, who was supposed to share his kingdom with his brother Sugriva, but following a misunderstanding, kicks him out.

This is not a geographical reference, rather a metaphorical indicator. In mythic vocabulary, north, the realm of the still Pole Star, is indicative of spiritual reality and south, the opposite, is indicative of material reality. And so, the farther one goes from Ayodhya to the south, the Ramayana reveals a gradual decay in the principles of dharma and the rise of man's animal and demonic nature.

Chitrakathi painting from Maharashtra of Surpanakha

A calendar print of Ravana abducting Sita

Dharma is about property rights as well as marriage rights. Ram and Sita are described as a couple who are eternally faithful to each other. Ram does not look at another woman, and Sita does not look at another man. They are the ideal couple. Their commitment to each other is repeatedly threatened by the world around.

When a Rakshasa woman, Surpanakha, seeks sexual gratification from Ram, he refuses on grounds that he is already married. The encounter turns ugly as Surpanakha, in keeping with her preference for the law of the jungle, tries to harm Sita. An enraged Lakshman cuts off Surpanakha's nose. Scorned thus, rather than tamed, Surpanakha complains to her brother, Ravana, who in outrage abducts Sita and carries her to his island-kingdom of Lanka, intent on making her one of his many wives. Sita, however, refuses to even look at Ravana. For her, there is no man but Ram.

In the forest, civilisation is gradually abandoned and rules are forgotten. Through force, a man can take his brother's property. Through force, men and women can disregard the marital rights of others. Neither Sita nor Ram let the forest erode their values. Wherever they go, they hold on to the principles of dharma. They may have left Ayodhya, but Ayodhya never leaves them.

In the forest, Ram encounters a monkey called Sugriva and helps him become king. In exchange, Sugriva offers to help Ram find Sita. Sugriva is bound by his word to help Ram. No such obligation binds another monkey called Hanuman. Hanuman serves Ram anyway. This spirit of generosity indicates spiritual awareness, a concern beyond the self for the other. Hanuman thus breaks free from Prakriti and becomes Purusha.

Calendar print of Hanuman building the bridge to Lanka

Calendar print of Hanuman revealing Ram in his heart

Animals are governed by their sexual and violent instincts. Humans can overpower these instincts because of their larger brain. Though animal, without the benefit of a larger brain, Hanuman practices celibacy and fights only for the benefit of others. This transforms him into an object of veneration. Though beast, he comes to be equated with God.

Under the leadership of Hanuman, the monkeys build a bridge across the sea to the island-kingdom of Lanka and launch an attack on Ravana's citadel. A king is supposed to be the provider and protector of his people. Ravan is neither; he is the archetypal alpha male for whom kingdom is nothing but territory. He is unwilling to give up Sita even if it means the destruction of Lanka. He sends his brothers and sons to their deaths, but refuses to part with Sita. He wants his way at all cost.

Ravana has ten heads and twenty hands. He is described as the son of a priest, well versed in the scriptures. He is also described as a devotee of Shiva. Despite all this knowledge, and all the powers bestowed upon him, he does not display wisdom. While the monkeys have transformed themselves into humans, Ravana descends from being human to animal. In fact, he is worse than animal, for his actions are not motivated by self-preservation or self-propagation. He is consumed by self-delusion and self-importance and that is ultimately his downfall.

After killing Ravana, Ram returns to Ayodhya with his wife Sita and is crowned king. This marks the dawn of Ram-rajya, the rule of Ram, considered the golden age when dharma is perfectly upheld.

But then, one day, Ram hears street gossip. The people of Ayodhya are embarrassed to have Sita as their queen, for having

Lakshman is asked to take Sita out of Ayodhya and leave her in the forest.

Sita is the innocent victim of street gossip and draconian royal laws that demand a queen should be above suspicion and gossip.

Chitrakathi painting from Maharashtra showing Sita being taken out of Ayodhya

Sita's twin sons, Luv and Kush, grow up with no knowledge of their father, and end up challenging his authority.

The royal horse is released by Ram so that all the lands it traverses unchallenged come under his rule.

Calendar art showing Sita's twin sons, Luv and Kush

spent several months as Ravana's captive she is a woman of tainted reputation. Ram promptly abandons Sita and has her sent to the forest, this despite the fact that she proves her fidelity by walking through fire unscathed. This is the controversial conclusion of the Ramayana. The obvious injustice is clearly at odds with the principles of dharma.

This episode draws attention to the complexity of dharma. Is Ram the king of Ayodhya first or the husband of Sita? As king, he is obliged to respect the wishes of the people of Ayodhya and the rules of his dynasty, that a woman of tainted reputation cannot be queen. But as husband, he is obliged to protect his wife. Ram chooses to be king first, sacrificing personal joy so that the integrity of the ruling family is never compromised.

One can argue that, as king, he should protect Sita who is, besides being wife and queen, also his subject. But one must remember that as king, Ram is expected not to make rules but to uphold them. This rule is the rule of his clan and he is obligated to uphold it. And Ram submits to it. This tale thus draws attention to the limitations of rules and traditions. The rules and traditions of the Raghu clan, which made Ram obey his father at the start of the epic, turn out to be draconian at the end of the epic when innocent Sita is rejected on grounds of tainted reputation.

But while Ram abandons Sita, the queen, he does not abandon Sita, the wife. He refuses to remarry. Instead he places beside him on his throne the golden effigy of Sita, a reminder that none can take her place. That the metal used to make Sita's image is gold, the purest of metals, is a symbolic representation of what Ram thinks of her character.

Every act in Hindu mythology has a consequence. And the

Kalamkari cloth painting of Ram;
it is unusual as it shows Ram with a moustache

abandonment of Sita has its consequence. After Sita is abandoned, Ram loses the only battle of his life. His royal horse is captured by Luv and Kush, Sita's children, born in the forest, who don't know that Ram is their father. They successfully fend off Ram's army, an indicator that dharma rests with Sita, not with Ayodhya.

Sita stops the war between Ram and his sons. Her victory is clear proof of her purity and chastity. The people of Ayodhya beg her forgiveness and ask her to return to the palace after reaffirming her chastity once more. So Sita asks the earth to open up and swallow her if she has been a faithful wife. The earth immediately opens up and Sita descends to the nether regions. It is in effect the return of Lakshmi to the land of her fathers.

Ram, as Vishnu, refuses to stay on earth without Lakshmi and so, after bequeathing his kingdom to his sons, walks into the river Sarayu and gives up his mortal body.

The final chapter of the Ramayana draws attention to the difference between dharma and niti and riti. Niti means law and riti means tradition. Laws and traditions are created in full earnestness to help the helpless. Sometimes they can end up being unfair and cruel. Sita's abandonment is a case in point. When law and tradition fail to uphold the principle of dharma, they need to be abandoned or changed. This thought is elaborated in the story of Krishna.

# 6. Krishna's Secret

*Know the thought behind the action*

Tanjore-style print showing the Krishna of *Bhagavata*

*T*he story of Krishna is spread across two epics: the *Bhagavata Purana* and the Mahabharata.

The *Bhagavata* refers to Krishna as the flute-playing, playful, lovable, mischievous, romantic cowherd who loves butter. Mahabharata refers to Krishna as the conch-blowing city-builder, warrior, leader, philosopher, statesman and charioteer covered with the grime of war. Together these two Krishnas create the purna-avatar, the most wholesome manifestation of God.

But Krishna is an unusual God. He challenges all conventional notions of divinity and appropriate social conduct. His name literally translates as 'black', challenging the traditional Indian discomfort with the dark complexion. He is visualised as either cowherd or charioteer, never as priest or king, a deliberate association with the lower strata of society. His mother is not his real mother, his beloved is not his wife, and the women he rescues are neither his subjects nor members of his family. His lovemaking is not really lovemaking; his war is not really war. There is always more than meets the eye. And so, only Krishna, of all the avatars, sports a smile, a mischievous, meaningful smile. There is always more than meets the eye, when Krishna is around.

While Ram is called Maryada Purushottam, he who upholds rules of society at any cost, Krishna is called Leela Purushottam, he who enjoys the game of life. Unlike Ram, who is serious and serene and evokes respect, Krishna is adorable and rakish, and evokes affection. Ram's story takes place in the second quarter of the world, the Treta yuga, when the bull of dharma stands on

A print of Parthasarathy of Chennai

three legs. Krishna's story takes place in a later, third quarter of the world, the Dvapara yuga, when the bull of dharma stands on two legs. Krishna's world is thus closer to the world we live in, the final quarter or Kali yuga, and shares the hazy morality and ethics we encounter today. In this world, the concept of dharma becomes even more difficult to express and institute. And this is most evident in the story of Yayati.

Yayati, an ancestor of Krishna, is cursed by his father-in-law to become old and impotent when he is discovered having a mistress. Yayati begs his sons to suffer the curse on his behalf so that he can retain his youth. Yadu, the eldest son, refuses to do so because he feels his father should respect the march of time and not feed on the youth of his children. Puru, the youngest son, however, agrees to accept his father's old age. Puru's sacrifice makes Yayati so happy that, years later, when he has had his fill of youth, he declares that the younger Puru will be his heir and not the elder Yadu. Further, he curses Yadu that none of his children or his children's children will be entitled to wear the crown.

Krishna, being Yadu's descendent, is therefore never king. Kingship passes on to Puru's descendents, the Pandavas and Kauravas, even though time and again they demonstrate their unworthiness to wear the crown.

What seems a good thing in Ram's yuga becomes a bad thing in Krishna's yuga. Ram's unquestioning obedience of his father transforms him into God. But Puru's unquestioning obedience results in the collapse of society. Dashratha requests Ram's obedience so that he can uphold his word. Yayati, however, demands the obedience of his children for his own pleasure. Yayati exploits the rule for his own benefit whereas Dashratha enforces the rule so

Devaki never nursed Krishna nor fed him butter, suggesting that this image is that of Yashoda; or the images of the two mothers are blurred; or in this image is fulfilled Devaki's desire to nurse Krishna.

The mother-child image alludes to Mother Mary and Jesus and according to local legend is the reason why this temple was not desecrated by the Portuguese rulers of Goa.

Krishna holds butter in his hand.

Print of Devaki Krishna enshrined at Marcela, Goa

that royal integrity is never questioned. The rule (obey the father) evokes dharma in Dashratha's case, but not so in Yayati's.

Yayati's conduct results in a society where the letter of the law becomes more important than the spirit of the law. This is the world of Krishna, a world where what matters more than the deed is the thought behind the deed.

⟨⚬⟩

The story of Krishna begins in Mathura, the city of the Yadavas. It is foretold that the eighth child of Devaki will kill her elder brother, Kamsa. Consumed by fear, Kamsa kills all of Devaki's children as soon as they are born.

The night Devaki delivers her eighth son, her husband Vasudeva takes him across the river Yamuna to Gokul. There, he exchanges his son for the daughter of Yashoda and cowherd-chief Nanda, who is born the same night. Yashoda wakes up to find Krishna in her arms. She assumes this is her son and raises him as a cowherd. Kamsa, meanwhile, tries to kill the girl he finds in Devaki's arms but the child slips out of his grasp, rises into the air, transforms into a goddess and informs him that his killer is safe. Kamsa fumes in frustration as he realises all his attempts to change his destiny have come to naught.

Krishna, as a consequence of his father's actions, ends up with two mothers: Devaki who gives birth to him and Yashoda who raises him. Devaki is a woman of noble rank. Yashoda is a common milkmaid. Devaki represents all the qualities one is born with. Yashoda represents all the qualities one acquires in life. Thus Krishna's divinity, rooted in Devaki's blood and Yashoda's milk, acknowledges both nature and nurture.

We are all a combination of what we are born with as well as

Butter is a symbol of love.

Mysore painting showing Krishna stealing butter

Clothes are the symbols of the masks we wear in society.

Nakedness indicates the truth of ourselves that we hide from the world as we adorn our bodies with clothes.

A south Indian temple wall carving showing Krishna stealing clothes

what we are raised to be. Our natural disposition is known as varna while the cultural indoctrination is jati. Krishna is by varna a nobleman but by jati a cowherd. Though nobleman, he can never be king. Though cowherd, he can always lead.

Our behaviour towards others is based on what we see and how we process our observation. But not all things can be seen. Jati can be seen but not varna. One can see behaviour but one has no access to beliefs. A man can dress as a cowherd and talk like a cowherd, but he may at heart be a prince. We will never know unless we open our eyes to this possibility.

In Krishna's narratives, butter, churned out of milk, is the symbol of love. The milkmaids of his village hoard the butter in pots hung high from ceilings, out of everyone's reach. They are only for sale. Krishna protests and demands its free distribution. And so, with a naughty glint in his eye, he climbs on the shoulders of his friends, reaches up to the pots and breaks them with glee, letting the butter of love flow out.

As Krishna grows up, the metaphor of love changes. Pots are no longer broken. Instead clothes are stolen. An embarrassing situation for the gopis bathing in the Yamuna and everyone hearing the story until we realise that in the language of symbols, clothes represent our public face. Krishna notices the sensitive hearts hiding behind each and every public face. This heart is sensitive, yearning to give affection and receive it.

Hearts resist and tongues complain, 'Don't steal our butter, Krishna. Don't steal our clothes, Krishna.' No one wants to be free with love. No one wants to expose the vulnerable heart. Everyone marches into Yashoda's house, demanding that Krishna be restrained.

Miniature painting showing the Maha-raas

Yashoda tries to stop Krishna but fails. She binds him to a drum, locks him inside the house, but Krishna remains the relentless mak-khan-chor and chitt-chor, he-who-steals-butter and he-who-steals-hearts. Until all defences break down, until there are no pots, no clothes, no stinginess with affection, only an open invitation to a heart full of buttery love.

⚬

When the heart is opened up, when love flows into it and from it, a sense of security prevails. With security comes freedom. There is no need to pretend. We can be ourselves. There is no desire to force our wills on anyone. We accept and embrace everyone, we include people, we allow them to be themselves, because we are accepted and embraced by God. The result is Maha-raas in the flowery meadow on the banks of the Yamuna, known as Madhuvan.

The Maha-raas, where Krishna plays the flute surrounded by a circle of dancing milkmaids, is a symbolic representation of absolute spontaneity. No formal relationship dictates Krishna's affection for the milkmaids. Unfettered by social restriction, it is created by emotions that are simple, innocent, with no underlying motive. That is why it takes the form of a circle, the most spontaneous of natural shapes. Between God in the centre and his devotees in the circumference only a radius of mutual unconditional affection prevails.

So long as the milkmaids love Krishna unconditionally without fetters, he multiplies himself and dances with each one of them, making each one feel completely and fully loved. But when they become possessive and refuse to share him with others, Krishna disappears and fills the women with despair. When realisation dawns and they beg forgiveness, Krishna returns to Madhuvan to

Kerala painting of Krishna taming the heron

Mysore painting of Krishna killing Putana

Odisha painting of Krishna subduing the serpent Kaliya in the river

Calendar art showing Krishna overpowering Kamsa

dance the dance of love.

The Maha-raas takes place outside the village, in the forest, at night, away from familiar surroundings. Yet the women feel safe. They are unthreatened by the law of the jungle. They have faith in Krishna and no fear. When Krishna plays the flute in the middle of the jungle, love — not force — prevails. The weakest, the most unfit, are not afraid. They can sing, dance and thrive in joyous abandon.

But Krishna's abode is not the jungle. First he lives in the village of Gokul, and later his parents migrate to Vrindavan, as Gokul becomes increasingly unsafe. These villages are domesticated spaces. Domestication of the land involves violence, the forcible removal or suppression of wild forces that threaten the settlement.

Krishna is threatened several times in his childhood. He is threatened by a wet-nurse, Putana, who carries poison in her breasts. He is threatened by natural forces: a whirlwind, a forest fire and torrential rain. He is threatened by animals: a wild horse, an errant calf, a ferocious bull, a python, a crane and a donkey. He is even threatened by cartwheels rolling down the street. As Krishna defends himself and protects his village from these various threats, he becomes violent. The demons are killed or driven away. The wild beasts are subdued and their spirit is broken as they are tamed. The forest fire is swallowed and a mountain raised to protect the village from the wet torrential downpour.

Thus Krishna acknowledges the violence that is implicit in human survival. More than the act of violence, what matters is the thought behind the violence. The demons seek to hurt Krishna because his existence threatens Kamsa; their violence is rooted in

A print of Ranchhodji Krishna enshrined in Dwarka

Kamsa's fear and his refusal to accept his fate. Such violence is adharma. Krishna's violence is defensive, rooted in the human need to survive and thrive; he does not want to hurt or exploit anyone. His violence is therefore dharma.

When Kamsa hears of this remarkable cowherd in Vrindavan who kills demons and tames wild beasts and holds mountains up with his little finger, he is convinced that this is his long lost nephew, his nemesis. Determined to change his fate and intent on killing him, he invites Krishna to a wrestling match in his city of Mathura, and sends a royal chariot to fetch him.

But things do not go as planned. The charismatic lad not only overpowers the mighty wrestlers of Mathura, he also kills the royal elephant, breaks the royal bow and finally attacks and kills the wicked king, to the delight of all the Yadavas who have grown tired of Kamsa's excesses.

The killing of Kamsa is unique because it is the only story in Hindu mythology where a father-figure is killed. Unlike Ram who submits to Dashratha, and Yadu who submits to Yayati, Krishna refuses to submit to Kamsa. This tale marks a shift in thinking where the younger generation refuses to suffer the tyranny of the older generation. This makes Krishna a radical hero in the Hindu spiritual landscape.

When the royal chariot carrying Krishna rolled out of Vrindavan for Mathura, the milkmaids had feared that Krishna would never return. Krishna had assured them that he would, as soon as the wrestling match was over. But after the killing of Kamsa, Krishna's true identity is revealed. He is Devaki's son, not Yashoda's. He is a Yadava nobleman, not a common cowherd. Destiny has other

Kerala mural of Krishna getting married

Mysore painting of Krishna with many wives

plans for him and he must submit to it. He cannot return to the land of milk and butter and cows and milkmaids, the land of his pleasure. His tryst with kings has begun.

Kamsa's father-in-law, Jarasandha, attacks the city of Mathura to avenge Kamsa's death and burns it to the ground. Rather than fight to the death, Krishna withdraws from the battlefield and takes the Yadavas westwards to the safety of the island-city of Dwarka, far from Jarasandha's influence. This display of discretion over valour is uncharacteristic of warriors and once again positions Krishna as an unconventional hero, one who accepts the inglorious epithet of Ran-chor-rai, the warrior who withdrew from battle. Krishna lives to fight another day.

Amongst all the milkmaids of Vrindavan, there is one who is identified as being closest to Krishna. Her name is Radha. Radha is said to be the wife of Yashoda's brother and she is older than Krishna. Theirs thus is a relationship that transcends custom and law. In their pure love, unbound by expectations, unanchored by conventions, there is music. It inspires Krishna to play the flute.

But when Krishna leaves Vrindavan, he enters a world of customs and laws, where no relationship is pure, where everything is fettered by expectations. The music stops. He gives up his flute and instead takes up the conch-shell of warriors. He goes about marrying women — not for love, but out of a sense of duty.

He elopes with and marries Rukmini, princess of Vidarbha, after she begs him to save her from a loveless marriage she is being forced into. He marries Satyabhama, who is given to him as a token of gratitude, when he identifies the killer of her uncle and recovers a very precious jewel, the Syamantaka, belonging to her family.

Calendar art showing the five Pandavas and their common wife, Draupadi

He ends up with eight principal wives and later gets 16,100 junior wives, women who seek refuge with him after he kills Naraka, the demon-king who held them captive in his harem.

Krishna is a good husband to all these women and a good father to their children. He multiplies himself several fold so that he can give each wife individual attention and no wife feels abandoned or excluded. But none of the wives sees the passion in his eyes that is reserved for Radha, nor do they dance around him as the milk-maids did in the forest. The relationship here is much like Ram's relationship with Sita, formal, dictated by custom, based on respect not passion.

Krishna does not receive love from his maternal uncle, Kamsa. But he ensures the same is not the fate of the Pandavas, his cousins. Their maternal uncle is Krishna's father, Vasudev.

Krishna finds his aunt, Kunti, and her sons in abject poverty, having been denied their inheritance by their father's brother, the blind Dhritarasthra and his hundred sons, the Kauravas. The only thing the five Pandavas have going for them is that they share a common wife, Draupadi, princess of Panchala, who is no ordinary woman, but Lakshmi.

When Vishnu is Parashurama, Lakshmi takes the form of his father's cow. In other words, she is his mother, providing him nutrition. When Vishnu is Ram, Lakshmi takes the form of Sita, his faithful wife, who stands by his side at all times. When Vishnu is Krishna, Lakshmi takes the form of Draupadi, not his mother or his wife, but a distant relative, barely connected by blood or marriage. Draupadi cares for Krishna as Radha does, without expectations. And that is why Krishna always watches over her, even

Modern painting showing Krishna replacing Draupadi's clothes
as the Kauravas try to disrobe her

though he is not obliged to.

With Draupadi as their wife and Krishna as their friend, the Pandavas demand from their uncle their half of the family inheritance. After much deliberation, they are given the forest of Khandavaprastha. With the help of Krishna, they transform this forest into the prosperous kingdom of Indraprastha.

With Krishna behind them, the Pandavas turn into a lethal force. Bhima, the mightiest Pandava, kills Jarasandha, destroyer of Mathura, in a duel. And Yudhishtira, the eldest Pandava, earns the right to declare himself a sovereign king.

Unfortunately, success goes to the head of the Pandavas. And while Krishna is away, they accept an invitation from the Kauravas to a gambling match. There they gamble away everything — not just gold and cows, but also their newfound kingdom, their own liberty and even their wife.

This gambling match is an indicator of the collapse of dharma for it shows kings treating culture as property. They have forgotten why dharma was instituted and kingdoms established in the first place: to create extra material resources so that man can look beyond survival and look for meaning.

That Krishna is not by their side when the Pandavas are gambling away everything indicates the lack of spiritual awareness. They become like Devas who lose Lakshmi.

Having managed to wrench away from the Pandavas everything they possess, the Kauravas, like Asuras, are consumed by megalomania. Instead of protecting the helpless, as kings are supposed to, they exploit the situation, like Rakshasas.

Draupadi, gambled away by her five husbands, now a Kaurava slave, is dragged by her hair, brought to the gambling hall and dis-

Mughal miniature showing Krishna negotiating peace with the Kauravas

robed in public. She demands justice, appeals to clemency, but no one comes to her rescue. Everyone hides behind the letter of the law. The spirit of dharma is totally forgotten as Draupadi screams in horror and raises her arms in utter helplessness.

This is when Krishna reveals his divinity. Miraculously, bending space and time, Krishna ensures that every cloth that is removed from Draupadi's body is replaced by another cloth. This is Vishnu acting as Govinda, the cowherd, protecting the earth-cow who is being abused by her so-called guardians, the kings. He promises to rid the earth of such unrighteous kings. He promises to wash her tears with their blood.

A pact is reached. The Pandavas and their wife will live in forest exile for twelve years followed by a year incognito. If in the final year they escape identification then the Kauravas promise to restore to the Pandavas all that they gambled away.

'Why can we not fight and take back what is ours right away? Why should we suffer thirteen years of humiliating exile?' demand the Pandavas. To this Krishna says, 'Because you have given your word. And because only this way will you be cleansed of the crime of gambling your kingdom away.'

For thirteen years, the Pandavas suffer the exile. During this time, their children live with Krishna. It is during such times of crisis that Saraswati returns to the Pandavas. Each brother admits their flaws and faults and emerges a stronger man. They meet sages and learn what the point of kingship is, what the point of material security is and the reason one must aspire for spiritual growth. It is during the exile, especially the final year spent living as servants in the court of King Virata, that the Pandavas make

Modern painting showing Arjuna before the war

Mysore painting showing Arjuna during the war

themselves worthy of kingship.

After thirteen years of exile, the Pandavas emerge cleansed but the Kauravas remain corrupt as ever, refusing to keep their word, refusing to even compromise. Krishna says, 'For the sake of peace at least give your cousins five villages.' But Duryodhana, the eldest of the Kauravas, refuses to part with even a needlepoint of land. It is then that Krishna encourages the Pandavas to declare war on the Kauravas.

This war is not for property. This war is about dharma. And dharma is about outgrowing the animal instinct of territoriality and discovering the human ability to share and care. The Kauravas refuse to share their wealth with their own brothers. They refuse to keep their word and use force to usurp other people's wealth. The earth cannot be burdened by such kings. They have to be killed.

Like the Maha-raas, the war at Kurukshetra is not what it seems. Both are paradoxes. The sexuality of the former is not about sex and the violence of the latter is not about violence. Beneath the unabashed clandestine sexuality of the Maha-raas is the absence of desire for any physical conquest; it is about perfect love and absolute security that allows married women to dance and sing all night in the forest with a divinely handsome boy. Likewise, the bloodshed at Kurukshetra is not about property or vengeance; it is about restoring humanity, outgrowing animal instincts, and discovering the divine.

Krishna does not fight in this war. He serves only as charioteer and guide. He can only encourage; the action is left to the Pandavas. It is their battle, their action, their decision. All he does, before the war starts, is to remind them that the war is not about property

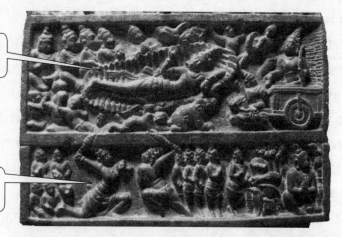

Bhishma lying on a bed of arrows, pinned to the ground.

The mace battle between Duryodhana and Bhima.

Karna and Arjuna showering arrows at each other.

Ghatotkacha, the son of Bhima, killed when Drona leads the Kauravas.

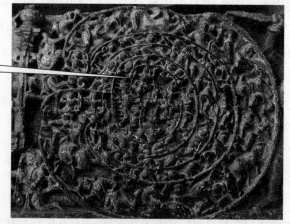

Abhimanyu, trapped in the whirlpool formation of Chakravyuha set up by Drona.

Temple wall carvings from Pattadakal and Halebid in Karnataka, showing scenes from the war at Kurukshetra

or vengeance. It is about restoring dharma and dharma is about sharing; about giving, not taking. The war is not about conquering material reality; that is a delusion for material reality can never be conquered. It is about realising spiritual reality through material reality. It is about questioning the very notions of property and identifying where from come greed, envy, rage and hate. It is about realising that in every human being is a frightened beast, seeking survival and significance, and knowing very well that humans can outgrow this beast as they empathise with others. This process of outgrowing the beast is the process of discovering God. This discourse of Krishna before the war is called the Bhagavad Gita, song of God.

The Kaurava forces are first led by the grand patriarch Bhishma who is like a father to the Pandavas. Krishna encourages his killing because Bhishma has abandoned ashrama-dharma. Like Yayati's son, Puru, he indulges the lust of his father, Shantanu, when he decides to give up sex so that his old father can marry the woman he loves. Though never married, he lives as a householder taking care of his nephews and his grandnephews. Even when the grand-nephews, the Pandavas and Kauravas, are old enough to take charge, in an overprotective zeal, he refuses to gracefully withdraw and continues to participate in worldly affairs.

When it emerges that killing Bhishma is impossible since he has the power to choose the time of his death, Krishna encourages the Pandava Arjuna to shoot a hundred arrows and pin the old man to the ground and immobilise him. Thus Krishna forcibly removes the incorrigible Bhishma from the arena of society.

After Bhishma, the Kauravas are led by their teacher, Drona, who is also teacher to the Pandavas. Krishna encourages Drona's

Kerala mural showing Parashurama, the warrior-priest incarnation of Vishnu

killing because Drona has abandoned varna-dharma. Though born in a family of priests, he functions as a warrior and even crowns his son king of a kingdom created by laying claim to one half of Draupada's land. As teacher, he teaches his students everything about war and nothing about peace. He teaches his students about taking property rather than sharing property. He teaches them everything about material reality and nothing about spiritual reality.

And so, Krishna encourages the Pandava Yudhishtira to tell a white lie and declare that Ashwatthama is dead. 'You will refer to Ashwatthama, the elephant, but he will assume it is Ashwatthama, his son. Heartbroken, he will stop fighting, and when he stops fighting,' says Krishna, 'Draupadi's brother, Dhristadhyumna, can sever his head from his body as he severed Draupada's kingdom of Panchala.'

After Drona, Karna is raised to the position of commander. Both Karna and Krishna know that Karna is the child of Kunti, born before her marriage to Pandu. He is therefore the elder brother of the Pandavas, Krishna's eldest cousin, who was raised amongst charioteers.

Karna manages to learn archery from Parashurama and becomes a renowned archer in the Kaurava court. Draupadi refused to let him contest for her hand in marriage because of his association with charioteers, and the Pandavas revile him constantly because of his low social status, but Duryodhana treats him like a prince. Draupadi's action costs her dearly. She rejects a charioteer only to end up marrying five men who gamble her away. Duryodhana's affection costs Karna dearly; he is forced to choose between a friend and dharma. Karna chooses his friend.

And so God turns against him. In the heat of battle his chariot

Photographs of Kathakali performances

wheel gets stuck in the ground. As he jumps down to release the wheel, Krishna encourages Arjuna to shoot the unarmed helpless Karna in his back. Arjuna protests but Krishna insists. A man who allowed the helpless Draupadi to be abused, a man who chose friendship over dharma, has no right to claim protection under dharma.

Bhishma, Drona and Karna are all students of Parashurama. Each one is taught warfare to uphold dharma. But each one remains silent when Draupadi is being disrobed in public. Each one of them justifies, however regretfully, their support of the Kauravas over Pandavas. Ultimately, they focus on rules rather than the spirit of dharma. Ultimately, they focus on their own helplessness rather than the consequences of their actions on society at large. That is why, as Krishna, Vishnu engineers the killing of his own students.

Krishna silently witnesses the killing of each and every Kaurava by the Pandava Bhima. He watches as Bhima drinks the blood of Dusshasana, Duryodhana's brother who had disrobed Draupadi. He watches Bhima wash Draupadi's hair, untied during that horrific incident, with Dusshasana's blood and tie it with Dusshasana's entrails. Thus a vile vow taken thirteen years ago in the gambling hall is fulfilled.

When it becomes difficult to kill Duryodhana, Krishna encourages the breaking of a war-rule: never strike the enemy below the waist. Bhima strikes Duryodhana below the waist and breaks his thighs.

With the hundredth Kaurava killed, the Pandavas are declared victorious. They are now masters not only of Indraprastha, the kingdom they built, but also of Hastinapur, the kingdom of their

The songs of the Ashta-Chaap poets, including Surdas, is sung for Srinathji.

Narayaniyam composed by Melpathur Narayana Bhattathiri is sung at Guruvayoor.

Songs of Haridasa devotional poets are sung for Chennakeshava.

Songs of Tukaram are sung in praise of Vithal.

Krishna enshrined in (clockwise) Nathdvara, Rajasthan; Guruvayoor, Kerala; Pandharpur, Maharashtra; and Udupi, Karnataka

ancestors that they should have inherited.

But victory comes at a price. Following the eighteen-day war, Drona's son, Ashwatthama, attacks the Pandava camp at night and kills the five children of Draupadi, mistaking them to be the Pandavas. As God, Krishna knew this would happen but he does not stop it, perhaps to remind the Pandavas of the consequences of any war, even one fought for dharma.

And so, in the end, Krishna has to console two women: Gandhari, the mother of the Kauravas, and Draupadi, the wife of the Pandavas. Both have lost their children.

Gandhari curses Krishna and his family. Krishna lets her. In that fit of rage, all the bitterness in Gandhari's heart gushes out leaving behind a soul once again pure for love. Gandhari then weeps uncontrollably for her imperfect children. Krishna holds her tight, feeling her pain.

Krishna also feels Draupadi's pain. The battle which avenges her humiliation also claims all five of her children. Draupadi learns that both vengeance and justice come at a price. Krishna asks her to forgive and let go. It is difficult. He holds her in his arms and gives her strength. Life is difficult and people are imperfect. Unable to cope with the vagaries of this world, everyone makes mistakes. True love is the ability to love people despite their mistakes.

In the final chapter of the Mahabharata, Yudhishtira is indignant when he finds the Kauravas in heaven. 'How can they — the cause of so much suffering — be given a place in heaven?' Krishna retorts, 'You killed them in battle and ruled their lands and still you hate them? You claim to have renounced the world but you have not renounced your rage. How then can you stake a claim to heaven?'

Rajagopalswamy from Tamil Nadu, Nayaka period

In the Hindu world, everything is God. Everything. Even the Kauravas. Everything in the world is a part of Krishna. Everything therefore can be loved and is capable of loving. He who has truly realised Krishna cannot hate the Kauravas. He cannot hate anyone. Krishna may punish the Kauravas for their misdeeds, but he never rejects them. His love makes room for the weakest, the cruellest, the most imperfect. This is dharma.

When we stop loving, we embrace adharma. We judge, condemn and reject people. Invalidate them in hatred. We stop being generous. Like the Kauravas, we become mean-minded, petty, stingy, clingy and possessive. Or like the Pandavas, we become clueless, confused, in search of direction and wisdom. We forget the path to Madhuvan. We entrap ourselves in Kurukshetra.

The earth weeps for us. Because in our inability to love, in our pursuit for power, in our lack of wisdom, we lose a golden opportunity to enjoy life, make life enjoyable for others and find joy in giving joy. That is why the Krishna saga begins when the earth-cow stands before Vishnu and begs him to save her children.

God listens. The cowherd turns into the charioteer. He disciplines the unruly horses of the head with verses of the Bhagavad Gita. The verses provide a true understanding of life, an understanding that prevents false interpretations of circumstances and false expectations from the world. Thus enlightened, the heart loses its craving for power and embraces love. We participate in life, not to control it, but to appreciate it.

The charioteer Krishna of the Mahabharata, lord of Rukmini, appeals to our head and helps us in times of crisis. He transforms our world from a battlefield into a garden. He leads us out of Kurukshetra and helps us return to Madhuvan.

Poster art showing Radha and Krishna

There we find the cowherd Krishna of the *Bhagavata*, lord of Radha, who appeals to our heart, and awakens a desire for celebration. Senses stirred, heart rejoicing in love, head filled with wisdom, we submit innocently to his music and take our place in his Maha-raas.

# 7. Kalki's Secret

## Allow things to wane

Two 19th-century Kalighat paintings from Bengal

*W*hen telling the story of the Mahabharata, parents often forget to tell their children a very important detail. That Balarama, Krishna's elder brother, refused to participate in the war. While Krishna led the Pandavas to victory on the battlefields of Kurukshetra, Balarama was away on a pilgrimage, unable to make sense of the carnage.

In some scriptures, Balarama is an avatar of Vishnu's serpent, Sesha, accompanying Vishnu when the latter descends on earth. But in other scriptures, especially those from south India, he is an incarnation of Vishnu, the ninth of the ten avatars. He is shown holding agricultural implements such as the plough and the pestle, unlike Krishna who holds implements of animal husbandry. This suggests that in early India, the two gods were gods associated with primary economic activities and that later, they acquired deeper metaphysical significance, but always complementing each other.

Through Krishna, Vishnu embraces worldliness or pravritti-marga, while through Balarama, Vishnu embraces monasticism or nivritti-marga. Though Balarama is the elder brother of Krishna, in the list of incarnations, he comes after Krishna, suggesting perhaps that in the lore of Vishnu, Balarama's approach is not as preferred as Krishna's.

Balarama is not a shrewd diplomat like his younger brother, nor is he the romantic rake. In the temple in Puri, Odisha, Krishna is worshipped as Jagannath, lord of the world, alongside his younger sister, Subhadra, and his elder brother, Balarama. While in the traditional narrative Balarama is married to Revati and has a daughter called Vatsala, in the Puri temple tradition he is treated

Traditional dolls of Jagannath and his siblings, brother Balabhadra and sister Subhadra

almost like an ascetic who, like Shiva, likes bhang, a drink made using narcotic Indian hemp, and shuns the company of women. This disengagement from women in metaphysical terms indicates a withdrawal from material reality. While Krishna struggles with the Pandavas to hold on to dharma, Balarama simply lets go. He goes away on pilgrimage and allows things to collapse. Balarama is thus more Shiva-like than Vishnu-like, and as the ninth avatar, after Krishna, he seems to herald the end of the world.

Like Shiva who supports Devas and Asuras equally, Balarama supports the Pandavas and the Kauravas equally. He trains both Bhima and Duryodhana in the art of fighting with a mace. Since he feels Krishna sides with the Pandavas, he tries to balance things by favouring Duryodhana over Bhima. On his return from his pilgrimage, he learns that Bhima killed Duryodhana by breaking a rule of mace-warfare: he had struck below the navel, and smashed Duryodhana's thigh. In fury, he raises his plough determined to strike and punish Bhima. But Krishna stops his elder brother, reminds him the war is over, and that for dharma, sometimes, rules have to be broken. Rules exist to protect the helpless; Duryodhana has misused the rules to abuse helpless Draupadi, hence has lost the moral right to claim protection under the rules. Balarama sees sense in Krishna's words and lowers his plough.

Balarama is a passionate god. He gets angry easily and is appeased as easily. He is also a simpleton. All these are also traits of Shiva. He does not understand the machinations of Krishna. He does not understand Krishna's complex logic, expressed in the *Bhagavad Gita*, justifying the war. He does not appreciate the notion of property. For him wisdom lies in renouncing property altogether.

But Balarama trusts Krishna. He knows there is wisdom in his

Images showing Krishna and Shiva in their distinctive stances;

Poster art showing the death of Krishna

younger brother's words. Perhaps there is another way to live, with property, by outgrowing the attachment for property. This can only happen not by shunning desire but by engaging with desire and exploring the roots of territorial behaviour.

In the Mahabharata, at the end of the war in Kurukshetra, Krishna is cursed by Gandhari, the mother of the Kauravas. Though Krishna has helped re-establish dharma, he has also broken a mother's heart by not sparing even one of her hundred sons. Gandhari curses Krishna that he will witness the killing of his own children and grandchildren and relatives and see his city fall.

The curse realises itself thirty-six years later. Krishna, and Balarama, watch their entire clan destroy itself in a mindless civil war ignited by an argument as to who was right and who was wrong in Kurukshetra. After this, Balarama loses all will to live; his life slips out of his mouth in the form of a serpent. Shortly after Balarama's death, Krishna dies too; he is shot dead by a hunter who mistakes his toe for the snout of a deer and shoots a poisoned arrow.

The hunter's arrow strikes Krishna on the sole of his left foot. Normally, in images, while playing the flute, Krishna always stands on his left foot and swings his right foot across. This is the opposite of Shiva's typical posture; Shiva stands on his right foot and swings his left foot across. The left foot represents material reality because it belongs to the side of the beating heart while the right foot represents spiritual reality because it belongs to the stiller, more silent, opposite side. Krishna stands firmly on the left foot, but also places the right foot on the ground, indicating grounding in material reality giving cognisance to spiritual reality.

Kalamkari print of Buddha

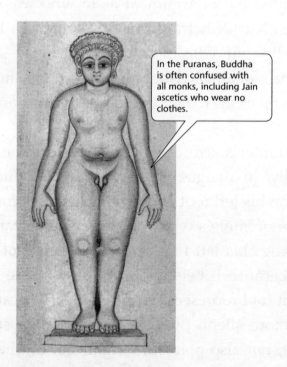

Mysore painting of Buddha

Shiva, on the other hand, balances his entire body on the right foot, indicating his clear preference for spiritual reality alone, making him Shiva-Ekapada, Shiva who stands on one foot.

At the time of his death, Krishna took an opposite stance; he swung his left foot over the right, exposing the left sole. In other words, as his time on earth as Krishna came to an end, Vishnu abandoned pravritti-marga represented by the left foot and embraced nivritti-marga represented by the right foot. The world-embracing that characterised his earlier avatars now had to wane because the Dvapara yuga had come to an end and the Kali yuga, the fourth and final quarter of the world, had dawned.

In the more popular list of the ten avatars of Vishnu, the ninth avatar is shown as Buddha, not Balarama. Some Hindu scriptures say Vishnu descended as Buddha out of compassion for animals to stop the practice of animal sacrifices and to promote non-violence and vegetarianism. Others say Vishnu took the form of the Buddha to distract people from Vedic practices, to prepare the world for its imminent destruction.

Buddhists do not accept either of these claims; they see it as an attempt by shrewd Hindu storytellers to make Buddhism a subsect of Hinduism. From a historical point of view, the inclusion of Buddha as an avatar of Vishnu does seem to have political motivation, but from a philosophical point of view, the Buddha-avatar indicates a step closer to the end of the world.

In the *Rig Veda* it is said that desire is the root of creation. Because spiritual reality (Narayana) desired to know himself, Brahma bloomed out of Vishnu's lotus and Brahmanda, Brahma's world, came into being. Thus Kama, or desire, is a living, giving force.

Three visual representations of Kalki in Mysore art

But in Buddhist mythology, Kama is Mara, the demon of desire. He is the root cause of all suffering. If one wants liberation from all suffering, one must abandon all desire. When this happens, all engagement stops, life ceases to be. This is the monastic path, the nivritti-marga which ultimately leads to what the Buddhists call nirvana, blowing out of the flame, an idea similar to the Hindu notion of moksha, liberation from the cycle of rebirths.

When there is no desire, Narayana would not wake up and Shiva would not open his eyes to the splendour of Prakriti. The Goddess would remain unacknowledged. There would be no Maya, no Brahmanda, no subjective reality, no human observation of nature, no flowering of human consciousness, just Prakriti without Purusha. This disengagement of the two metaphysical realities is described as destruction.

While Buddha and/or Balarama represents destruction by passive withdrawal from the world, Kalki represents active destruction of the world. He is the tenth and final avatar of Vishnu, visualised as a warrior who rides a white horse and brandishes a flaming sword.

The story of Kalki starts appearing in Hindu scriptures at the time when India was overrun by a whole host of foreign marauders from Central Asia. These were brutal and barbaric tribes such as the Huns and later the Mongols. The story was a clear response to their brutality. These new invaders were destroying the old way of life and it was hoped that Vishnu, as Kalki, would destroy the new ways, and restore life to the old ways. Kalki was probably inspired by messianic thoughts that is prevalent in Judaism, Christianity and Islam. He was the deliverer and the saviour.

Across India, there are many folk heroes who ride a horse and

The priest who takes up arms, Parashurama.

The prince who gives up his kingdom and his wife, Ram.

The cowherd and charioteer who brings wisdom, Krishna.

The hermit who withdraws, Buddha.

The final warrior, destroyer and saviour, Kalki.

Bronze images of the traditional five human avatars of Vishnu brandish a sword much like Kalki. He is thus almost a guardian god in folk imagination, but in the scriptures, he is the one who will close the Kalpa, the world-cycle, so that a new one can begin.

Even the Buddhists had a similar idea, of a Bodhisattva of the future, Manjushri, who yields a flaming sword. In the Tibetan Buddhist tradition, this wrathful manifestation Manjushri is called Yamantaka. Yamantaka is an epithet associated with Shiva in Hindu tradition and means the destroyer of death. Thus, metaphysically, Kalki will destroy everything, even death. He will destroy all structures so that none exist. In other words, he will herald Pralaya.

Material reality is impermanent. It has to change; in other words, it has to die and be reborn. So everything that has form and name has to eventually wither away and die. In the lore of Vishnu these transformations of Prakriti are not random; they are organised and predictable. They take the form of yugas, or eras. Just as every living organism goes through four phases of life — childhood, youth, maturity and old age — so does the world. Krita yuga marks the childhood of the world, Treta yuga marks the youth, Dvapara marks the maturity of the world and Kali, its old age. Parashurama heralds the end of Krita, Ram the end of Treta, Krishna the end of Dvapara, and Kalki the end of Kali yuga. Pralaya is death, death before rebirth. Pralaya is when Vishnu goes to sleep, becomes Narayana. Pralaya is when Ananta becomes Sesha, infinity becomes zero and Yoga-maya becomes Yoga-nidra.

Vishnu thus acknowledges the end of the world, engages with it, even participates in it. While as Parashurama and Ram and Krishna, he struggles to hold on to dharma, despite the corrupting march of time, as Balarama and finally Kalki, he lets go and allows

Calendar art showing milkmaids weeping as Krishna leaves Vrindavan

Photograph showing the Ratha-yatra festival of Puri, Odisha

the world to collapse. This is wisdom, knowing when to act and when to withdraw, knowing when to stop fighting and allowing age to take its toll.

The idea of things ending recurs in the three great epics of India: Ramayan, Mahabharata and *Bhagavata*. In the Ramayan, in the end, Sita returns to the earth whence she came from and Ram walks into the river Sarayu, never to rise up again. In the Mahabharata, in the end, the Pandavas have to renounce their kingdom and walk up the mountains, seeking heaven and ultimately facing death. In the *Bhagavata*, Krishna leaves the village of cowherds, Vrindavan, and makes his way to the city of Mathura. He leaves on a chariot whose charioteer's name is Akrura, one who is not cruel. The milkmaids beg Krishna to stay back but Krishna moves on to the next phase of his life, abandoning his parents and friends and lovers. That the charioteer is 'not-cruel' is a clear communication that one must never begrudge the march of time. Like Yashoda, who raised Krishna with love and affection only to watch him leave her and go to Mathura, we must all ultimately learn to let go.

In a way, Akrura is Yama, the god of death, described in mythology as dispassionate. Yama evokes fear in all of us. But Yama himself does not seek to frighten; he has no feelings. He is merely doing his duty as the one who separates material reality from spiritual reality. The journey which begins in the mother's womb ends with the arrival of Yama. In the mother's womb, thanks to Kama, the god of love, spiritual reality interacts with and is wrapped in material reality. But a time comes when Yama must unwrap the material reality and release spiritual reality.

Both Kama and Yama are forms of Vishnu, doing their duty,

Kama, god of love, shoots an arrow that will inflame the five senses.

Yama, god of death, rides a buffalo that moves steadily towards all living creatures and will eventually catch up with them.

Miniature painting of Kama

Cambodian stone carving of Yama

The wheel and the mace associated with inevitability and pain are symbols of Yama in Vishnu's arms.

The conch and lotus flower associated with water and life are symbols of Kama in Vishnu's arms.

Benarasi wooded doll of Vishnu

preserving the cycle of rebirths. Kama ignites life. Yama ignites death. Kama ensures death is not permanent; Yama ensures life is not permanent. There are typically no temples dedicated to Kama or Yama but their images are sometimes seen in Vishnu temples. Kama is depicted riding a parrot and holding a sugarcane bow in his hand; Yama rides a buffalo and holds in his hand either a book of accounts or a staff or a noose. Kama arouses the senses, makes Brahma succumb to the power of Maya; Yama ensures that all actions are repaid, thus maintaining the account book of Karma.

The symbols of Kama and Yama are found on the image of Vishnu. Vishnu holds in his hands four symbols: Shankha (conch), Chakra (wheel), Gada (mace) and Padma (lotus). Shanka symbolises communication; Chakra marks the wheel of time; Gada the demand for discipline; Padma the nectar of joy. Shankha and Padma are water symbols; they affirm life and love and so are associated with Kama. Chakra and Gada are fire symbols; they affirm the rhythm of nature and the rules of culture and so are associated with Yama. Together, Kama and Yama preserve life. Together, Kama and Yama make up Vishnu.

A little known character in Hindu mythology is Vadavagni, a mare which breathes fire and stands on the ocean floor. This submarine mare causes the sea water to evaporate and turn into mist, thus preventing the sea from ever overflowing on to land. It is said that at the time of Pralaya, Vadavagni will stop doing this, causing the ocean to expand and submerge the earth. The fire of the submarine mare will burst forth in the form of volcanoes. Everything will be destroyed by lava and water.

The origin of the fire-breathing mare is interesting. According

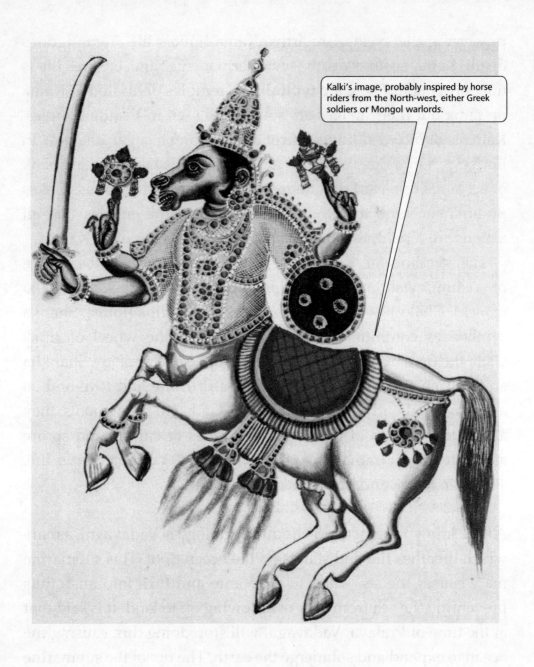

Kalki's image, probably inspired by horse riders from the North-west, either Greek soldiers or Mongol warlords.

South Indian painting of Kalki

to one story, Kama, the god of love, once tried to arouse desire in the mind of Shiva. Shiva opened his third eye, released a missile of fire and destroyed the god of desire. But without desire, the world cannot function. Hence, Vishnu caught the fire of Shiva's third-eye, turned it into a mare and hid her under the sea.

The horse is a highly revered animal in Hinduism right from Rig Vedic times even though, strangely, the horse is not a native Indian animal. It does not thrive in the subcontinent except in parts of Gujarat and Rajasthan. Since the horse came into India from the North West frontier, along with traders and marauders, Vishnu's horse-riding form, Kalki, has been associated with warlords who overran India in medieval times.

Vishnu not only rides a horse. He also becomes a horse. One form of Vishnu with the head of a horse that is highly revered especially in south India is Hayagriva. This form of Vishnu is associated with education. From the horse's head emerges Saraswati, goddess of knowledge.

Vedic mythology is full of tales where wisdom reaches the world through horse-headed beings. The sun, for example, appeared with a horse's head to reveal the wisdom of the Veda to Rishi Yagnavalkya. Rishi Dadichi replaced his human head with a horse's so that he could share Vedic wisdom with the Ashwini twins.

What is this Vedic wisdom? Vedic wisdom is the realisation that there is more to life than material reality that is perceived through the senses. It is wisdom that liberates us from the limitations of nature. It enables man to break free from Prakriti and realise Purusha. Prakriti makes us mortal and restless, Purusha makes us immortal and serene. The journey from Brahma to brahman, from the finite to the infinite, is the song of Hayagriva.

Patta painting from Odisha showing the horse-headed
Hayagriva and his consort, identified as Lakshmi

When Brahma was born, the first emotion he experienced was curiosity — who was he and why was he? Curiosity was followed by fear, because he found no answers. This fear is different from the fear of animals. Animals are afraid of scarcity, animals are afraid of predators, but these are real fears. Human fear is born of imagination — imagined scarcity, imagined predators and more importantly an imagined idea of self-worth. This self-worth is determined by possessions, 'what I have' rather than 'what I am'. Self-worth rises as one possesses more wealth, more power over others and more information.

Hayagriva draws attention to the fact that the notion of property is not an objective reality, but a subjective truth, a cultural construction of human beings, not a natural phenomenon. In other words, they are creations of Maya and components of Brahmanda. If man does not exist, there would be no property to possess. Nature does not need man; man needs nature. It is a delusion of man that it is the master of nature, and the owner of nature's wealth and information.

When we self-aggrandise ourselves by being territorial and dominating other human beings, Hayagriva reminds us that we are still animals, displaying animal instincts of survival, and that we have not evolved despite a larger human brain. Vedic wisdom is that which enables man to break free from the animal and discover the human. To break free from fear and discover faith. For that, we have to surrender to the idea of spiritual reality, to Purusha, that which exists beyond Prakriti.

Vishnu lore tells us the story of the elephant-king, Gajendra, who was sporting in a lotus pond with a herd of cow-elephants who adored him. Suddenly, a crocodile caught hold of his foot and

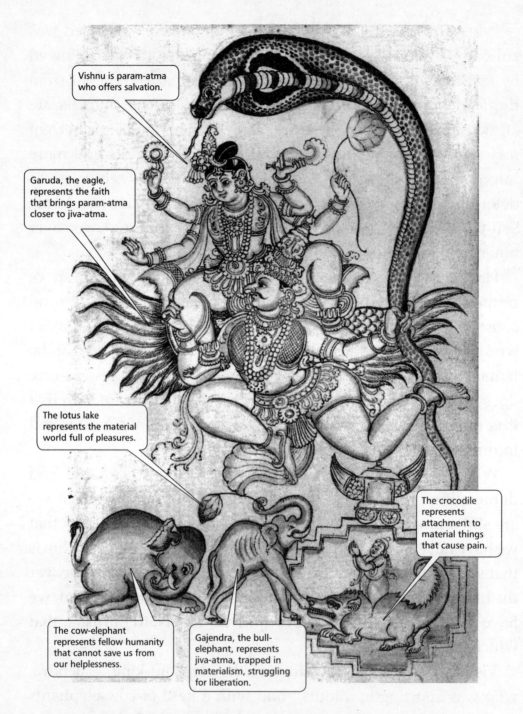

Mysore painting showing Vishnu liberating the elephant Gajendra

began dragging him underwater. Gajendra thrashed about in the water and tried to get rid of the crocodile but the crocodile did not release his grip. The cow-elephants tried to rescue him but failed. He was helpless until he picked up a lotus and begged Vishnu to come to his aid.

The story draws attention to the human condition. We are all Gajendras. Sometimes, like Devas, we crave for material security. Even when we get it we become insecure. Insecurity breeds hedonism or may transform into complacency and cynicism as one finds oneself bereft of any purpose. At other times, like Asuras, we crave for material growth. It becomes the sole purpose of existence. When we grow materially we become arrogant and feel invulnerable, until circumstances turn against us. In misery, we thrash about like Gajendra trying to get rid of the crocodile. No one comes to our rescue. No one can come to our rescue. We become restless and anxious. Liberation from this state will come only when we surrender to the wisdom of Vishnu, revealed through his stories, symbols and rituals.

# Symbols in this book

## Symbols in *7 Secrets of Shiva*

 The coiled, hooded serpent represents stillness and awareness.

 The sprig of three bilva leaves represents the merger of three worlds: social, physical and psychological.

 The turtle represents withdrawal from worldly life, which is the trait of a hermit.

## Symbols in *7 Secrets of the Goddess*

 The footprints of Lakshmi, which bring fortune in the direction they point.

 The downward pointing triangle evokes the womb of the Goddess, which is nature itself that envelops all life.

 The spread-eagled stick figure of Lajja-gauri (?) evoking fertility, popular in Bengal.

## Symbols in *7 Secrets of Vishnu*

 The vertical mark of Vishnu represents the material growth (central upward pointing red mark) contained within spiritual thought (the white sandal paste cup).

 The conch draws attention to water as well as wind that sustains life.

 The elephant-headed fish (Capricorn or Makara) represents spring and love and growth.

# Acknowledgements

I would like to thank all those who helped me in the making of the book, including:

- R.N. Singh and Dharmendra Rao of Ramsons Kalapratishtana, Mysore for their unwavering support. Most of the handicraft images in this book were provided by them.

- Harsha Dehejia for helping me with the image of Balarama and Yamuna.

- Satya Banerjee, for giving me access to his vast collection of Goddess images and permission to use them.

- Ayan Chaudhuri, for his photograph of an image of Durga.

- Pramod Kumar K.G, for giving me access to rare images from his library.

- Dhaivat Chhaya and Swapnil Sakpal, for designing the book and helping with the artwork.